C000247066

Marygrove

EX LIBRIS

270.92
SulF

270.92
SulF

MAN OF SPAIN

Francis Suarez

THE MACMILLAN COMPANY
NEW YORK · BOSTON · CHICAGO · DALLAS
ATLANTA · SAN FRANCISCO

MACMILLAN AND CO., LIMITED
LONDON · BOMBAY · CALCUTTA · MADRAS
MELBOURNE

THE MACMILLAN COMPANY
OF CANADA, LIMITED
TORONTO

MAN OF SPAIN

Francis Suarez

by

JOSEPH H. FICHTER, S. J.

AUTHOR OF "ROOTS OF CHANGE"

New York

THE MACMILLAN COMPANY

1940

Cum effuderis esurienti animam tuam, et animam afflictam repleveris, orietur in tenebris lux tua, et tenebrae tuae erunt sicut meridies.—ISAIAS.

CONTENTS

MAN OF SPAIN

Francis Suarez

I

Maternity

ON A SOFT, MELLOW NIGHT in the Spring of 1555 Mary Tudor was brought to bed of a prospective heir to the English throne. She wanted a child, preferably a son. Maternity was the cherished goal of long fruitless years, and a lusty royal son would be the infant she hoped to present to her husband, Philip of Spain. All England was agog at the news; but none rejoiced more merrily than the Queen's Catholic subjects. They knew that the heir of devout Mary and of Catholic Philip would bring back a religious security that had not existed since the early years of Henry VIII's rule.

At the time of Mary's accouchement Philip was a strong and virile twenty-eight, but he had his own thoughts about all this hubbub over a child's birth. His wife was eleven years his senior, no beauty by anyone's measuring stick, and with "thin, sandy, reddish hair; no eyebrows; almost colorless eyes; a wide flattish nose and a big mouth." [1] As he walked the halls of Hampton Court that night, interrupted now and then by the assurances of the ladies of quality who buzzed about in anticipation, he genuinely doubted that there would be any son of this English Queen, and even entertained misgivings that there would be an offspring at all.

The following day was Saturday, an apt day for the announcement of momentous happenings. Rustics mingled with town folk at the bazaars and stalls, and typical English people welcomed the word from London: the birth of a prince. Churches

[1] Loth, David: *Philip II of Spain*, New York, 1932, Brentano's, p. 76.

1

were crowded; thanksgivings were offered to God for this benign favor; people everywhere took a new interest in the Spanish noble who had travelled all those miles simply to beget a sovereign for them. Their antipathy to anything foreign was for a day softened and they congratulated each other on the astuteness of "Bloody Mary" in capturing the young and handsome Philip for the service of England. Their merriment, however, lasted hardly till nightfall.

The announcement was premature. Mary had feverishly tossed the night in convinced anticipation that her time had come— only to have the pains pass with the breaking of dawn. A further month of prayer and preparation still found her in anxiety, restive over the delay. Not enjoying the experience of Philip, who already had children of his own, she could not be shaken of her delusion. The Spaniard became coldly cynical about the whole affair and strained to get back to his country and his father, the Emperor Charles. As the weeks passed he successfully persuaded Mary that she had been deluding herself and that there was to be no child; but she clung to her hope.

Announcement followed false announcement until the citizenry, in its blunt Anglo-Saxon way, made lewd songs about the confinement of the Queen. Gentlemen about the town of London endangered their liberty by scoffing at it, and two of them were sent to the Tower for disrespectful ribaldry. The retinue of Spanish nobles whom Philip had brought with him was even more outspoken than the English. They had never cared about the northward trip in the first place, found the women of England little to their taste, and could not get on at all in the "barbaric" language of the Island. They were discontented in the North.

Among these followers of Philip was a scion from each of the most prominent families of Spain. The troops in his train had been despatched to join the Emperor's army in France, but the grandees and a few fine ladies went on to the royal court of

England. Naturally, the ancient Suarez family, of Toledo and Granada, was represented in the cortège, and it was this young man who could bring back to his relatives an account of the things going forward among the English. Obscurely he and the others followed the English interlude, for Philip pointedly ignored his own people to show every kindness to Mary's gentry and nobles. Services at table and in the bedchamber were handed over to strangers; processions, banquets, and all court functions, which the Spaniards had been accustomed to oversee in the grand manner, were centered about the Queen. Justly was it muttered that the son of an Emperor was bowing too low and serving too slavishly.

But the patience of Philip gave out eventually, though he made a great show of love and protestation upon his departure. Mary was as broken-hearted when he convinced her that he must leave to attend his affairs on the continent as she had been when he finally persuaded her that wishful pregnancy was not sufficient to ensure a child. During the summer of 1555 she had become reconciled to the latter fact, but she still clung to the hope that her royal romance with this dashing husband and lover would somehow remain intact. Finally, near the end of August, Philip sailed away to the south and left her forlorn.

As Catholic Mary stood there in her tower window watching her husband's barge slowly float down the Thames she probably did not realize that here was closing an irrevocable chapter in the history of Old England. She herself was to die in a couple of years and the succession would go to treacherous and capable Elizabeth, daughter of Mary's own father, Henry VIII, and of his mistress, Anne Boleyn. She must have seen that the Spanish strain of Catherine of Aragon would depart from the Tudor line. Catherine had desired as frantically to present sons to Henry, as Mary wished to have them from Philip, but in the providence of God there was disappointment for both mother and daughter.

Her father, whom history has come to know as the monarch of many wives, had begun the ruination of the ancient religion before he died in 1547. Her half-brother, Edward VI, had proselytized almost half the kingdom in the brief six years of his reign. She herself had only five years of agitated rule in which to regain the lost ground—an impossible feat. Thirty years after her death, this youthful Spanish husband of hers would send the Invincible Armada, partly for the purpose of restoring the Catholicism which they both cherished. Over the vista of years she may have envisioned its destruction and the triumph of Elizabeth. At any rate she herself had made the hopeless gesture of returning her people to the religious rule of Rome.

With Philip by her side, and in the midst of the Lords and Commons of the realm, Mary had asked Cardinal Pole to receive the English people back into the true Church. The ceremony at Whitehall meant that the little nation of about two million souls was again officially counted among the traditional Catholic countries of Europe. Sincerely the Queen believed that she had done a great work for God; secretly the Spanish gentlemen thought that she was doing it for love of her husband. Philip had no need to urge her to the step. Unhesitatingly, however, he offered the necessary moral support to stand in the face of opposition on the part of powerful subjects. The deed had been happily done and Mary felt that for all time the English throne, which in the person of her father and half-brother, had fought the papacy, would now be its strong right arm.

As she turned from the window there in the gathering evening dusk, Mary could not foresee that the royal English champion to take her father's place against Rome was not yet born. The future Scottish King, James I, would come into life in 1566 and into English power in 1603. Then another battle would rage, a battle more bitter, more interesting, more colorful than the one she had sorrowfully watched in her youth between her worldly father, Henry VIII, and her spiritual father, Clement VII. The new battle would take place after Elizabeth's death, when the theologically inclined James would argue fiercely and futilely with Bellarmine and with another who was even then a young boy in Granada. That seven-year-old subject of her husband, Philip, was busy about the things of a child while Mary pondered her failure to give a Catholic King to England and thought gloomily of what life would be without Philip.

The whole tenor of English history would have changed had a son been born to Mary and Philip. Much would have been gained; suffering and disloyalties would have been fewer; but something would have been lost too. England would have been subject for a long time to the dominance of Spain had their son grown to take the royal place of the Queen. But the glory that was Suarez, and the enlightenment which flowed from his mind and pen, might have been greatly shaded. There would have been no controversy between a dictatorial divine-right King and a humbly devout and democratic Jesuit.

The presence of the young Francis Suarez in Spain at that time was not unknown to Philip. The Suarez family had been in the intimate service of the Spanish kings long before the glorious reign of Ferdinand and Isabella. But Philip was in danger of losing these ancient contacts with his fellow countrymen, at least with those who stayed at home to keep the peninsula in readiness against his return. After leaving Mary he went to his father, Emperor Charles V, in Flanders, and spent most of his time fighting the French. About a dozen weeks in the following year were all he could afford to spend with his wife, and in December he had the sorrowful duty of celebrating funeral obsequies for the pitiful little Queen of England. A week later, on December 30, 1558, the Emperor himself was buried in Brussels, and Philip found himself the absolute ruler of about half of Europe and of vast territories beyond the seas.

Far different from the sickly, self-deluded Queen of England, was the healthy and beautiful woman who had born Francis Suarez. Pregnancy and childbirth were no novel experience for Antonia Vasquez, the wife of Gaspar Suarez, leading citizen of Granada, friend and intimate of both Philip and his father Charles. Antonia had already been delivered of John and was to have, in all, eight sturdy children, four boys and four girls. They were a vigorous and fecund race, these Spaniards, and theirs was a high disregard for the weakness or policy of northern peoples who would not or could not bring large families into the world.

To moderns it is something in the nature of a social phenomenon that people of the Latin race insist upon the pleasure and duty of raising numerous offspring. To Antonia and Gaspar Suarez it was a clear fulfillment of the meaning of marriage. The size and good fortune of their family was a manifestation of God's blessing upon their union. They were lavish, too, in giving their children to the service of the Church; another attitude that is amazing to people of less penetrating religious beliefs. In the immediate Suarez clan, Francis and his brother Gaspar entered the young Society of Jesus. Pedro died in boyhood, and three of the girls became nuns. John remained to carry on the family name and tradition.

Francis was born on the fifth of January, 1548. That is a simple statement of fact which would prove amply satisfactory for any fact-searching modern historian. But historians, particularly hagiographers of the seventeenth century, could not let it go at that. Typical of the times in which he wrote and of the men who wrote in those times is Bernard Sartolo's account of the birth, published in 1693. "The year 1548 had just begun;" said he, "the Church was governed by Julius III, the Society of Jesus by its founder, St. Ignatius; the Spanish monarchy by Charles V who had united under the same yoke the Lions and the Eagles.

This very time God had chosen to give a new Sun to the world, glorifying it by the birth of Francis." [2]

The same author continues by pointing out the wonder that had come into the world with Doña Antonia's son, and the omens and portents which hovered about the Suarez residence on the evening of that cold winter day. "The morning of January 5th, the Vigil of the Epiphany of Our Savior, dawned a happy one for the Church, for Spain, and for the Company [of Jesus], for it was to give to the Church militant a valiant champion who would defend her with an invincible pen, to the Spanish people a great man whose glory would be reflected in them, to the Company of Jesus an excellent Doctor who would shed luster upon it by his incomparable wisdom. Heaven shared its joy with earth that day. A large and brilliant star appeared in the sky after sunset inundating both the house where the child was born and the neighboring streets. It was a presage of the brightness that Francis was to shed on the world." [3]

The relation of prophetic circumstances of this kind always detracts from the historicity of any event. The child was born; that is an established fact. Historical investigation, after the rejection of other tentative dates, has established also that the birth occurred on the fifth of January of that year. Regarding certain prodigies and signs there is nothing but an untrustworthy, pious belief, harmless in itself, it is true, but not contributing anything significant to our present knowledge.

About one of Francis' sisters, however, there seems to be a doubtful chronicle. Her name was Catalina, the youngest member of the family, and it is not certain whether she entered the convent or married. She is generally identified with the Catalina de Frillo who for thirty years, as Coleridge remarks, "was in the

[2] Sartolo, Bernard, quoted by De Scorraille, Raoul: *François Suarez, de la Compagnie de Jésus*, Paris, 1911, Lethiellieux, vol. i, pp. 13–14.
[3] *Ibid.*, p. 14.

habit of visiting daily the poor villagers of a hamlet that lay
under the shadow of the castle in which she lived, laden with
food, clothes, and medicine to relieve their necessities." [4] Others
believe her to have been a relative of the Suarez family. At any
rate, she was closely connected with them, and is important here
only for the gentle aura of benignity which seems to emanate
from the whole family circle.

. There is no particular need to demonstrate that the Suarez
family was supremely above the average of Spanish piety of
those days. Nor can we preclude the evidence that there were
saints as well as rake-hells in most sixteenth-century families.
There were both holy and unholy Spaniards in that age just as
there were holy and unholy men in every country and every age
since the world began. The young men who went off to the many
wars that Charles and Philip waged were on the average no
better nor worse than soldiers everywhere. The men and women
who stayed at home in Spain to administer the peaceful pursuits
of the nation were much of a patch with those of other nations.
There was this one difference: Spain was at that time the most
thoroughly Catholic people in the world; and a thorough Catholic
is more guilty because he always knows when he is doing evil.

Francis Suarez grew up to become a man of great personal
integrity, an eventuation which may be attributable to his family
surroundings in early years. But, "good and pious as were all
the members of this family," writes Coleridge, "it is probable
that Spain had hundreds of noble families at that time of which
the same account might be given." [5] What other factors entered
to form the character of Suarez remain to be demonstrated, for
he was assuredly a man of outstanding gifts. His ancestors had

[4] Coleridge, H. J.: "Francis Suarez," *The Month,* London, January, 1865,
vol. ii, p. 53.
[5] *Ibid.,* p. 53.

been prodigious warriors and capable administrators, but there is undoubtedly more than one ghost lurking in the ancestral closets which it would be neither possible nor profitable to raise. The effort that has been made to whitewash the Spanish nobility on all scores has been as futile as would be the attempt to besmirch it.

If Antonia stood in the casement of the Suarez home which still exists in Granada and which fortunately escaped the ravages of the recent Spanish war, she probably entertained none of the false hopes and misgivings which assailed Mary Tudor meditating in her tower near the Thames. She, too, watched her husband, Gaspar, frequently depart on long missions of a royal nature, and commended him to the providence of God. Watching her children at play she may have fancied that they would serve God in their own capable ways but even that fancy of the future must be inscrutable. Antonia was a serene and stately person. She cherished the laudable hope that her sons and daughters would follow in the footsteps of their ancestors, some of whom had been statesmen, others soldiers, still others men and women in the priestly and religious life. How could she possibly guess that this very house in which she now lived would some day carry an inscription praising her second son to all the world?

The inscription is still there on that ancient building, for it was appended only in 1896 by the officials of the city of Granada. Antonia, if she were in the city of Granada to-day, would stand outside her old home in the street which has been renamed in his honor: *Calle del Padre Suarez*, and, with her back to the Convent of the Franciscans, would read the encomium which men of the nineteenth century wrote of her son. According to this tablet he was a "famous philosopher, profound theologian, distinguished lawyer, so eloquent a defender of the Catholic faith that he merited to receive from the Holy See the title of *Eminent Doctor*, the glory of the Church, the light of the Society of Jesus, the honor of Spain and one of the most illustrious sons of this city." [6]

. All of these titles were to come to Francis with the passage of the years, most of them after both Antonia, his mother, and Gaspar, his father, had died. Added to them are two modern titles, which it would have pleased the heart of both son and parents to hear. He is frequently called the "King-Baiter" because of his verbal tilts with King James, and the "Democrat," because of his espousal of popular sovereignty. Allegiance to the king was a virtue in the Spain of those years, but that allegiance did not blind people of the Suarez strain to the fundamental rights of their lowliest servants and retainers. Basically, at least, they practiced the theories which Francis himself was to formulate so carefully in later years.

The men and women who frequented the grand Suarez residence were taken aback by this attitude of Spaniards who, like themselves, were fighting for the maintenance of Andalusia. All about the neighborhood were the Moors, traditional enemies of Christianity, former conquerors and now subjects of the Spanish nation. The mother of Francis Suarez queened it over these unfortunates with a more gentle charity than Mary of England used in governing the subjects of her own race and religion. For Moor and Christian alike, the Suarez family group—and many other straight-thinking Christian families for that matter—had a sense of equality that must have seemed strange even to the down-trodden.

Hidden in various Spanish annals there is a host of stories

[6] The composer of this inscription is Canon Joachim de los Reyes, professor at the University of Granada, and Director of the Institute of Technology. His nephew, Felix Campos, owned the ancient Suarez residence in 1917, when he had it thrown open to the members of the convention then celebrating at Granada the third centenary of the great theologian's death. Cf. Dudon, Paul, "Le Congrès de Grenade et le troisième centenaire de la mort de Suarez," *Etudes*, Paris, November, 1917, vol. 153, p. 412.

telling of Gaspar's humane treatment of subjects who came under his sway, and of Antonia's solicitude for the least of these despised people. Some of the stories are undoubtedly apocryphal, but their prevalence is indicative of an attitude which must genuinely have existed. It is no source of wonder, then, that Francis got an early start in the definite way of thinking which would oppose him to the authoritarian and dictatorial theories of most of his contemporaries. His mother set the example of universal charity and his father that of universal justice; and the combination of these two was the thread which ran like a belt of gold throughout the whole of his life.

The King who, many years later, was to order Francis to his favorite University of Coimbra in Portugal, was seldom seen in Spain during the first decade of the boy's life. Francis knew mainly from hearsay that Philip was concerned about the solidification of Spain's far-flung provinces. Philip was hardly aware, certainly not over-concerned, about this child of one of his trusted friends. He used the Spanish people during most of these years as a steady source of the revenue he needed to wage his conquests—and often enough to lavish on undeserving courtiers. Spaniards were financially crippled for many years afterwards because of his fiscal policy, and it was this extortion which prevented the family of Suarez from gathering even more wealth than it had.

If heredity means anything at all it means that in the case of Suarez there should appear an abundance of generosity, of intellectual stability, of traditional Christianity. As for material prosperity, which is sometimes a good, more often an evil, the boy himself could later assure the Jesuit questioners that his father's fortune was estimated at well over thirty thousand ducats. When his name was entered in the novitiate annals of the Order he was described as "the son of distinguished and wealthy parents."

The story of Gaspar Suarez' rise to the eminent position which he held in southern Spain at the time when Francis was born, is a story dependent upon the exploits of his ancestors. That account turns back the pages of Spanish history several centuries and explains the background upon which Francis Suarez painted his remarkable career.

CHAPTER II

Approach to Granada

THE SOUTHERN SPAIN into which Saurez was born was a mosaic of rival civilizations. The Visigoths descended in hordes upon the land in the early fifth century. They mingled their customs and morals with the Roman culture which had existed there since before the time of Christ. The Vandals swept a hurricane of destruction through the country and left their name there in Andalusia. Then the conversion of Recaredo to Christianity changed the color and tone of life somewhat to normalcy. This man was, says Louis Bertrand, "rich, cultured, and a lover of luxury. He made Seville and Toledo regular centres of study—what are rather pompously called universities." [1] The rule he instituted lasted about three hundred years, till the beginning of the eighth century, the time of the Moslem invasion.

The nature of the Moorish domination is still a matter of debate among historians; some claiming that there was no such thing as Moorish culture, civilization or art. At the outset they were considered cannibals. Upon their first invasion the Mussulmans from Africa deliberately spread a reputation of terror by cutting to pieces their captives and boiling them over fire. Added to these exploits was the fact that they zealously proselytized among the Christians for their prophet Mohammed. Theirs was not only a barbaric invasion. It was an armed conflict between religious ideologies.

[1] Bertrand, Louis, and Petrie, Charles: *The History of Spain*, New York, 1934, Appleton-Century, pp. 5–6.

But the charge of outright barbarism does not square with the historical records of Spain. Had the Moslems been nothing more than another horde of savages, such as the Huns, Visigoths, Vandals, and others, their influence would not have remained, as it did, even to our own time. It would have been absorbed by the higher native culture, and therein vanished. The truth is that even long after the age of Loyola, Borgia, and Suarez, this influence was strongly felt. To-day in the Spanish peninsula it is not yet completely dead.

With the passage of time the science and philosophy and art of the invaders culminated in a period of brilliant expansion. From them the Christian scholars of the great Middle Ages learned deeply and wisely.

Christopher Dawson, one of the most penetrating of modern thinkers, significantly opines that "at the very moment when Christendom seemed about to succumb to the simultaneous attacks of Saracens, Vikings and Magyars, the Moslem culture of the Western Mediterranean was entering on the most brilliant phase of its development. In the tenth century, under the Khalifate of Cordova, Southern Spain was the richest and most populous region of Western Europe. Its cities, with their palaces and colleges and public baths, resembled the towns of the Roman Empire rather than the miserable groups of wooden hovels that were growing up in France and Germany under the shelter of an abbey or a feudal stronghold." [2]

Granada, the birthplace of Suarez, was in that tenth century an insignificant place. It was somewhat to the southeast of Cordova and even more deeply immersed in Moslem territory. The center of all things Islamic was Cordova, the largest city of Europe, with the exception of Constantinople, containing about two hundred thousand houses and probably a million residents.

[2] Dawson, Christopher: *The Making of Europe*, New York, 1934, Sheed and Ward, p. 167.

Its library is said to have held about four hundred thousand manuscripts, and its governors and princes were noted for their patronage of scholarship and the fine arts.

The tenth century then was the peak of power and prestige for the Moors in Spain. In comparison the rest of Europe was extremely backward. The more advanced civilization of these foreign invaders overshadowed the whole culture of Western Europe. "It was not until the thirteenth century, after the age of the Crusades and the great catastrophe of the Mongol invasions, that the civilization of Western Christendom began to attain a position of relative equality with that of Islam, and even then it remained permeated with oriental influences. Only in the fifteenth century, with the Renaissance and the great maritime expansion of the European states, did the Christian West acquire that leadership of civilization which we regard to-day as a kind of law of nature." [3]

All through these centuries of Moorish control the Spaniards themselves were dreaming their dreams of reconquest. The movement to oust the foreigners gradually took definite shape in obscure Asturia, in the northernmost part of Spain. This movement was slow, alternating victory with defeat. But the rise was perceptible. From an almost completely dominated race the Spaniards came to be the conquerors of most of the world. They became the greatest rulers, colonizers, explorers; and then began gradually to sink again to that oblivion to which the "intellectuals" of the nineteeth century have consigned them.

During the long period leading up to the heroic reconquest of the Peninsula the ancestors of Francis Suarez took a prominent part. According to an ancient genealogy presented to King Charles II in 1685 by John Suarez of Toledo, grand-nephew of Francis Suarez, a document which received the royal stamp of approval in 1688, the Suarez clan was at war with the Moors

[3] *Ibid.*, p. 168.

almost from the beginning. This record of the family covers a
period of six centuries, that is, roughly from the middle of the
eleventh to the middle of the seventeenth, a period during which
the most profound changes took place in Spain.

The history of Castile, one of the five independent and mutu-
ally jealous kingdoms of Spain, is especially replete with the
names of Suarez' forebears. This central part of the peninsula
was a battleground over which waves of Moslem armies and
Christian armies passed and repassed. Each approach of the
Mussulmans, however, seemed to carry less force. Each counter-
attack of the Christians was more telling, until gradually the
invader was pushed southward and out of Spain.

It was in Castile that the early progenitors of Suarez made the
family name redoubtable not only in warfare but also in the
affairs of Church and State. They were prominent leaders in civil
and ecclesiastical life as well as capable military men. Most
intriguing, however, to the casual reader is the active part they
took in the exhaustive conflict with the Moors. Out of these conquests which thus successively took place they won their family
estates and their titles to nobility.

In the middle of the eleventh century we find a relative of
Suarez, Count Munio Adefonso, fighting under the same king
and in the same army with the historically renowned and romantic figure, the Cid Campeador. Ferdinand I and his Queen,
Sancha, were the Christian rulers of Castile and Leon, and in
their campaigns against the Moors and even against other Christian princes, Munio Adefonso is reputed to have distinguished
himself as a brilliant leader. The fabled Cid clearly outshone
him, but the same characterization can probably be given to both
Cid and Adefonso: that he was "not merely a good Christian, but
even a devotee, and that he was so throughout the whole of his
life, in Castile no less than in Saragossa and Valencia, scrupulous
about celebrating religious festivals, observing Lent as a Mussul-

man observes Ramadan, and making donations to monasteries and churches." [4]

The successor of Ferdinand I was Alfonso VI who became King of Galicia as well as of Leon and Castile. The Cid was at first suspect in the eyes of Alfonso even though he protested to his dying day that he had always been faithful to his monarch. At any rate he was not present at the siege of Toledo in 1085, in which another member of the Suarez family took part. This was Alfonso Muños, son of Count Munio Adefonso. After the capture of the city the King handed over to this young man the estate of Ajofrin, formerly the property of a Moor, and added to this the title of nobility. From that time onward Toledo became the native place of all the Suarez family, and each member even down to the time of Francis appended the words, "de Toledo," to his name. Alfonso Muños pushed onward in the campaign against the Moors and finally died of a wound received in battle, but he had left his children and his reputation well established in Castile.

Alfonso VI proceeded southward and the growth of his power struck terror into the hearts of Andalusian Christians as well as those of the Mussulmans there. In his train, just after the turn of the century, was Munio Alfonso, son of the first Lord of Ajofrin, who lost his life in one of the sporadic battles in which the King engaged on the march. The story goes that he was one of the most valiant of the Christian warriors, known and esteemed by the Moslems, and when he fell they cut off his head to exhibit it as a kind of relic of heroism. They are supposed to have carried the gruesome trophy through the South of Spain and into Africa, demonstrating everywhere the evidence that they had made an end of this fearful enemy.

But the twelfth century was a lamentable one for the fortunes of Spain. The tide turned again in favor of the invaders as they

[4] Bertrand and Petrie, *op. cit.,* p. 176.

learned the important lesson of unified effort. The Christians had been defeating them, they believed, because of their own loosely joined confederacy and the jealous strife among their leaders. In 1146 the Caliph Abd el Moumin started a counter-move to the north and was little by little rewarded with success. During the next fifty years still greater progress was made, and in 1196 Alfonso VIII of Castile was badly defeated in the battle of Alarcos. Steadily the enemy encroached until Madrid and Guadalajara were captured, but the turning point came again in 1212 when the Moslem forces were completely routed at the battle of Las Navas de Tolosa.

Again the ancient chronicler takes up the thread of the Suarez-ian family story in the account of this pivotal battle. The sixth Lord of Ajofrin, Pero Ruis, one of the paternal ancestors of Francis Suarez, while carrying on the bloody work of killing Mussulmans, is supposed to have seen a vision of a cross in the sky. It is not certain whether this portent of victory appeared in the sky or whether he was inspired by the cross on a banner which a priest carried unharmed through the ranks of the enemy. At any rate Pero decided at this time to commemorate the event by adding two silver crosses to the family coat-of-arms. Whether or not the story is true we cannot know. The fact is that the escutcheon of the Suarez family, divided into four parts, carries a silver cross in an azure field in upper left- and lower right-hand corners. The other corners display a purple castle on a field of gold.[5]

In the thirteenth century another great Spanish leader arose to regain much of the lost territory, and to push the Moslems into their one last stronghold, the Kingdom of Granada, where they

[5] This escutcheon is still preserved in the Granadine home of the Suarez. Cf. Dudon, *op. cit.,* p. 412; where he remarks: ". . . the venerable old gentle-man was justly proud to show his visitors the old shields carved in wood which still bear the arms of the family which the wish and the benefits of the Catholic Kings established at Granada immediately after the conquest."

stayed until within two generations of the birth of Francis
Suarez. This great hero of mediæval Spain is the storied St.
Ferdinand III, King of Castile and Leon until his death in 1252.
But Mohammed Al Ahmar, who ruled the Kingdom of Granada
for forty-two years, was able to keep full control of these rich
southern districts against the tired Christian armies. He made
peace with the Spanish rulers and took advantage of this long
period to convert the city on the banks of the Darro into a Moslem show place. He gained undying fame as the architect of the
Alhambra, the palace of the Moorish kings.

Proud and cultured Syrians from Damascus had once made
Granada their residence. Then the early Arab invaders of the
peninsula conquered the place and developed it into a center of
their own peculiar civilization. Now that Cordova had declined
Al Ahmar decided that Granada was to be the cradle of a revivi-
fied Islamic culture. Alfonso X, surnamed The Wise, was content to live with these Moslems as his friendly neighbors and
loyal allies. And so it was for several decades. Wilberforce has
written of Al Ahmar that "he collected at his Arab court a great
part of the wealth, the science, and the intelligence of Spain. His
empire has long ago been broken up; the Moslem has been
driven out; there is no king nor kingdom of Granada. But their
memory lives in the great palace fortress whose red towers still
rise over the sparkling Darro, and whose fairy chambers are still
to be seen in what is, perhaps, the most celebrated of the wonder
works of the master builders of the world."

For almost two centuries after the great Al Ahmar's death in
1272, neither Christian nor Moslem could make much headway
against each other. Both sides had their own internal difficulties
—a series of struggles among the Moslem leaders prevented the
Kingdom of Granada from expansion, while disunion among
the Spanish groups rendered them incapable of driving again

toward the south. But when Isabella and Ferdinand united Castile and Aragon by their marriage in 1469, the end was at hand for the Moors. The last king of Granada was Abul Hassan, who came into power in 1466, and whose rule ended when his wife, the Sultana Zoraya, turned against him. Her son, Abu Abdallah, or Boabdil, took over the authority of the kingdom and saw it through to the bitter end.

The generation which witnessed the fall of Granada was that of Francis Suarez' grandparents. Among his relatives fighting under the Christian standard were a Lopez, an Alvarez, and his great-uncle John, all holding their permanent residence and estates in Toledo.

Before investigating the gallant careers of these close relatives of Francis Suarez we might well call into question the supposed glory they bequeathed to the great theologian's name. The constant drives against the Moors in Spain were no exceptions to the butcheries and savageries of all marching armies and, strictly as such, they would add no glory to the ancestry of Suarez. War is generally a horrible thing and the exploits of war are generally much less glamorous than ancient chroniclers would have us believe.

But the cause for which Spanish Christians fought during those centuries, like the cause they fought for against the recent Communists, gave an entirely different color to their hostilities. Suarez was himself the most gentle and peaceful of men but even he defended the justice of a righteous war and contended later that warfare was not incompatible with the precept of love for one's enemies. "For he who wages war honestly does not hate the persons but their works which he rightly punishes."

No one now living can possibly judge of the complete justification of Christian warfare against the Moslems. Certainly no one would attempt to prove that the actions of Spanish individuals were performed always in the spirit of charity. The deception and brutality of leaders likewise frequently overshadowed whatever just motives they may have formulated for themselves. On the whole, however, the forcible expulsion of the Moorish hordes from Spain remains as one of the few examples of a plausible case for the justice of war. There were greed and selfishness, reasons of economy and of state, as well as religious motives, which prompted the reconquest. Defense of the Faith was the inspiration of the warriors, but the lands and treasures in the hands of the enemy constituted their practical aspirations.

Among the men who hoped thus to profit personally were Lopez, Alvarez, and John Suarez, all of whom marched in the armies of his Catholic Majesty Ferdinand. The first of them did not proceed very far before he covered himself with glory in the Portuguese war at the battle of Toro. He continued on with the armies but nothing more is heard of him in the line of military prowess. King Ferdinand was learning the military business in those early days and he was in great need of individual heroes who would cover up the results of his own rashness.

Garcia Alvarez saw a great deal more action than Lopez. He was with Ferdinand in 1482 when the armies of Old Castile were disastrously defeated at Loja and pursued by the Moslems to the gates of Cordova. He was with him in a dozen different battles, some of which the Spaniards won, and some the Moslems, until four years later, when the first humiliation of Loja was vindicated. After many days of long and bloody fighting the troops "battered down the walls, and entered the city in triumph, while the whole army cried 'Castile! Castile!' and knelt, saying the *Te Deum*." [6] Among the men who received estates for their services on this occasion was Garcia Alvarez. He was an authentic and valorous warrior, but he did not live long to enjoy his re-

[6] Walsh, W. T.: *Isabella The Crusader*, New York, 1935, Sheed and Ward, p. 187.

ward. A short while later, in the seige of Baza, he was killed
by the Moors.

In the meanwhile John Suarez of Toledo, the great-uncle of
Francis, had become an officer close to their Catholic Majesties.
When Isabella and Ferdinand were encamped at Santa Fe, awaiting the capitulation of Granada, he gained their especial notice
and commendation. Years later, in 1509, when the great Cardinal Ximenes was preparing an expedition against the Moors in
Africa, Ferdinand still remembered the ability of John Suarez.
In a personal letter to him the King wrote ". . . since we know
that you are the type of man this war demands and that you can
make yourself useful in the service of God Our Lord and of Ourselves we command and order you to join the Cardinal and
depart with him."

When the Catholic rulers finally pulled up their armies before
Granada in 1491 they had been conducting a regular campaign
with large troops and artillery forces for more than a decade.
These ten years had shown that the Moor was by no means a
senile and debilitated warrior, and it is quite probable that the
Christians could never have taken Granada by direct assault.
There was some misgiving about taking it at all, but Ferdinand
and Isabella, who travelled with the troops, made up their minds
that the back of Moorish domination must be broken once and
for all. There was neither vanquished nor vanquisher at Granada, for Boabdil was strong enough to treat with Ferdinand on
a basis of equality.

Despite the historic facts of the fall of the city, there has appeared a vast literature of song and story recounting Spanish
deeds of valor at the occurrence. Actually, the Christians did not
completely surround the city, and a constant source of supplies
came into Granada which could have made it possible for the
Moors to hold out indefinitely. The Spanish army sat down on a
hill overlooking the city, first in an ordinary encampment and

then in a permanent city which they named Santa Fe. Its buildings of stone and mortar were built after a fire had destroyed many of the tents and much of the equipment of the temporary camp. The rôle of Isabella in this construction is a story in itself.

Alonso de Toledo, the brother of John Suarez and grandfather of Francis, was present at the siege and "performed important functions for the Catholic rulers, who did not show themselves ungrateful toward him." [7] What these functions were we cannot clearly know, but they were probably of an administrative rather than a belligerent nature, for there was not much fighting going on. He was major-domo (steward) of the royal household. Whatever his duties were they repaid him amply for his trouble and they were the reason why he permanently shifted his place of residence from Toledo to Granada.

Granada opened its gates to the Catholic sovereigns on January 2, 1492, and the surrender was conditioned by an agreement containing fifty-five specific articles. Among these articles it was stated that the Moors would be permitted to retain all of their property, movable and immovable, that they would have complete freedom of conscience and the right to public worship in their fashion, that they would continue to possess their mosques, minarets, and muezzins. To these and similar generous conditions Ferdinand and Isabella affixed their royal signatures solemnly bound by the words: "We assure, promise and swear by our faith and royal word that we will observe, and make observed, everything herein contained, everything and every part, now and hereafter, now and forever."

But deception was as much a policy of the Christians as of the Moslems, and it was a policy as prevalent then as it is in modern diplomatic and international circles. Ferdinand simply did not keep the agreement. Moorish properties were made prizes for his best officers. Mosques were purified according to the Catholic

[7] De Scorraille, *op. cit.,* p. 7.

formulae and re-dedicated to the service of the true God. The "conquerors" took over the booty and recompensed themselves for their trouble in the "conquest." Thus by a personal declaration Ferdinand and Isabella handed over to Alonso de Toledo, grandfather of Francis Suarez, an estate which he and his heirs were to possess forever. "Thus we make over to him by this present act," wrote the sovereigns, "the houses, vineyards, lands, olive groves and baths, which the Moor Mohammed Abenandid possessed in the estate of Zubia, in the territory and jurisdiction of this city." [8]

With this royal gift in his hands Alonso decided to sell the seignorial domains in Toledo and Tocenaque and to establish permanent residence among the Moors and Christians of Granada. This grandfather of Francis Suarez was as active physically as his grandson was active intellectually. For many years he had the duty, always a trying one in war-impoverished Spain, of finding the money necessary to maintain royal armies around Granada. As a combination of quartermaster and military treasurer, Alonso was continually busy in the whole Andalusian province. Besides that he was also charged with the direct supervision of the palace which Charles V ordered built in the Alhambra.

While performing all of these things he found time to father three sons at his new home in Granada: John, Balthazar and Gaspar. The first entered the Franciscan Order and became a canon at Granada. Balthazar joined the army and was actively engaged as an officer in the conquests of Oran and Navarre. Gaspar, who was born in 1500, remained at home, became an advocate and lawyer, and carried on the titles and estates of his father. He was forty-eight years old and one of the most prominent Granadines when his wife Doña Antonia gave birth to Francis.

[8] *Ibid.*, p. 8.

Roughly then, and in a direct line of father-to-son relationship, the immediate ancestry of Francis Suarez is this: (*a*) Pedro Lopez, *contador mayor* of Don Juan, the father of Ferdinand the Catholic; (*b*) Alonzo Suarez, officer for King Henry, the brother of Isabella the Catholic; (*c*) Alonso, major-domo of Ferdinand and Isabella; (*d*) Gaspar, the father of Francis Suarez. Gaspar breaks with the long line of practical warriors and takes up a distinction which is as foreign to theirs as anything could be. Certainly they were not theologians or philosophers; nor were they particularly outstanding for their piety. Whatever it was they contributed to Francis by heredity, it cannot always be discovered in their actions.

CHAPTER III

Like Father, Unlike Son

IT IS A PITY that more is not known about Gaspar Suarez, the lawyer of Granada. His practice was a lucrative one especially during that half-century when the Moors and Christians were trying to absorb each other, become accustomed to the idea that property must pass from one to the other, satisfy themselves that a Christian lawyer would treat fairly with both Moor and Christian. He had to have the habit of looking at things twice, and if he showed any of the legal qualities which later appeared in his son he must have been able to judge with decent perspective both angles of his cases.

Suarez' father leaned over the cradle of his second-born son and generously dedicated him to whatever profession the Lord should elect. Piously some believe that he promised him there and then to the service of the Church, and designed his education accordingly. Perhaps he did. If so, it was a good guess in the dark, for children thus prematurely dedicated have had a way of bringing disrepute on themselves, their families and their Church. The usual custom among good Catholic parents was to arrange careers for three sons: one to the Church, one to the army, and one to carrying on the family line. What a fourth son would do in life is anyone's guess. One of the four Suarez boys died in childhood and the problem was avoided. But two of them became Jesuits, and that left the family without a Suarez in the army.

Hindsight easily attributes to men like Suarez every kind of

26

gracious youthful quality: innocence and devoutness, seriousness of purpose and docility. Foresight on the part of parents of such men—in the form of memoirs or a diary—would undoubtedly disillusion the breed of biographers of many imaginative descriptions. If Francis Suarez was innocent, devout, serious and docile as a child, he was remarkably different from children of every race and every age; and he must have been a paragon to his brothers and sisters. In the lack of evidence we are forced to assume that the child was normal. In the face of his later scholastic difficulties we must say that he was less apt intellectually, and of a more phlegmatic character, than his brothers and sisters.

Gaspar was a middle-aged father—forty-eight—when Francis was born; and such fathers make notoriously poor companions for their sons. He was a busy man too, long arrived on the road of success, and the circles in which he moved gave him the benefit of more diverse experience than he could possibly digest, or could possibly hand on to his sons. Still, he was a hearty person, confident that his children would inherit his own qualities and those of the wife of his bosom. Spanish children were brought up close to the family patio and he himself would be to them the beacon of the outside world. He must have seen, before Francis was two feet high, that this son was too slow-witted to reflect that beacon.

There is a laudatory letter, written more than a hundred years later by John Suarez, the proud grand-nephew of Gaspar's son. In it he boasted to Descamps, Suarez' first biographer, that his uncle "always showed a great inclination to virtue, much reflection, reserve and modesty, and so from his tenderest years was dedicated by his parents to the service of the Church." So there the matter stands. According to this nephew the fond parents, Gaspar and Antonia, watched him intently during the first decade of his life and then decided that he was cut of the cloth from which priests are made.

The boy's schooling was not exactly a hit-or-miss affair. Probably the more important part of what he learned before going off to school at Toledo and Salamanca was largely acquired by keeping his eyes and ears open to what was transpiring at home. In winter the house which still stands on the street named after him, and in summer the villa just outside the city, were frequented a great deal by men of affairs. Royal and ecclesiastical messengers and ambassadors had to deal much with Gaspar Suarez. Those of the Moors who still remained prominent came as guests to his home. Relatives who were in the army and others who had been across the sea to Spain's universal provinces, men who knew what was going on in the world because they were themselves fashioning that world; all of these made conversation flow interestingly at the Suarez table.

Informally the youngster learned one bit of great wisdom from his father and his father's associates: to trust not so much in the words as in the actions of men, not to be too puffed-up when things went well, nor too dejected when they went ill. His subsequent doings proved that he learned that one lesson by heart. His father did not teach it to him in sweet platitudes which are common property, and thus too often overlooked, but by the even balance of his own life and actions. At times he had the control of hundreds of thousands of ducats in his hands, at others he held the destinies of men, friends and enemies alike, in his decisions. But he had grown wise with the experiences of a half-century: his worldly outlook was as serene as his family life.

Suarez was different from most other young boys by becoming the recipient of an independent income when he was ten years old. The income was from Church property in the form of two benefices which were at the disposal of the Suarez family and were considered as much their right as were the estates and houses taken from the Moors. On September 9, 1558, the vicar general, Fonseca, acting in the name of Pedro Guerrero, archbishop of Granada and intimate friend of the whole Suarez clan, turned over these nominal chaplaincies to the boy. With them went the clerical tonsure which was carefully noted on the Jesuit records upon his admission to the Order: *Es de primera corona.*[1]

The money from these offices went into the family coffers and was thus of little personal influence on the boy. He may have used some of it to defray the cost of his schooling. Certainly he did not enjoy the privilege of benefices very long, for he had to renounce them when he became a member of the Society of Jesus. The result of a system of ecclesiastical benefices is not in general a nice thing to behold throughout the history of the Church. Abuses were only too common, especially when some ennobled family obtained the office as a sort of hereditary patronage. It was somewhat like the practice of allowing kings and emperors to dictate the appointment of the hierarchical membership. Secular considerations took precedence over the works of the Lord; and in the end those works always suffered.

Modern objectors to the mediæval custom of benefices are likely to find fault, too, with the consecration of children to the service of the Church. Suarez was definitely set on the road to that service when he received the tonsure, and your proponent of self-expression will cry to heaven that the boy's freedom was taken from him, and that he was pushed into the Church. Obviously, Francis was much too young to make up his own mind on so important a step, and the conclusion is that his inspiration was derived from either his parents or his three uncles who were priests. In either case it makes little difference; he was a mature man before he became a priest and had more than enough time to change the course thus marked out for him.

Dedicating children to the altar is not really the anti-social, inhuman thing which it may at first seem. I dare say that a larger

---

[1] De Scorraille, *op. cit.*, p. 17, remarks in a footnote that it was impossible to discover in the archives of the Archdiocese of Granada the official documents relating the event. The registration of such appointments and ordinations did not begin until 1576.

percentage of genuine vocations resulted from the practice of
those times than comes at present from the custom of allowing
children to reach adolescence, and beyond, with no pointed training. Similarly, the European habit of arranging marriages for
sons and daughters has more often than not proved that parental
wisdom was more selective than adolescent love. In this same
sixteenth century the Council of Trent gravely approved the acceptance of very young applicants for the Church's seminaries,
and it is probable that the greater number of clerics had at that
time been guided and influenced by others toward an ecclesiastical career.

Suarez himself, when he came to the mellow age of sixty,
looked back at this boyhood event and saw that the choice was
good. He knew, of course, that his parents had made the correct
decision for him and was convinced that such influence, in the
long run, did tremendously more good than harm. In his work,
De Religione, he enumerated a list of the advantages of clerical
life and pointed out that influence in that direction was always
genuinely helpful. There are exceptions, of course, and they are
accounted for by parents who, to make up for their own sins, wish
to offer a vicarious sacrifice in the persons of their children; others
have the mistaken notion that the clerical life is a sinecure which
will ensure a comfortable old age for both parents and children.

Besides this incident, which set him apart from other youths
of his own age, there was another which reinforced that separation, or at least determined him to become a priest. It was a
murder perpetrated in a fit of passion before his very eyes; and
it occurred on one of those narrow streets for which Granada was
notorious. There was hardly room enough for two men to walk
abreast between the houses, and when another youth, coming in
the direction of Suarez and his companion, refused to step aside,
the latter argued for a little while and then plunged his dagger
into the other's breast. The letting of human blood is always a

horrible thing and one need not be particularly squeamish to be deeply affected by it. Suarez saw the sinfulness as well as the stupidity of this murderous action, and sometimes talked of it as a turning point in his young life.

In the pursuit of a more formal education Suarez spent three or four years in laying a groundwork of language at the University of Granada. Of course, that language was Latin without which you could no more become an educated man than you could cross to New Spain without a ship. The studies were designed for a liberal education, that is, one which fits a man to a fully-rounded life; and these fundamental drills in grammar were necessary for any profession. Latin was the language of the day, spoken by the most vacuous courtier as well as by the most serious bishop. It was the tongue familiar to university professor and college student. There simply was no way of doing without it.

The foundation in grammar melded into the study of rhetoric. Descamps says that Suarez took his rhetoric under the master, John Latin (*Jean Latino*), who taught at Granada for sixty years and who could work the roughest schoolboy composition into a polished piece of literature. This "John Latin" is probably an apocryphal name, suspicious because of its very sound, but the person to whom it applied undoubtedly existed. What his name was matters little; the important fact is that he helped to give Suarez an apt medium for his future writings. These Suarezian productions are written in an easy-flowing, precise style, a pleasure to read and interpret even to-day. More enthusiastic commentators have called his style limpid, elegant, simple, correct.

If we go out of our way to note the boy's early work in school, we may be sure that his teachers and parents did not waste too much praise upon him. It was not that they were afraid of spoiling him by overindulgence or by letting him think he was an infant prodigy. Sober history tells us that he was not intellectually quick in the accepted manner of bright youngsters. When twelve years old, and for many years afterward, he must have seemed discouragingly dull to those who pinned roseate hopes to his scholastic tunic. He found study very hard work, much harder than did his brother John who took all the prizes for his ability in class, and all the bows for his ingenious wit at home. John was cut out to be the follower of his father in the business of convicting or exonerating accused persons. Francis was simply to be the prayerful man of God.

The boy was not an apt learner in the very matters in which he later became one of Spain's greatest teachers. But as he kept his ears and eyes attuned to the affairs transpiring among his father's friends, he became aware of a tremendous wave of new enthusiasm which had been spreading in the Church from northern Spain even down to this Andalusian province. The minions of Loyola, later called the "Jesuit Wolves," the "Machiavellians" and a thousand other names, were gathering their forces for the assault on untruth. They were on the march all over Europe, in Italy, Germany, France, and Spain, and were spreading out into the Asiatic continent. Only fourteen years after their constitutions had been approved by the Pope they opened their first residence at Granada.

Long reputed as the educators of Europe during the seventeenth century, the Jesuits were, first of all, apostolic men. The house which Miguel Torres, provincial of Andalusia, set up at Suarez' native place in 1554, was nothing more than a center for the apostolic ministry. First, arrangements for their coming had to cut through certain legal technicalities, and Suarez' father was the logical person to handle the details. Francis was a chap of six when Torres came to take over the Granadine house for his Order, and the tremendous impression made upon the youngster by this personage is difficult for us to understand.

The least that can be said about the modern Jesuits is that they are simply another of the active Orders working for the glory of God and the advancement of His Church. The least that could have been said about them in the youth of Suarez is that they were the defenders of the papacy and the vanguard of a whole new order of things. Under the inspiration of Ignatius Loyola they descended on the world like a whirlwind cutting a swathe through the middle of the sixteenth century. When Ignatius died in 1556 the Jesuits were known wherever Christianity was known, and they were really only beginning their work.

The Jesuit picture of the previous decade and a half has been modestly painted by Thomas Campbell in his brief history of the Order. He writes that Ignatius during his fifteen years as General (1541–1556) "had seen some of his sons distinguishing themselves in one of the greatest councils of the Church [Trent]; others turning back the tide of Protestantism in Germany and elsewhere; others again, winning a large part of the Orient to the Faith; and still others reorganizing Catholic education throughout regenerated Europe, on a scale that was bewildering both in the multitude of the schools they established and the splendor of their successes. Great saints were being produced in the Society and also outside of it through its ministrations. Meantime its development had been so great that the little group of men which had gathered around him a few years before had grown to a thousand, with a hundred establishments in every part of the world." [2]

The superior of the Jesuits at Granada at this time was a certain Pedro Navarro, a sparkling personality, friendly, genial, saintly, combining the qualities which would captivate even an unimaginative boy like Suarez. He often came on business to the family home and in 1556 brought with him the new provincial, Father Bustamente, who wished to sound out the elder Suarez on the

[2] Campbell, Thomas: *The Jesuits*, New York, 1921, Encyclopedia Press, p. 96.

advisability of moving the Jesuit Novitiate from Cordova to Granada. That was the customary Jesuit procedure: to learn the temper of the inhabitants toward them and the possibilities for success in whatever venture they were contemplating. Many moderns have the idea that they rashly rushed in to start a work and then depended solely on the good providence of God to see them through. Nothing could be further from the facts, and the reasonable Jesuit procedure is demonstrated in the case of Granada where they waited almost thirty years, till 1583, to found their college of San Pablo.

But all was not smooth sailing for the Jesuits at Granada. The charge of breaking the seal of confession was made against one of them, and before it was over Gaspar Suarez had ample opportunity to practice his habit of looking carefully at both sides of a contention. His son, too, was able to profit in his own way in that trait of looking at things twice before judging. The case in question was that of a woman who told a Jesuit that a notorious priest made an improper proposal to her; worse still, he had made the solicitation in the confessional. She refused to abide by the Jesuit's decision when he told her that she must make the thing known to the archbishop; and he in turn refused to grant her absolution. In her loquacious feminine way she spread the calumny that the Jesuits freely broke the seal of the sacrament of penance and that they obliged their penitents to name accomplices in sin.

A wave of opposition and recrimination broke over the city. Of course, the Jesuit priest had acted completely within his right and duty in giving such advice. The affair was not settled even when the archbishop publicly pronounced in his favor and vindicated the conduct and teaching of the Order in this regard. Suarez' uncle, Pedro Vasquez de Utiel, the brother of Antonia, was busily engaged in the controversy because of his position as archdeacon of the city church in Granada, but his intercession,

while it brought the Jesuits and their problems closer to the
Suarez family, could not avail to put an end to the calumny.

Finally, another cleric entered the dispute, a certain John
Ramirez, already a famous preacher, who was appointed by his
superiors to give a series of lectures at Granada to explain and
justify the Order's conduct and doctrine. He performed his task
so brilliantly and so charitably that he left a lasting impression
on the city in general and on Francis Suarez in particular. Later,
when the youth was a student at Salamanca, Ramirez was the
most popular preacher there, and Suarez had the opportunity of
taking up again the threads of friendship with him. Aside from
his father, who made it possible for him to make contacts with
such men, there was probably no other more influential person in
Suarez' young life.

The affable Ramirez was an added inducement for Suarez to
travel to Salamanca for his higher studies. His father, Gaspar,
had himself studied both civil and canon law at that university
and was anxious that his sons take advantage of the legal opportunities there. He knew that the professors were probably the
best to be found in their fields in Spain, and that both of his
sons, the eldest, John, and the second, Francis, would not fail
through lack of able teaching. Their spiritual development would
also go on apace for there were relatives living near Salamanca
who would keep a watchful eye on them, and there were likewise
priestly friends always at hand. Of the latter Ramirez would be
the most watchful.

Thus the two boys started off on their journey to the University of Salamanca in the autumn of 1561. Suarez was only
thirteen and a half years old, and his brother John about fifteen,
but both had finished their literary studies and were now ready
to prepare themselves in actual professional and specialized
studies. As the boys walked away from their home in that narrow street of Granada, Gaspar and Antonia watched them with

mingled feelings. About John they had no worries; he was the bright one, the quick-witted maker of repartee. He would undoubtedly compile a brilliant scholastic record. Of Francis they were more hopeful than confident; he was far behind the other in scholarly promise or achievement. Perhaps he would be a failure.

CHAPTER IV

Salamanca Schoolboy

THE NORTHWARD TREK of the Suarez brothers to the ancient University of Salamanca must not be thought of as a merry jaunt to a diverting collegiate life such as we know it to-day. Nor was it toward the romantic rioting and fabled ribaldry for which mediæval students and schools were supposed to be notorious. Salamanca was a precise and orderly place; its halls and corridors a comfortable, likeable jumble, but its intellectual activity as straight and clear-headed a thing as could be found anywhere.

Salamanca was not then as international in personnel as Paris, Bologna and Oxford, nor as it has since become at various times. But in its scheme of learning it was of a piece with the whole system of the Christian mediæval intellect. Whatever subject it taught, that subject was universal—for such is the very nature of a university. It transcended national and racial boundaries, local prejudices and personal vanities. What Sargent has said of Oxford was true of Salamanca: "They were clear-headed men, practised in disputation, and merciless in their logic, . . . mists that existed in adjoining regions disappeared. Fairy tales could not enter it. Enthusiasms found themselves there sorely chastened. Precipitancy was rebuked." [1]

The scholastic work here was a continuation of that which had been started by the two brothers at Granada. There were no fanciful and willful excursions into special realms of research until all the rounded scheme had been traversed. The reality of

[1] Sargent, Daniel: *Thomas More,* New York, 1933, Sheed and Ward, p. 11.

a substantial foundation had to be firmly made of the various stones which even back to the age of Cicero had constituted the edifice of the liberal arts. They were seven in number, the first three unalterable: Grammar, Rhetoric and Dialectic; the four others insisted upon with more or less severity: Arithmetic, Geometry, Music, Astronomy. These had been taught at Granada as well as at Salamanca, as indeed in every university of Europe in those centuries. The thing now in hand was to follow those studies, which, for reasons of a practical kind, were flourishing at that time. First of all, Philosophy, and then, if one was to become a cleric, the supreme citadel of Theology, or if not a cleric, the study of Political and International Law.

Since John was to follow in the legal footsteps of his father he inscribed his name in the register of the Faculty of Civil Law. At this point he is pretty much lost sight of. That was in November, 1561, and in the following November he signed up again for the same course; but he seems soon to have tired of the place and returned to complete his studies in his native town of Granada. The records of the university show that Francis Suarez attended the lectures of the Faculty of Canon Law for three years before he entered the Novitiate of the Jesuits. His accomplishments were anything but phenomenal; in fact he barely got through the examinations.

The success or failure of a student was not the fault of the university or its professors. Suarez' life span covered the midway point, and extended on both sides, in the two centuries that have been called Spain's Golden Age. It was the flourishing period of Spanish expansion and hegemony which, as Bertrand remarks, "coincided with an extraordinary intellectual, literary and artistic development. This great movement maintained its impetus for nearly two hundred years, and its influence extended all over Europe and even to the New World. At this period a number of universities was founded, side by side with the old university centers of Alcalá and Salamanca. There were more than thirty of them in the Peninsula." [2]

The influence of the Jesuits was already being felt in the colleges and universities of Spain, and this influence extended beyond those schools then being opened all over the country. Even the ancient schools of Salamanca and Alcalá received the impetus of Europe's newest educators. Modernization was taking place in the art of teaching, and it was the Jesuits who were responsible for it "by giving a larger place in it to the study of the humanities and by reviving the study of classical antiquity. Colleges of theirs were established in the principal cities of the kingdom. In Spain, as elsewhere, they educated generations of humanists." [3]

Even before the advent of Suarez to Salamanca the following cities of Spain welcomed the opening of Jesuit colleges: Gandia, where philosophy was being taught as early as 1546, Cordova at the end of 1553, and in chronological order: Medina del Campo, Burgos, Plasencia, Monterey, Murcia and Ocaña. All of these resulted from the work of that supreme organizer among Jesuits, Jerome Nadal, and of other competent men, among whom was Suarez' friend and adviser, John Ramirez. Loyola had sent Nadal to the peninsula with instructions that "he should introduce the method followed in Italy into the new Spanish and Portuguese colleges, particularly in the more important centers and where he saw there was hope of doing the most spiritual good."

But the university to which Gaspar Suarez had sent his sons was almost three and a half centuries older than any of the Jesuit colleges in Spain. The Order opened a simple and unpretentious college of its own at the University of Salamanca in 1595, but did not inaugurate its large and famous College of the Holy

---

[2] Bertrand and Petrie, *op. cit.,* p. 350.
[3] *Ibid.,* p. 350.

Spirit until twenty years later when Philip III presented it.[4] The ancient university traced its beginnings back to 1212 when Spain was much at odds with the Moslems and in the very year that Alfonso IX administered to them a rousing defeat at Las Navas de Tolosa. Gratitude for this victory prompted him to found a seat of learning for the glory of God. His son, Saint Ferdinand III, and his grandson, Alfonso X, called "The Wise," followed out his wishes in concentrating much time, energy and money in its building.

But there were other matters more urgent than learning, in the following century, with the necessary result that the progress of the university was slow. The site of the school filled the requirements of an ancient Spanish law decreeing that a university city "should have a healthy climate and pleasant surroundings" so that both masters and scholars should "in the evening find pleasant diversions." But weather and environment are not the most important assets of learning, and the school languished somewhat until the beginning of the fifteenth century when Pope Benedict XIII enlarged and enriched it to such extent that he was called its second founder. Ferdinand and Isabella likewise had a hand in its attainment to preëminence among European universities. About the time that the Saurez brothers attended, the university had what was probably its record enrollment, approximately sixty-eight hundred students. The annals for the year 1822 showed only four hundred and twelve, and in later years even this number was decimated.

So the young canonist was there at the height of the school's reputation and glory, and when it was living up to the words officially inscribed on its device: *Princeps omnium scientiarum*

---

[4] His wife, Margaret of Austria, died in 1611 leaving a large donation in her will for the foundation of the College. Philip added more money to the bequest, and the cornerstone was placed in 1617. Cf. Astrain, Antonio, *Historia de la Compañía de Jesús en la Asistencia de España,* Madrid, 1916, vol. v, pp. 31–38.

Salamanca docet. Forty-three colleges, twenty-one monasteries and seventeen convents were grouped around the university, forming its nucleus and making it a cocoon of intellectual advancement. And the purpose of it all was never lost sight of. Suarez himself is the apt embodiment of the thought which Pope Alexander IV expressed when he declared that he approved the courses at Salamanca "because in the multitude of their wise men is the security of nations, and their governments are maintained as much by the advice of the prudent as by the energy and bravery of the strong."

Up to the time of Francis Suarez, bodily strength was a particular ancestral quality. Stretching back down the centuries from his grandfather's time there were more soldiers than scholars in the family line. By their energy and bravery they had made secure, in their own individual ways, the nation of Spain, but this was an age of another kind of strength. With the coming of Suarez there was an achievement of intellect rather than of brawn, and by the advice of the scholars who followed the prudence of Francis, there was, at least in theory, a possibility of national security. What held true of the age following him holds true in this, our own day, and the attention which is now being paid to his teachings is an unflattering reminder that the best of international and national theories have not been discovered in the twentieth century. Even though force seems predominant in modern times, there will ever be a harking back to the need for wisdom.

When you talk of Spanish universities you cannot mention Salamanca without, in the same breath, bringing up the name of Alcalá. It was founded somewhat later that Salamanca, but in the student days of Suarez it was highly favored by Philip II who sent his rascally son, Don Carlos, to blight the lives of students and professors there. Philip's predilection for Alcalá is probably accounted for by the fact that the great Cardinal Ximenez, former prime minister of Spain and trusted friend of Ferdinand and Isabella, had practically rejuvenated the school. It was the Cardinal's idea that the students, instead of the professors as at Salamanca, should yearly elect the rector, and this decision led to some riotous happenings at Alcalá.

Suarez was not faring well with his books in the Spring of 1562 but Carlos at the University of Alcalá had other things than books on his mind. Philip's son by his first wife, Maria of Portugal, was three years older than Suarez and was just entering that age when young men engage in what has been called the "sowing of wild oats," but what the English envoy preferred to term "the hasty following of a wench." Carlos, his cousin, Alexander Farnese, later the Duke of Parma, and his uncle, the famous Don Juan of Austria, were all about the same age and were supposed to be following the lectures at Alcalá. Don Carlos had the misfortune of falling down the stairs of a public stew, was mentally injured more than his royal father cared to admit, and thenceforth became more recklessly self-indulgent and criminally vicious than before.[5]

Don Carlos died in 1568 after causing his father and the royal court, as well as the men who tried to teach him at the university, more trouble than usually comes from a single headstrong youth. Incidents such as those for which he was accountable put the schools in ill repute and give much credence to speculations about town and gown rivalry which dated back even to the early days of the University of Paris. Undoubtedly there was gaiety in student life, and a great deal of viciousness. Insubordination was no new thing at Alcalá, where the wrangling between students and townspeople and between students and professors, had to be harshly handled more than once. As a matter of fact discipline had got so far out of hand there that the faculties seriously considered, in 1518, removal to Madrid. But the kings

[5] Loth, David, *op. cit.*, pp. 154–155.

of Spain took such personal interest in the place during the six-
teenth century that the thought was abandoned. At its height
Alcalá never had more than about a third as many students as
Salamanca.

As far as we can find out Francis Suarez never even approached
the excessive antics which Don Carlos was given to in student
days. It was not that the opportunities for such adventure were
missing in his own university town. The school was under better
control but the town was as wide open as any other notorious
locality of the times. Nor was it that Suarez had no taste for passing pleasures. The necrologist who wrote his obituary shortly
after his death, remarks that in his student days "he was completely given over to the pleasures of his age and asked nothing more than to have a good time." For the edification of pious
ears, however, he cautiously adds: "But he never fell into bad
ways."

Even if this statement were taken at its face value it would not
necessarily lead us to the conclusion that Suarez was a young
debauchee. Being "completely given over to the pleasures of his
age" might mean anything from the most innocent frivolities to
the most wicked libertinism. Happily there is no need to read a
low meaning into it. Had he sinned occasionally and grievously
as a youth he would not have been totally ostracized from the
company of his contemporaries. Other men and women, who
were later raised to the altar as canonized saints, admitted more
heinous offenses than this unsupported and meager testimony
of Suarez indicates. But the same commentator relieves our speculation regarding his youthful purity by remarking that "an unusually delicate modesty safeguarded his innocence, and in these
matters he blushed at trifles."

During these three years at school Suarez developed an
amiable nature even if he did not become a wild young man
about town. The world was opening for him in a way that it

never could through his books; books to which he still had an
instinctive repugnance. His talent for companionship made him
an admirable friend to fellow students just as it later made him
deeply loved by the boys who studied under him. A talent for
music, too, was somewhere hidden among his qualities, for he
enjoyed "falling asleep to the sound of the mandoline and
waking to that of the merry voices of the students." The whole
large world was certainly not his oyster, but he was able to pry
open the delights of the little part of it in which he moved.

The concomitant of amiability is too often thought to be
wealth, and in the case of Suarez there was more than sufficient
of the latter. He was not, nor had he any need to be, the literary
starveling who is frequently alluded to as a typical result of early
university life. His father's wealth and position, the ancient
reputation of his family, the qualities of his own friendly nature,
all of these made popularity among the students a foregone conclusion. Although he was only a little more than sixteen when
he entered the Jesuit Order, he had really lived beyond his years.
The youths of that time developed faster, and this was especially
true of the southern and Mediterranean section of Europe. It is
no wonder then that Suarez could count a host of friends and
intimates to bid him adieu when he left the pleasant world for a
higher way of life.

But that decision to leave the world was slow in forming. His
early tonsure meant that he was considered a cleric, but many a
cleric never went beyond that initial step toward the priesthood.
He recalled his family's aspirations for his priestly vocation, but
thoughts of this nature were not always uppermost in his mind.
Above and beyond all that the most serious obstacle confronted
him here and now. To become a worthy priest one had first to
be a worthy student, and Suarez was anything but a lover of
study. All of these things passed through his mind, and in order
to dispense with them he frequently went to the room of his old

friend, Ramirez, whenever that priestly Jesuit's assiduous labors allowed him time for consultation. There were friendly, if unsatisfying chats, between this experienced man and this eager boy, but the spark of divine grace did not seem to catch fire until the Lent of 1564.

John Ramirez was not a particularly learned man as learned men then went, but like so many men who have mastered a few things perfectly he had a way of divulging his convictions that made others conform to his ideas. Coleridge calls him "a plain and severe man, who had great influence over the young men of the university." [6] He appeared so in his official public rôle, but Suarez knew him in a more genial and intimate capacity. His sincerity and humility were the most influential things about him.

As a fully matured priest who had been a popular preacher even before he entered the noviceship of the Society of Jesus, Father Ramirez could be affable with the most hardened sinners. He could speak tenderly of the love of Christ to prostitutes who had known only carnal love before; and he could bring a score of them to repentant knees, as he did on one occasion, by the preaching of a single sermon. He could relate majestically the heroism of those who gave their lives entirely to Christ's service, and could bring five hundred applicants to religious orders by a series of Lenten sermons.

Just before coming to Salamanca for the Lent of 1564 he had been preaching with great success at Saragossa. When the assignment came to take the Jesuit pulpit in the university town he humbly protested that a more scholarly and capable man should be sent in his place. His own sermons were the kind that "suit popular audiences, without any great polish or refinement. He was afraid of the fastidious tastes of the academic critics of Salamanca. He might seem to them either commonplace or too

[6] Coleridge, *op. cit.*, p. 55.

free." These legitimate objections were overruled by his superiors with the result that he talked his way into the hearts of his new audiences.

Suarez was one of the most eager listeners there. What he liked most of all about the preacher was his uncompromising attitude on matters where there could be no mistaking the right. Women's dresses, especially the low bodice of the period, were something of a scandal in the town and Ramirez bluntly told the women to cover up. His denunciation of more important scandal, the sin of uncharitableness in deception and lying, was of an even more vehement nature. This placing of the sin against charity as one of the most offensive wrongs of men shows a nice discrimination on the part of the preacher, especially in an age when less discerning men were heaping brimstone and ashes on sins of the flesh, and allowing injustice and uncharitableness to go unheeded. He was utterly convinced that there were two all-important commandments, and both of them began with the imperative: Love. Like Christ, and like the Eagle of Patmos, he could not but teach that command.

. The effects of the Lenten sermons at Salamanca were incredible. "Manners became so much improved that street-rows were at an end; the professors sometimes suspended their lectures at the times of his sermons, and crowded round his pulpit along with their scholars." [7] But on the positive side the result was even more astounding—approximately one-twelfth of the whole student body made application to enter various religious orders.

The number of religious vocations suddenly blossoming at this time is staggering, and really taxes one's credence in the fact-grubbers of those times. There seems, nevertheless, to be some unanimity among them regarding the tremendous wave of zeal which occurred after Ramirez' talks. About two hundred

[7] *Ibid.*, p. 55.

are supposed to have been received into the religious novitiates within four months of Easter, and three hundred more before the end of the year. Round numbers like these are always suspect, and suspicion grows when a third round number appears, that of the fifty boys who asked admission into the Jesuit Order. The truth is probably found in a number somewhat below those given, but there can be no doubt of the fact that an unusually large group of men and women became members of religious orders that year because of Father Ramirez.

But quantity does not beget quality and of all of those who went off to monasteries and convents from Salamanca in 1564 none ever achieved even a shadow of the vogue which came to Suarez in his own generation. Francis was as deeply moved as any of them and felt that the time had come for his first step along the highroad that leads to spiritual sublimity. After all, as Ramirez had pointed out, this was a dangerous age when continuous wars were depopulating Europe and sudden death came from unconquerable diseases. There was only one thing to do: give back to God the body and soul He had created, and give them back in such manner that they could be used to His greater glory and to Francis' ultimate sanctification.

The promise was easy to make to himself for he was, as a cleric, more or less conditioned for the spiritual life, but when he came to apply for admission he made the unflattering discovery that the Jesuits did not want him. He might try another place where the entrance requirements were not so high, but only serious and capable students need apply to this new Order! No one who "fled from the very sight of books," and who "seemed incapable of overcoming his repugnance for them," could conceivably gain admittance to this group of intellectual men who were changing the teaching habits of Europe. Perhaps Bartholomew Fernandez, rector of the Jesuit house at Salamanca, told him a great deal more than this. Undoubtedly he was suavely gentle, but he was nonetheless adamant in his refusal.

So the boy was turned away—the only one of the fifty who had applied; and it was because he could not satisfy the triple qualification which is still a *sine qua non* to the priesthood. Morally, intellectually and physically, a youth must be of priestly timber before he can be admitted to a seminary or novitiate. Suarez was morally fit, for he had no vicious habits. He was told, however, that his talents were not of a high enough grade for one who would have to study and teach all the rest of his life. For this too he would need a more robust physical constitution than he possessed. Perhaps if his body were fatter and his mind leaner he would be allowed to enter.

At this point in the story of Suarez all of his biographers stop to ask the question: How could it be that one of the most brilliant intellects in the Society of Jesus was at first refused admission for lack of talent? None of them answers the question but all agree that he was refused because he appeared too stupid to make the grade. They say the event is inexplicable, but they forget that nothing is inexplicable and nothing impossible in the providence of God who, more often than not, selects the weak to confound the strong.

There was nothing that Suarez could do about the decision of Father Fernandez at Salamanca. But there was something he could do at Valladolid, and at the advice and recommendation of Ramirez he went there to interview the Provincial of Castile. This was John Suarez, of the same name but of no kinship whatsoever with Francis, who had recently been installed as head of the newly created province. He listened patiently to the boy, questioned him again according to the formula that Francis had gone through at the university, called in the consulters and examiners and asked them to test the candidate. When it was all over he gravely shook his head. He was very sorry indeed, but there was simply no place for a lack-wit like this.

CHAPTER V

Into the Spiritual School

YEARS AFTERWARD Francis Suarez could look back with something like humor in his eyes at the grim heartache he suffered through this double refusal. Then he was known as the greatest theologian the Jesuits had ever produced, and the learned Lessius could write to Bellarmine that "Suarez is a man of shrewd intelligence." Then Pope Paul V wanted him to remain at Rome after successfully solving knotty theological problems and King Philip II demanded that he come to the University of Coimbra to lend prestige to that place. But all of that was in the dim future, and neither Suarez nor his examiners at Valladolid could have believed that such a picture could ever be painted by the brush of time.

The boy insisted on hanging around the headquarters of the Jesuit provincial. He refused absolutely to go home to Granada or to return to school at Salamanca. He knew what he wanted: to enter the religious life, to give himself completely to the service of God and the Church; and he definitely wanted to do that in the Jesuit Order and in no other. His could not have been an obnoxious persistence, for men of the caliber of the reverend provincial can usually make short shrift of such annoyance, if they wish to.

Evidently, then, Father Suarez did not dismiss the case of Francis Suarez forthright from his mind. One of the early Jesuits testifies that this superior was an excellent judge of character, a man of more than ordinary spiritual attainments, and a careful

49

director of young people. He pondered the matter for a few days, again called his consulters together and told them that he felt the young Granadine should be given a trial. "Your advice is very wise," he said, "and if I followed it I would be following my own judgment. But I cannot. Some interior power inclines my will in the opposite direction."

Men who are in a position to direct the destinies of a Jesuit province do not act merely upon some vague inner urge. We can be sure that he had a rational conviction that it would be worth while at least to give the importunate young man a chance to prove himself of that stern stuff which is the raw material of which priests are made. The necrologist later wrote that Francis had studied for eight years "but without success, and little hope could be entertained of his future work." As for his physical equipment, De Scorraille comments that "his appearance was always somewhat frail and he may have appeared even more so at an age when his body had not reached its full development." [1]

Certainly in the eyes of his consulters the provincial was thrusting himself in the way of coming trouble. The status of the Suarez family, the position of the parents, the reputation of Suarezian ancestry—and all of these counted for much more in those days than they do in ours—must have raised a warning. If the boy did not make good he would have to be sent home, and that would be a disgrace to a Spanish family of proud rank. In the face of these hurdles the provincial made his decision, gave the boy some cheerful encouragement and sent him back to Salamanca with a letter for Father Fernandez.

Francis hurried back to the university town in a gleeful state of mind. Nothing could hinder him now from becoming a Jesuit; the ticket of admission was in his possession. He would not even take time out to journey southword for a last farewell with his parents at Granada, even though this omission meant

[1] De Scorraille, *op. cit.*, p. 44.

that he would never see them again. Arriving at the Jesuit
rectory in Salamanca he thrust the provincial's letter into the
hands of Father Fernandez, who was still somewhat dubious
about the whole thing but who dutifully followed his superior's
recommendation.

Suarez wished to become a priest and to enter the noviceship
with that wish clearly understood; but it was not so easy as he
thought. According to the Constitutions of the Order, as drawn
up by Ignatius Loyola, superiors were to protect themselves
against just such questionable recruits as Suarez. When they
were not sure that a young man could fulfill the conditions required, or felt that he might make a better lay brother than a
priest, the Jesuit superiors were to accept him as *indifferent*. In
other words, he was not promised anything definitely for the
future. He would have to content himself with accepting whatever choice might be made for him: to continue toward the
priesthood, to remain a teaching cleric, or to become a lay brother.

The boy was accepted at the Jesuit residence as *indifferent* on
June 16, 1564, and for twelve days he made a study of the rules,
regulations, constitutions, and so forth, of the new life he was
entering upon. This is still the custom for all who enter the
Order: they are given an opportunity to see at first hand just what
they are expected to do, the kind of discipline they must submit
themselves to, the vows and promises they must make. The
Order, at the same time, is enabled to look over the candidate
as a preliminary to the more detailed scrutiny he will receive
during the novitiate training period. Suarez passed through all
this before receiving his cassock.

An entry on the old registers of Salamanca informs us where
he was born, who his father and mother were, that they were
"amply provided with means of subsistence," how many brothers
and sisters he had, and how many years he had studied. It states
further that "He has not yet promised to renounce his possessions.

Having read the Bulls and the Constitutions and the Examen which summarizes them, he finds that he is bound by no impediment, and he declares that he wishes to conform to them in all things with the help of God. He was examined as *indifferent*. In testimony of which he has signed his name on June 28, 1564."

Besides the signature of the novice, Francis Suarez, there is also that of the rector, Bartholomew Fernandez. In still another handwriting there is appended the remark that "He has made the renunciation concerning his possessions." And in the margin near the entry, probably scrawled there years later by some unknown but observant person, is the terse and telling sentence: "This is the celebrated author."

When asked whether he was satisfied to be received in the rather uncertain and unflattering status of *indifferent*, Suarez declared that he had but one desire: to be allowed to enter the Society of Jesus, and to live therein for God alone, in any position at all. As a matter of later history he actually asked to remain in the Order as a lay brother since he himself was convinced that he could not successfully complete even the fundamental courses in philosophy. Thus he was in perfect accord with the common opinion of his superiors and his other contemporaries. And that accord has frequently been alluded to by his admirers as a mark of supreme humility and of utter disregard of the human respect that he, as a member of the ancient Suarez family, could rightfully expect.

If true humility is a recognition of truth—and it is nothing more than that—the boy was sincerely humble. The common, modern misapprehension is that humility is a cowering thing; that the humble person is an ignoble character. But the modern definition is terribly awry. It requires real courage to look squarely at the facts in one's own case and to come to the honest conclusion that certain qualities are present and such and such others missing. Psychologically it is a bold stroke when one acts on those conclusions; and it is a paradox that only through such self-revelation can one gain a tractable self-confidence. Suarez had ample time to arrive at a self-analysis in the novitiate, even if he had not had ample opportunity to realize it from the considered judgments of others about himself.

The provincial had in the meanwhile come from Valladolid to Salamanca to look over the current crop of prospective Jesuits. There were six others besides Suarez and none of them seemed to satisfy the complete and rigid requirements the Society demanded of its recruits. He wrote in the third week of June to the Jesuit general, Lainez, at Rome that "We have just received seven subjects of middling worth and shall probably admit five better ones soon." It is improbable that this screed pleased Lainez. He was the immediate successor of Loyola and had his spiritual master's intense distaste for human mediocrity within the Order. In about six months he would be replaced by another Spaniard, Francis Borgia, who was likewise averse to "subjects of middling worth."

At any rate Suarez was in, and he intended to remain in. The novitiate was at Medina del Campo, just outside of the city, and he stayed there an uncommonly short time, from July until October of that year. The period of probation, which Loyola had set for those who would enter the Order, was two years, longer than that of any other Order or congregation in the Church, either then or now. But Suarez did not pronounce his vows until 1566. In the meanwhile he returned to study philosophy at the University of Salamanca, still retaining the title of *indifferent novice.*

Biographers have tried to make out a case for the spiritual influence of the famed Alphonse Rodriguez on Francis Suarez. The facts in the matter are that Rodriguez was at this time the appointed spiritual director at the Jesuit house in Salamanca, and that the novice master at Medina del Campo was Antonio de

Avendaño. Thus it is patent that the young tyro came under the direct instruction of both of these men, of the latter when he went through the Spiritual Exercises of St. Ignatius, and of the former when he returned, still a novice, to his studies at the university. The importance of both men, and the importance of both experiences, cannot be glossed over in the light of what was yet to occur in the life of this future celebrity. The Exercises, in the form of a retreat, were, and still are, a kind of spiritual revolution of the individual. The Jesuit art of spiritual direction, in the person of Rodriguez, was, and still is, a kind of standard pattern.

Francis Thompson has called the Spiritual Exercises "the Excalibur of Ignatius . . . which he had evolved from his own experience at Manresa, a graduated process of religious preparation based on subtle spiritual psychology, a turnstile through which only the fit and few could pass." [2] They were a new idea which broke away from the rigid formalism of the past and made possible a novel spiritual athleticism. Men had always believed in taking physical exercise for the benefit of their bodies; Ignatius in his simple way taught that spiritual exercise would be a tremendous good for their souls. The theory and its practice have since been as much a part of the Society as its constitutions and rules.

Because of its extraordinary influence in bringing about a regeneration of soul—when used in the hands of a competent director—perhaps no other book its size has ever evoked similar commentaries. From the ridiculous assertion that "haggard men practice spiritual and physical orgies in subterranean caverns" to the sublime praise which Popes and saints have heaped upon it, this diminutive volume has undergone every grade of criticism. Actually, it is no mysterious mumbo-jumbo of incantations, as Suarez and thousands of other people since his time have discovered. It is simply a logical sequence of related facts which

[2] Thompson, Francis: *Saint Ignatius Loyola*, ed. by John Pollen, London, 1909, Burns, Oates and Washbourne, p. 33.

must be fully grasped by the exercitant—and then put into action. "Its very simplicity excites suspicion;" writes Campbell, "its apparent jejuneness suggests all sorts of mysterious and malignant designs." [3]

Suarez was no exception to the custom which all Jesuits still follow in the matter of the Exercises. Each must go through them for thirty days in the noviceship and again for the same period of time when he has completed his course of intensive training. During the summer months the Exercises are given by priests in condensed form of an eight-day retreat, or even in three-day retreats for the laity. The exercitant is guided toward Christian piety and devotion by the consideration of fundamental truths: creation and the goodness of the Creator to the individual, the reasonableness of avoiding sin, the perfection of following Christ's counsels, the happiness of loving God completely. The psychological effect is the strengthening of one's will to act in accord with one's rational conclusions. When people emerge to act as different men they are thought to have undergone some strange metamorphosis at the manipulation of Jesuit intrigue.

The effect on the young novice of Medina del Campo was exactly this. He was even more fully determined that he should remain forever a religious. Previous to his retreat he had been unshakable in that resolve. Superiors had not been able to dissuade him from entering; now only their direct command could have convinced him that his high ideal was impossible for him. Any trial they could now devise for him in the probationary period would not discourage him. He was pious, zealous and humble, for the life which he was now living was a continual endeavor toward the most perfect virtue. Coleridge opines that "if he had not been so renowned afterwards as a theologian, his name might still have been handed down to us as that of a reli-

[3] Campbell, *op. cit.,* p. 13.

gious of remarkable sanctity even in those days, when saintly souls were plentiful." [4]

The habit of life that Suarez now entered was poles apart from the merry student life wherein, as some have suggested, he may have been an easy-going loafer. There was a goad which pricked him on to careful performance of detailed duties. It was the will to please God in all things, through the commands of superiors, and to make the most of the trials purposely designed to temper the novice. Martindale, writing about Aloysius Gonzaga, who was to enter the Society and die in it before the end of that century, says that "the noviceship is a tissue of minutiæ. Save the general upshot of the training, nothing matters really. But since everything does enter into a general training, each thing matters very much, for it would be a frightful thing to reject the ordinary life to which men are called, embark upon a training which has no object whatsoever but to produce a certain character, and then not to do that training properly. Not only would that character not be created, but the character which sound worldly experience would have been creating, would have escaped the grasp; . . . It is a very serious thing indeed to enter a novitiate." [5]

Novices are always masters of minutiæ. They are letter-perfect in the performance of all those little duties which follow each other in the rapidly mutable schedule of the day. Put any one of them, after he has been through the Long Retreat and has got the feel of the thing, out among his former companions and they will awfully whisper of him that he is a saint. The danger is always present that a certain external woodenness will be mistaken for virtue, that the scrupulous observance of every regulation will develop a stultifying and rigid exterior deportment at the expense of a spiritually rich and pliable character. That is where

---

[4] Coleridge, op. cit., p. 57.

[5] Martindale, C. C.: *The Vocation of Aloysius Gonzaga*, London, 1927, Sheed and Ward, p. 141.

the importance of the master, or director, of novices can be appreciated in making or breaking some of his charges. He is the one
who shows to them the meat and meaning in otherwise trivial
actions.

"It cannot be denied," remarks Foley, "that each master of
novices does give his own impress to the precious heritage St.
Ignatius has left his sons. One will emphasize this phase of
Jesuit spirituality, another will prefer to insist on that." [6] In this
respect Francis Suarez was extremely fortunate, for he had the
master of masters as his spiritual director during more than a year
of his noviceship. When he came back to the Jesuit house in
Salamanca after several months at Medina del Campo he found
Alphonse Rodriguez there in the official capacity of Spiritual
Father to the Community. This author of the famous *Practice of
Christian Perfection* was still a young and vigorous priest at the
time Suarez came under his direction. His peculiar emphasis on
Ignatian spirituality was such that his work has become a tradi-
tional part of the novice-training, not only in the Society, but in
many other religious Orders as well.

Rodriguez was then thirty-nine years old, born twenty-two
years before Suarez in the city of Valladolid. He came to Salamanca in 1546 and was one of the first to join the Society of
Jesus at that place. He had begun to teach moral theology shortly
after completing his course of studies and it was his duty also to
deliver the spiritual exhortations which are given weekly in
Jesuit houses. Shortly after Suarez' departure from Salamanca
he was sent to Montille in the province of Andalusia, where he
spent most of the rest of his life as master of novices. The book
on Christian perfection, the only work of his pen ever published,
appeared in 1609, became immediately popular, and has endured
till this day. It enjoyed more than twenty-five editions in the

---

[6] Foley, Albert: *A Modern Galahad, St. John Berchmans,* Milwaukee, 1937,
Bruce, p. 75.

original Spanish, sixty in the French translation, twenty in Italian, ten in German, eight in Latin, and several in English, as well as in several languages of the East. Rodriguez died in 1616, just one year before his most prominent spiritual son.

Nothing can give us a better picture of the scheme which Suarez was following during his noviceship than a scrutiny of Father Rodriguez' book. It was compiled from the notes he used in giving talks to the Jesuit community and in shaping the religious neophytes along the lines of Ignatian spirituality. Given to practical men who would have the very practical job of remodeling the stiff stuff of men's morals, these talks purposely avoided lofty flights of mysticism. They take concrete cases as models in place of abstruse speculation. They show the psychological approach to perfection as well as the manner in which personal perfection can redound to the wholesome benefit of one's neighbor. Adverse criticism can be given them only on the score that they abound in allegories and metaphors, an ancient Eastern influence among religious writers that is now happily archaic.

Particularly applicable to the position of Suarez, in the otherwise deadening routine of the novitiate, is Rodriguez' advice concerning the performance of minute actions. "And this is the difference," he told the novices, "between a good and perfect religious and an imperfect and tepid one; the difference lies not in the doing of more or different things in this case and in that, but in doing what one does perfectly or imperfectly. For this reason is the one a good and perfect religious, that he gets these things well done; and for this is the other imperfect, that he does them with much tepidity and negligence. And the more a man lays himself out and goes forward in this particular, the more perfect or imperfect will he be." [7] There is no straining for literary effect in these pages of his printed work, no suasive-

[7] Rodriguez, Alphonse: *Practice of Perfection and Christian Virtues,* translated from the original Spanish by Joseph Rickaby (in three volumes), Chicago, 1929, Loyola University Press, vol. i, p. 96.

ness in attempting to paint over the hard spots in complete religious observance.

The hard reality of the spiritual life, not only in the matter of personal advancement but also in that of the social phase, was brought out by this master when he spoke of mutual relationships among men. The religious who scrupulously performs every small action may still be a thorn in the side of his fellows. Rodriguez insists on the great fundamental virtue of charity. "I say, then, that we ought to have a good opinion of all our brethren and not believe they are so thin-skinned as to be angry for any small matter; but this does not exempt us from using as much caution and moderation in dealing with them as if they were more brittle than glass and the weakest creatures in the world, not giving them on our part any occasion of annoyance or irritation, however weak or imperfect they may be. And this caution we should keep for two reasons. One reason touches ourselves; it is that, however much virtue another has, that does not make our action cease to be our fault; and again for a second reason, touching our neighbor, that not all people on all occasions are so well disposed, or so well in form, as not to be sensible of the offenses we commit against them." [8] There is much more in the same strain of this careful wisdom, and its common sense has made of the work a popular Christian guide book for more than three centuries.

Suarez was young and impressionable during the two years he spent under the influence of Alphonse Rodriguez, imbibing fully these sound words of advice and putting them into practice. His strides toward the Jesuit ideal, at a time when that ideal was being exemplified by saints like Kostka, Borgia and Bellarmine, were long and sure. Men who lived with him at that time remarked that his observance was letter-perfect and, what is more important, seemed to exhibit a perfection of spirit. His personal

[8] *Ibid.,* p. 222.

probity is more apparent in later life when there is a great deal more testimony concerning it, but in retrospect his contemporaries declared that there was in him a perceptible growth in holiness during the time of his probation.

There is always one important consideration that must not be overlooked when we are discussing the members of a young religious congregation or order. Benedictines, Dominicans, Augustinians, all of the Orders of the Church, show in their early years a kind of flame that is hard to define from a natural point of view. Later on, the members do not perform less laudable work, but they seem to lack the zealous fire which suddenly flared high at their inception. Perhaps this is an illusion brought on by the proximity of men around us to-day. Perhaps distance lends a perspective which was not available to men living in those days, and a perspective of three hundred added years may put us moderns in a better light than we now admit to ourselves. At any rate, we are more or less convinced that giants walked the earth in other times and that the men who immediately followed in the footsteps of a religious founder were more zealous, capable, and holy than are our moderns.

The aura that surrounds the name of Suarez is one that gives meaning to such consideration. His later accomplishments of a spiritual nature bespeak the reputation for holiness which he earned in the noviceship. But one problem looms large before us: the about-face which occurred in his intellectual activities. Everywhere else we find slow, natural growth, a gradual evolution from earlier indications to the complete flowering in mature years. Rationalize as we will, we cannot escape the fact that only a supernatural force could have changed Suarez from a mediocre incompetent to one of the most dazzling intellects of his time. At this point the provincial still believed that he was of ordinary intelligence, and Suarez himself, discouraged at his failure to make progress, wished to become a lay brother.

CHAPTER VI

The Birth of Brilliance

WHILE SUAREZ was struggling with the fundamentals of philosophy in the Autumn of 1564 the whole Jesuit educational scheme was still a fluid thing. The *Ratio Studiorum* or, as Dr. Allan Farrell renders it in English, the Jesuit Code of Liberal Education, was being experimented with in Italy, Spain and Portugal. To the ultimate formulation of that code Suarez himself was to contribute no little of his time and knowledge thirty years later. And now he was learning through inevitable experience some of the things which he would then recommend as techniques in studying and teaching. In the meanwhile plans had been drafted and sent to all the provinces, and in the years 1561 and 1562 Jerome Nadal himself came to Spain to investigate educational program and progress.

In the many drafts of the preliminary Code which had been contributed from the Jesuit colleges all over Europe there were endless specific suggestions and regulations. In practically all of them, however, there appeared one fundamental rule, regulative of Jesuit studies even before Suarez entered the Society. It was the one which the young Spaniard now attempted to follow most religiously. It told the student to "pray to God for knowledge; but meanwhile study as if He would not grant your prayer without hard, studious effort on your part." [1] It is the rock-bottom explanation of that educational phenomenon which some have

[1] Farrell, Allan: *The Jesuit Code of Liberal Education*, Milwaukee, 1938, Bruce. Photostatic facsimile of manuscript, facing p. 431.

been pleased to call Jesuit genius. And the modern result of that dictum is not far different from the result which occurred as a startling change in Suarez.

The first scholastic block that seriously stumbled the youth was the abstract study of logic. No one who has not been thrust suddenly from the more practical pursuits of the work-a-day world into the rarefied atmosphere of abstract thinking can fully appreciate his situation. Most students get over their bewilderment after a short period of careful reflection, but Suarez seemed to get more entangled the more he studied the subject. He asked foolish questions of his professors and then realized that his queries were stupid mainly because he himself did not even know clearly what he wanted to ask. His nickname from the first was the Dumb Ox just as St. Thomas's had been centuries before him, but like Thomas he eventually lived down that ignominious title. While he laughed at himself he inwardly became oppressed with a sense of intellectual inferiority.

His professor, Father Andres Martinez, was an exception to the brilliant breed of educationists who cannot stomach stupid students. He went out of his way to be of help to Suarez, gave him personal instructions, and appointed one of his best students to repeat the daily matter of the classes with him. The marked ability of this classmate tended to make the youth even more conscious of his own inability. The more he studied and prayed the less he seemed to grasp of the class matter. Rather than become panicky over the thing, as many another has done, he decided to lay the matter before his superior and to ask for work more suitable, in any corner of the Society that should be assigned to him.

The superiors Francis had during his course of philosophy, and with whom he freely discussed his intellectual ineptitude, were several in number. Father Fernandez left for Rome in the Spring of 1565. Suarez' old friend, Ramirez, took his place for

a short time and then departed for his favorite work of preaching. Father de Segura was appointed vice-rector only to be sup-
planted by Pedro Sanchez. Finally, Martin Gutierrez, the man
most instrumental in Suarez' metamorphosis, became rector, but
that was only in 1568 when Francis was already pursuing the
course of theology. So Gutierrez was not the superior when this
vast change took place in the young novice. Like Ramirez he was
one of the advisers with whom the boy frankly discussed the
problem of cramming knowledge into a sluggish brain.

A wise prescription in the Jesuit Order provides that a scholastic may go for advice to any of the priests in the same community. Even for the purpose of receiving the sacrament of
penance he may choose the one in whom he has most confidence.
Thus it happens that an adviser, whether spiritual or scholastic,
is best able to diagnose the case of his confidant and to suggest
means of overcoming obstacles. After the departure of Ramirez,
Suarez found Father Gutierrez most to his liking and somewhere
in the first year of his study went to him with his major difficulty.

Suarez told him that he was in a hopeless muddle over the
intricacies of philosophy. Humbly and honestly he told the priest
that God could not want him to continue toward the priesthood
since He had evidently not given him the intellectual equipment
for that state of life. His true vocation must be that of a lay
brother; and with a smile he added that surely there must be
some compensation for the lack of mental ability. There must
indeed be some aptitude in him for work with his hands since
there was so little for work with his brain. He told the priest of
the troubles he had experienced in gaining admittance to the
Society in the first place, and that his examiners were undoubtedly correct in their first estimation of him. The only course left
open was that of petitioning superiors for a change of status to
that of lay brother.

This self-depreciation was no false humility on the part of

Francis. Work and prayer were the order of the day for him.
The counsel that the religious student should pray as though
everything depended upon God and work as though everything
depended upon himself was one which he intently followed.
When he declared that he had done his best, it was truly his best;
but the whole subsequent procedure is merely another proof that
the best a man can do is still far removed from what God can do
for him. The very fact that the boy proposed to give up his
dream of the priesthood rather than leave the religious life is
proof sufficient that he was not looking for sugary sympathy from
Gutierrez. What he wanted was advice and approval for his step.

But Gutierrez would not give that approval though he did give
wholehearted advice. In his eyes this was heroic submission to
the will of God, and he was himself a heroic person. The
Huguenots in France later proved that to their own satisfaction
when they tortured and killed him on a journey to Rome; but
heroism can show itself in a variety of ways. The grander thing
for Francis Suarez would be to return to his books as before, and
to return to his prayers, not as before, but with special emphasis
on petitions to the Blessed Mother of God. He praised the
youth's attachment to the religious vocation, appreciated his spirit
of sacrifice in wishing to give up the priesthood, told him that
his prayer to God from now on must be through Mary.

This was sound spiritual advice. But it was advice, too, of a
peculiar psychological significance. Suarez' preoccupation with
his own scholastic shortcoming was one which has occurred, and
which will occur, to almost all students of a less brilliant ability.
It was undoubtedly his habit to "fight the books" in a determination to wrest knowledge from them. Like so many others who
have not learned the secret of calm meditative study, he gritted
his teeth, gripped the book with both hands, frowned darkly at
the page, and hunched over his desk in a do-or-die attitude. All
of this may be the outward sign of intense concentration but it is

a hopelessly inadequate approach to learning unless the mind is clear of worry and the thought-processes flow with a certain freedom. A student in this frame of mind is very much like a muscle-bound athlete. Every attempt at improvement is as awkward as it is futile.

I do not mean that Francis' change from a dullard to a student was due more to psychological than to spiritual forces. Improving one's method of study may and does achieve wonderful results but more than that is necessary to lift one from a fourth-rate student to a first-rate scholar. Suarez himself always attributed the change to the good graces of the Blessed Virgin. People on the sidelines talk glibly of the physical factors present in such things, but Suarez knew his own case. He was the subject in whom the change took place and if anyone knew what brought it about it was he. In a recent article on Suarez, Dr. Magner wrote that "he agreed to abandon scholastic ambitions, should his superiors deem it wise. *Heaven intervened.* His powers appeared *rather suddenly* during his course in philosophy. Suarez had a *remarkable devotion to Our Lady.*" [2]

I have italicized the important words in Dr. Magner's remark because they coincide perfectly with the admission of Suarez himself and with the belief of all his biographers. Because of this remarkable devotion to Our Lady, allusions to which are peppered through his writings, God intervened to change him rather suddenly into a mental giant. Call it a miracle if you will, call it a peculiar coincidence if miraculous is too high a word. Whatever it was, the historical sequence cannot be overlooked. First, Suarez is for seventeen years considered stupid or at best mentally backward, the poorest in whatever group of students he moved. Secondly, after studying and praying fervently with no scholastic improvement he switches the searchlight of his prayers

[2] Magner, James: "Suarez in the Political Controversy," *The Catholic World*, New York, May, 1930, vol. CXXXL, p. 157 (italics added).

almost exclusively on Mary. Finally, he is discovered by his teachers to have changed "rather suddenly" into the most brilliant student in the class. All of this appears fortuitous to the complete rationalist. To the completely rational person it appears the work of a powerful intercessor before God.

Happily, in this twentieth century the vogue of rationalism is passé. It has run its devious course, and we can now get down to true explanations of spiritual phenomena. There is nothing contradictory in the thought that God holds in His hands the intellect, as well as the will and body, of a human being. We are *entirely* His creations; all our faculties come from Him. If at Lourdes, through the intercession of His Mother, He can make the blind to see and the halt to walk and the deaf to hear, why can He not perform miracles in the intellectual order? The case of Suarez is not without parallel. Thomas of Aquin, the greatest Christian philosopher that ever lived, was thought stupid at first. Albert the Great said that what knowledge he had—and it was encyclopedic—came as a gift from the Blessed Virgin. Duns Scotus, most subtle of logicians, asked her frequently for aid in untangling the maze of thought in which he found himself.

It is a commonplace teaching of Scholastic thought that all souls, that is, intellects, are a *tabula rasa* at birth. There is nothing in the intellect itself which marks one man off from another; the differences come from the conditioning each intellect receives during life. Now Suarez was inept. He made a botch of his early studies, and the conditioning which his intellect underwent was not equal to that of, say, a prodigy like Macaulay. But there is no difficulty in believing that God Himself gave inspiration to the mind of Suarez by the simple expedient of improving the conditions under which knowledge is assimilated. Whatever gift God gives there is a providential reason for it, and the gift which Suarez now received was to be used constantly for the furtherance of God's work on earth.

Divine gifts are spread about with a prodigality which far exceeds any human liberality, but often enough they are presented as a reward. In the case of Suarez this intellectual acumen was probably the reward of virtues he had learned to practice: prayer, humility, and above all, obedience. Years later he was to write in his work, *De Religione*, that the vow of obedience supersedes those of poverty and chastity. "But through obedience a man offers his soul, intellect, will, his whole being completely. Indeed, it is a more extensive oblation for through this vow man subjects himself to God, offers all his possession, pleasures, all his other actions together with himself in a perpetual service." [3] In another place he asserts that the vow of obedience in the Society of Jesus is found in its most perfect form, *perfectissimo modo*. [4]

While no one, strictly speaking, deserves a reward from God, the divine goodness often manifests itself in the nature of an unexpected gift. There could be no doubt that Suarez was the recipient of something which he had not enjoyed before, and which he himself had not been able to attain by his own unaided efforts. That acumen, that grasp of subtle studies, came to a young novice whose outstanding virtue was his willingness to give up every wish of his own in order to follow implicitly the dictates of obedience as expressed by superiors. It may be that it is only when one abandons himself wholly to the will of God through the hands of superiors, when he has tried everything of his own personal command, and found it to fail, when he has reached the end of his own rope, and can find no human way out of his difficulty—it is only then that God shows His power. The gift is a reward for entire submission and for complete admittance of human helplessness.

Your materialist will stand baffled at such occurrences, but will

[3] *De Religione,* 3, X.   [4] *Ibid.,* 3, X, 9, 9.

at the same time sneer at such explanations. Nor will he understand the Christian concept of Mary as the channel of all graces,
the hand by which all divine gifts are dispensed. Be that as it
may, the historical significance of certain interrelated things cannot be ignored by the simple will to disbelief. The Jesuits at
Salamanca were no mere visionaries. They were hard-headed in
the logical doctrine of Mary's power and virtue, and the still
extant record of the college tells us that in 1559 they had "bound
themselves by common consent to defend with all their power,
whenever an occasion offered, the Immaculate Conception of the
Most Holy Virgin." When all of Spain resounded with his fame
as a theologian, not the least famous of Suarez' teaching was that
"the Blessed Virgin, Mary, received perfection from God at the
first instant of conception."

Francis was a devotee of Mary, the Mother of God, and as a
result became a very intelligent student. Many another student,
both in religion and out of it, has taken a leaf from his experience, prayed incessantly to Mary—and the result has not been
the vast intellectual improvement expected. If the method works
in one case why will it not work in another? The explanation is
an easy one. These are free gifts of God given through Mary,
and only God knows whether a man will be benefited or hindered
by them. Many another student would become inordinately
proud of himself if he were an intellectual genius, and human
pride is the one thing which is least helpful in performing the
will of God in obedience. The gift may not be used to the divine
glory. In that case the gift is a punishment and would be better
left unaccepted.

It may seem like an undue bludgeoning of the stake at issue to
insist so fully on this marvellous change in Suarez' abilities.
Without a thorough understanding of it, however, the impact
of his life is lost. The whole gamut of his years is colored and
toned and harmonized by it. The following lengthy opinion of

Coleridge is, therefore, a significant key to Suarez' future fame. He writes that intellectual powers "bring with them, as their shadow, the temptation to pride and self-complacency, and the greatest blessing that can be attached to them is the circumstance or condition that acts as a safeguard to the humility without which they so often prove the occasion of the greatest ruin. . . . In the case of Suarez, his whole life bears witness that he never forgot the lesson that had been taught him at the outset of his career as a student. That the change that came over him was a sudden one is proved by the fact that, when a youth of singular promise, afterwards known as Gregory of Valencia, came to the college at Salamanca for his studies in the same year in which Suarez had returned from Medina del Campo, the latter was already sufficiently distinguished among his companions to be selected as the instructor of the newcomer in philosophy. In fact he at once took the position of a student whose future career was marked out for him in the schools of theology. His early piety, and the conviction that he owed the illumination of his mind to the intercession of our Blessed Lady, gave a turn and color to some of his earliest efforts, which were not abandoned as he grew older and more famous." [5]

The illumination of Suarez' mind was almost absurdly abrupt. It happened literally over-night, for on one class day he handled the philosophical subject with his usual clumsiness and on the next he clearly grasped its subtleties. The story goes that he went as usual after class to the room of his tutor, the student whom his professor, Father Martinez, had assigned to help him. After the student had explained the difficult matter Suarez repeated it thoroughly and brilliantly and not at all in his usual bungling fashion. As an enthusiastic biographer tells us, he "went over

[5] Coleridge, *op. cit.*, p. 59. The author is mistaken about the date of Gregory's advent to Salamanca as a Jesuit scholastic. He came in the Autumn of the year following Suarez' return from Medina del Campo.

the whole question and developed it in such manner as manifested full comprehension. He even added solid considerations which the professor had passed over, and solved difficulties which had not been touched upon; in short, he spoke more like a master instructing his pupils, than one of those pupils." There is really nothing more to say about it, except that his abilities were from that day forward recognized by every teacher and superior with whom he came in contact.

In the following year, when Gregory of Valencia entered the Society of Jesus, Suarez, in turn, was made his tutor. Gregory was two years younger than Francis, of a fine mind and excellent temperament, and there began between them an association which lasted for over thirty-five years. Thereafter their careers ran almost parallel; while Suarez taught philosophy at Segovia and theology at Rome, Alcalá and Coimbra, Gregory was teaching philosophy at Rome and theology at the University of Ingolstadt. Both of them became famous as Europe's foremost writers and theologians at the end of the sixteenth century. Both of them took part in the famous Jesuit-Dominican controversy regarding grace; and both received high papal commendation for their work.

There was never again a question of Suarez' aptitude in the matter of studies. What had previously been his greatest trial now became the easiest thing in the world for him. He was released from the drudgery of unprofitable study and now dedicated himself to the divine monotony of profitable speculation. Where he had found himself the laggard of the class and the student for whom special explanations had to be given, he now fell into the danger of impatience with those who could not keep up with the pace he set. There is probably nothing so personally satisfying as intellectual insight and nothing so aggravating as the slowness and stupidity of others. Suarez was in a position to appreciate both aspects of the learning process.

This personal experience with the pain of slow learning was a tool in the hands of Suarez when he came to be a teacher. It is the reason why he is painstakingly clear in every sentence of his voluminous writings. It is the reason, too, why his students always found his lectures full and accurate when he spoke from a professor's platform. Men who appreciate the difficulties of gaining knowledge are most apt to be perfect teachers, just as the doctor who has experienced bodily pain is himself most gentle with his patients. When he was appointed to assist fellow students, even before he had finished his course of studies, he was more capable of overcoming his impatience at their slowness. The danger of making flip remarks was always there in such circumstances but there is no record whatever of his succumbing to that temptation.

The fact is that Suarez, besides becoming a brilliant student in the process of his novitiate, became also a holy man. Following the precept of *ora et labora,* which the Benedictines had observed for centuries and which was rendered by the pointed Jesuit formula of prayer and study, he could not help but develop into a remarkable religious. Too often, in discussing men like Suarez, Bellarmine, Canisius, and others, people stress one characteristic at the expense of the other. Unless the lineaments of the picture include both mental agility and spiritual rectitude the picture itself is badly drawn. Others have been canonized. Suarez has not even been beatified. But there are happenings in the life of Suarez which seem as remarkable as those in the lives of men who have been raised to the altar for our admiration and veneration. What the official pronouncements of the Church may yet be in regard to his holiness cannot be foretold. This, however, we do know: he became a model of religious Jesuit conduct for his younger brothers in the Society.

Preliminary tests being brought to a close, Suarez pronounced his first vows of perpetual poverty, chastity, and obedience, in

August, 1566, when he was eighteen years old. These are called the simple vows and are made in the Jesuit domestic chapel, in contrast to the solemn vows which are pronounced in public after the long years of training are complete. Thus the capacity of Suarez for the religious life had been sounded thoroughly for two years, and the soundings had satisfied his superiors on the three necessary qualifications for the priestly vocation. He was considered physically fit for the arduous years his body would have to spend in the confining work of the lecture hall. He was mentally alert now for the deep study his intellect would be forced to perform. He was spiritually prepared to cope with the assaults which the world, the flesh and the devil would make against him.

If there were any obstacles standing in the path of Suarez, his superiors did not deem them sufficient to keep him from pronouncing the promises which bound him to that life forever. The vows themselves were a means for avoiding the main hurdles which would possibly confront the young religious. Years later, when he could reflect maturely on his own experience and on his observation of others, he wrote that "in them [the vows] are virtually contained all those things which are conducive for removing obstacles and for making a perfect oblation of oneself and one's possessions to God." [6] All the counsels of Christ are therein observed and an opportunity is given every religious person for the achievement of that perfect life to which he aspires.

That Suarez used these vows as a shield for his own protection becomes increasingly clear as we watch his progress, his disappointments, battles, successes and failures through the years. The shield of the religious vows acts effectively as a wall against outside intruders but to a man of Suarez' parts there was in them a much more positive purpose. That purpose was their use as a means of ascending closer to God. He knew from the start that the avoidance of prohibited things had to be supplemented by the

[6] *De Religione*, 3, II, 2, 16.

performance of recommended things. One cannot spend his life negatively, that is, concentrating his whole attention on the avoidance of faults. If he does this—and refuses to go actively about the business of the Lord, even where that work might lead him into spiritual danger—he is as useless to his religious family as he would have been to his natural family had he remained in secular life.

Of course, vows and promises, like New Year's resolutions, are not kept automatically. A spiritual automaton is as much an impossibility as a physical automaton. This affair of salvation and the service of God is one that has to be worked at continuously, and the device that will make that work easier is prayer. Again and again we must return to the combination of intense work and devoted prayer to explain not only how Suarez kept his vows but also how he was able to keep his productive capacities at their top speed. Good intention and good will are essential in good actions, but the action is that which comes after one has made up his mind. This action was for Suarez mainly intellectul speculation and literary composition in his later years. His output was prodigious but the number of hours he gave to prayer is incredible. So convinced was he of the necessity of prayer that he often remarked he would willingly renounce all the knowledge he had, as well as all the world's human knowledge, rather than give up an hour of prayer. With that thought continuously in his mind, the religious life which he began with those vows in the August of 1566 could not but be successful.

CHAPTER VII

Lessons in Divinity

IN THE FOUR YEARS from 1566 to 1570, during which Suarez studied theology, events struck him at every angle from which they can possibly strike a man. In his own personal family he lost both mother and father. In his spiritual family, the Society, there was trouble enough to keep his mind occupied. Philip of Spain was having difficulties with rebellious subjects at home and with jealous princes abroad. The new Pope, Pius V, was making a vigorous sweep for complete reform throughout the Church. It was, indeed, a hectic time for a man who was supposed to ponder the most sublime studies in prayerful and unruffled calm.

Spain was in the midst of European affairs at that time; and Salamanca was in the midst of Spain. The Jesuit theologate was not cut off from the world in which it existed as religious novitiates are cut off from their surroundings. There were comings and goings of men who did mighty deeds for their country, their Order and their Church. The house of studies was the hot-house from which there would soon emerge men who would themselves carry these burdens, undertake journeys, preach and teach in public, advise and counsel in private. These Jesuit theologians could not be left out of the stream of quickly happening changes; they had to know what was going on; they were too perilously close to public performance to be allowed to slip behind the times.

All during those years they were talking about the preponderant influence which Philip II had, sometimes for good, other times for evil, in the most intimate ecclesiastical matters. He is

74

supposed to have insisted that only one Cardinal, the Dominican Michele Ghislieri, would be acceptable to him at the papal election early in 1566. Borromeo wanted to show the independence of the electors, and put forth Cardinal Sirleto, but in the end it was Ghislieri who was elected.

As a matter of fact the new pope was really the man for the times. Philip had sent certain instructions to his ambassador, Luis de Requesens, "in which the election of the Pope was touched upon, and in which he stated that the one thing necessary was to elect a Pope who should be pious and a lover of peace, or in other words a Pope who would not make political complications for the Spanish king, and who would have the reform of the Church at heart." [1] He was a good and holy man, one who would not be turned from his purpose, and who lived to inaugurate one of the strictest reforms Rome or the Church has ever experienced. Philip, if his nomination had the weight it is said to have carried, did the Church a good turn in proposing the man who became Pius V.

The action of the new Pope which most immediately affected Suarez and the other theological students and professors at Salamanca was his practical furtherance of the doctrines of Thomas of Aquin. It was a determination of his that Scholasticism must not only be kept in the Christian schools, as had been so capably done by the learned Dominicans, but it must be enthusiastically forwarded. To this end he gave five thousand scudi for the reprinting of the works of St. Thomas, an edition of seventeen folio volumes which was prepared by the Spanish Dominican, Tommaso de Manriquez. To keep the memory of the great Thomas fresh, he ordered that the date of his death, March 7th, should be celebrated throughout the Church in the same way as the feasts of the four doctors of the Church.

[1] Pastor, Ludwig: *The History of the Popes,* St. Louis, 1929, Herder, vol. xvii, p. 12.

It was an important event for the Church in general and for those interested in theological studies in particular, when the Pope made Thomas of Aquin the fifth doctor of the Church. He conferred this dignity by a special bull on April 11, 1567, when Suarez was nearing the end of his first year of ecclesiastical science. It was an honor which put the stamp of approval upon the author whom the Jesuits, following the example of their teachers, the Dominicans, had taken to their hearts. It confirmed, too, the great work of the Council of Trent, in which the Jesuits, Salmeron and Lainez, had taken a leading part and in which they had relied most deeply on the doctrines of Thomas.

Only the mighty Greek intellects of the early Church had been given the honor which now belatedly came to the saintly representative of Scholasticism. As Pastor aptly remarks, "Not only did the Church herself take the science of the Middle Ages under her protection against the hostility of the Protestants and even of some Catholics, but she also recognized the teaching of Aquinas as the richest fruit of an earlier scientific evolution, and as an imperishable treasure, but at the same time she proclaimed that she recognized her own doctrines in those of the great schoolman. At the same time the line for further theological development was clearly traced out." [2]

The further tracing of this line of development was precisely the task which Suarez was at this time preparing to perform. He immediately caught the spirit of the thing; and it is the spirit of Scholasticism which counts for most in its enthusiastic perusal. There is nothing else quite like it in all the long and varied series of subjects which fall under the scientific scrutiny of man. Perhaps only a few favored minds are able to keep at white heat the fire which is enkindled by the spirit of the Scholastic system. Suarez was one of these. He delighted in this new edition of the *Summa* particularly, and immediately began to make notes

[2] *Ibid.*, pp. 201–202.

against the time when he should compose his own commentary
on it.

His own remark to Gregory of Valencia, when they were both
studying Thomas almost exclusively, was a harbinger of the attitude he maintained all his life. "We must put St. Thomas," he
said, "in a fresh light, so that people of our own day may find
in his works all the rich treasures of Christianity." In the event,
neither Gregory nor Suarez followed Thomas slavishly; but before they departed from his doctrine on any point they knew
thoroughly and exactly what the Angel of the Schools had taught
about it. Thomas was always the source and inspiration of his
theology and the Suarezian commentaries were interpretations
rather than changes in the master's doctrines. He included also
the opinions of numerous other philosophers in these interpreta-
tive works, but fundamentally they are all carried upon the
Thomistic framework.

The Neo-Scholasticism, which the Pope encouraged and which
Suarez now studied, was as much a method as a system. In our
own way of looking at it the term is usually applied to philosophy,
but in the present seminaries of the world it is used to designate
both a doctrinal system and a pedagogical method for the cognate
studies of theology and philosophy. The distinctive feature of
Scholastic theology, as followed by the students at Salamanca,
was its speculative exploration of the premises of revelation,
mainly through the assistance of philosophical methods. The
Schoolmen themselves distinguished between positive theology,
which coördinates the data of revelation, and speculative theology, which philosophizes about the findings and draws from
them theological conclusions.

But all of this was not kept in the high-blown atmosphere of
mere theory. Suarez, like Bellarmine and Canisius, was one of
those who kept theological feet on firm ground even while he
was dealing with the most abstruse problems. He had entered

the religious and studious manner of life in order to save souls, and here in his theological course he was intent on turning speculative investigations to practical use. Like all true Scholastics he theorized a great deal, but primarily to assist both himself and his fellowmen to lead fuller Christian lives.

Otten has written that Thomas "ranges over the whole field of philosophy and theology, apologetics and exegesis, and proves himself a master in every subject he treats." [3] He showed himself particularly masterful in his *Summa Theologica,* the last and most polished of his works. When the new edition came out in 1567 the Jesuit students at Salamanca avidly pounced upon the *Summa* for detailed work. Other editions at hand were few, very old, and frequently misleading because of printers' errors and the rough handling of generations of students at the university. Here at last they had the master himself, and although they were constrained to use the book only as a reference work they felt sure that when they consulted the source they would find Thomas' doctrines relatively unpolluted.

For theological purposes this *Summa* is in many ways ideal and it remains even now the fundamental text for Catholic seminarians. Thomas wrote it near the end of his life for the purpose of putting in the student's hand a compendium of the whole of Christian theology. Unlike the *Summa* which Suarez himself wrote, it was never completed, but was ended, in the middle of the treatise on the sacrament of Penance, by the author's death. There is evidence that Suarez began even as a student the plan of commenting on Thomas' words, explaining and amplifying for contemporary purposes, and arranging his own teachings, if not with the same dialectic exactitude, at least along the same general lines. The work of Thomas might be called a jumping-off place for Suarez, and at the same time a safe and solid foun-

[3] Otten, Bernard: *A Manual of the History of Dogmas,* St. Louis, 1918, Herder, vol. ii, p. 17.

dation to which he could always return for proof and verification of his own theses.

Suarez at Salamanca was in a peculiarly fit position to get the very training he needed for his future work of writing. Scholarly Jesuit theologians were appearing here and there in Europe, but there were not yet enough of them to staff the faculties under which students of their own order were enrolled. So it happened that the young men at the Jesuit College at Salamanca attended classes in theology at the University where the eminent Dominican, John Mancio, filled the post which the Schoolmen would call *magister scholae*. In earlier terminology this would have been synonymous with the title *scholasticus,* but now this latter word was more frequently used to designate a particular student appointed by the *magister* to help other students. In the capacity of *scholasticus* for some of his fellow Jesuits, Suarez had to understand perfectly the lectures of Mancio so that he could in turn explain them to the others.

Like Father Gutierrez at the college, Mancio at the university is supposed to have seen and pointed out the intellectual perspicacity of the young theologian. Only a couple of years previously when Francis was still the despair of his teachers, Gutierrez is quoted as having remarked: "You see that Brother: well, he will be the honor of the Society and a light to the Church." They did not laugh in his face for he was in a position of authority. But now when Manico admitted that he must always be on his guard when Suarez proposed a problem in class, and when he told some students: "You see that young man: he will turn into a prodigy," they suspected that there was a great deal of truth in the prophecy.

Perhaps in no other university in the world is there to be found so brilliant a succession of professors as that which filled the principal chair of theology at Salamanca during the sixteenth century. Suarez' teacher, Mancio, was the fifth of the line which started

with the great Francis Vittorio in 1526, and ended with the controversial Dominic Bañez in 1604. In the order in which they
followed Vittorio these outstanding Dominican scholars were:
Melchior Cano, Dominic de Soto, Peter de Sotomayer, John
Mancio, Bartholomew de Medina, and Dominic Bañez. All of
these men enter intimately into the life of Francis Suarez; those
before Mancio, his teacher, because of their influence on his own
development; those after Mancio because he knew them personally and was sometimes at odds with them.

After the Council of Trent the center of theological activities
shifted from France to Spain, and the main reason for this is the
learning of the Spanish Dominicans, especially of Francis Vittorio. In the twenty years of his professionship at Salamanca Vittorio took St. Thomas as his text, adapting the principles and
solutions of the *Summa* to the needs of his times, emphasizing
the positive aspects of theology, making extensive use of the
Scriptures and the writings of the Fathers. "He replaced the
idle speculations of decadent Scholasticism by a theological system that was at once thorough and comprehensive. He is justly
regarded as the founder of Neo-Scholasticism, which is little
else than the Scholasticism of the thirteenth century brought up
to date and developed along positive lines." [4] He died in 1546,
when one of his most able disciples, Melchior Cano, took his place
at Salamanca.

Cano gained his renown through a new treatment of the
sources of arguments for fundamental theology, a method which
Suarez was to utilize not only during his student years but during
the rest of his life. The book was called *De Locis Theologicis,*
the ten sources to which the theologian must go for his arguments. In a separate book he discusses each of them: Holy Scripture, oral tradition, the Catholic Church, the Councils, the
Fathers, the Roman Church, the Scholastic theologians, science,

[4] *Ibid.,* p. 480.

philosophy, history. He was succeeded in 1552 by the famous Dominic de Soto who, together with Sotomayer and Mancio, used the ideas of Vittorio in the system of Cano.

These men can be truly called reformers of the divine science whose influence so greatly helped the Church in the Reformation. Their big contribution lay in the fact that they made theology more theological. They stripped it largely of the time-wasting habit of refined subtlety in argumentation, and gave back to it the solidity and authority which are inherent in it. They welded the positive proofs of reason with the erudition of the sacred writings. It is unfortunate that of these men Cano who, with De Soto, had been a theologian at the Council of Trent, should tarnish his reputation through a petty opposition to the Jesuits. There was indeed much trouble abrewing, and Suarez would be in the midst of it. These advanced studies were but a fundamental prelude to the part he would take in later controversies.

There is little of the anecdotal to be reported of Francis' four years in the work of theology. His biographer Descamps glowingly remarks that he put in a great amount of profound meditation on the treatises of St. Thomas, that he studied religiously all the other great theologians, voraciously read the history and opinions of other schools of thought, and did all of this with a wise independence of judgment which was as necessary for a great thinker as it was novel in a student so young. One of his teachers in a minor subject, Father De Acosta, was so impressed with Suarez' dogged perusal of the books and with his brilliant performance in the lecture hall, that he considered him "the master of his professor." [5]

The ordinary work assigned to the university students following the lectures of the theological faculty was not enough to keep Suarez occupied. To help him use up his time profitably Mancio selected a long list of specialized problems for his inves-

[5] Descamps; also Sartolo, quoted by De Scorraille, *op. cit.*, pp. 95–96.

tigation, some of them deeply theological, others in the field of philosophy. As a sort of side line the young man gathered data for that future time when he himself would publish a work on metaphysics. He thus coördinated the two main sciences of Scholasticism, reason and revelation, which in the last analysis were meant to be treated in their reflection upon each other. It was a preparation too for the "Grand Act" with which Suarez climaxed his scholastic career at the University of Salamanca.

The Grand Act, which is not performed so frequently now as it was in the earlier history of the Society of Jesus, is an individual performance by the most gifted student in the college. The matter in which he is to be examined covers the whole field of philosophy and theology, from which various theses, conclusions and propositions may be drawn for his specific defense. It is a battle of wits, carried on in the strict argumentation of the Schoolmen, in which the student must match his own knowledge and skill against those of professors, visitors and adversaries. He must be ready to answer all questions and solve all difficulties proposed to him in two public sessions held on the same day.

Suarez was the first to represent the young Jesuit college at the University of Salamanca in this difficult rôle. The disputation took place some time in the Spring of 1570, and was presided over by the Dominican Mancio, friend and professor of Suarez. Mancio had tried to dissuade him from including, among the theses to be defended, one which proposed to prove the supereminence of grace of the Mother of God. Both he and Suarez had to sign the list of theses to be defended, which list would then be posted in a public place on one of the bulletins of the university. Upon seeing the proposition in defense of the Blessed Virgin, Mancio demurred at placing his signature below it.

His objection was not to the thesis itself. It was rather that the audience would consider it a novelty, a strange innovation in the traditional teachings, and perhaps even a dangerous doctrine. Mancio declared that it was to Suarez' own interest to omit it. This was the young man's first public defense; and it was no time to leave the beaten track in order to defend an opinion which St. Thomas himself [6] did not hold. Suarez modestly assured his professor that he could uphold the proposition by relying mainly upon the writings of the Fathers. He argued well his case; and Mancio finally signed the paper, warning him that it would probably end in a public humiliation, but promising that he would help all he could in his capacity of chairman.

The Grand Act was performed with more than usual aplomb that year. Something of a local reputation which Suarez had among the students and professors spread also among the towns-people so that the disputation hall was jammed for both sessions. This was the debut of the Jesuits, and they were out in full force for the affair. Ramirez scurried back to the city from his preaching tour. Gutierrez, Francis' superior, was among the prominent guests. Francis Borgia himself, third Jesuit general and intimate friend of Pius V, was expected at Salamanca about this time. Actually he did not arrive until the following year, but until the last moment the students hoped for his arrival on time for the performance. Suarez' two brothers, John and Gaspar, came up from Granada for the occasion. The official report of the proceedings has it that Suarez did not disappoint his audience but "explained and defended his doctrine with such erudition, penetration, presence of mind, and at the same time with such good grace and modesty that he won the admiration and approval of the whole assembly."

The suave and sober way in which Suarez conducted his Grand

[6] Thomas was at first in favor of the doctrine but later pronounced against it. His difficulty was in explaining how the Redemption could affect Mary if she were immaculate. Cf. *Summa Theol.*, III, q. xxvii. There has been much controversy over the meaning of Thomas' words. Cf. also the article "Immaculate Conception," in *The Catholic Encyclopedia*.

Act is in strange contrast to the eloquent, flowery and stylish "act" which a young scholar named Edmund Campion, had recently put on for Queen Elizabeth at Oxford University. Charmingly and in Latin he said: "One thing only reconciles me to the unequal contest, which I must maintain single-handed against four pugnacious youths; that I am speaking in the name of Philosophy, the princess of letters, before Elizabeth, the lettered princess." [7] There was much more in the same vein, spoken by a youth who was of an age with Suarez, but with a background as different as anything could be. But he died a Jesuit martyr, defending with his life the very teachings which would make his Spanish contemporary famous in Catholic countries, and hated in England.

Both of these men had an extremely fond regard for Mary, the Mother of God. Campion, in the bluff and hale way of all that grand group of English Catholics, practiced a profound devotion to her that always had something of the romantical about it. Suarez' love was a penetrating thing that swept both his heart and his head into the service of the Queen of Heaven. That it was reciprocal is a belief that came out of a beautiful vision.

Father Gutierrez was one of the leaders of that band at Salamanca that promised to further the doctrine of the Immaculate Conception. To him Mary appeared one day while he was in prayerful contemplation of the wonder of her creation. She thanked the priest for having advised Francis Suarez "to throw all the light he could on the excellence of grace that raised me above the whole world of creatures. I am grateful to him also for having consecrated his talent with such eagerness and filial piety to the manifestation of my glory."

The occurrence of Mary's visitation is recounted in the Jesuit

[7] Waugh, Evelyn: *Edmund Campion*, New York, 1935, Sheed and Ward, p. 11.

annals at Salamanca and appeared in a published biography even during the lifetime of Suarez. Gutierrez was holy enough to deserve a martyr's death; to him were vouched several other heavenly visitations. The important point in this particular happening is the time when it took place: just after Suarez had covered himself with laurels in the defense of Mary, and just before his reception of Holy Orders. From then on the Jesuit was to lean heavily on the help of the Mother of God.

CHAPTER VIII

Family Affairs and Ordination

SUAREZ AND HIS BROTHERS AND SISTERS were caught in the backwash of King Philip's political swamp. Shrewd as a horse-trader in some things, the monarch was a terrible bungler in others. He was artless enough to think that he could successfully and alone stick his finger into the hot English contention between Mary Stuart and Elizabeth, put the heretics to rout in Central Europe, watch over papal affairs in general, guide and guard his far-flung colonies, ensure domestic peace on the Peninsula. Here and there he succeeded in these universal activities but with the Morisco question he failed; and in that failure there tumbled the ancient prestige and fortune of the Suarez family.

The King's relations with the saintly Pius included everything from the suppression of bullfights to the reformation of the religious orders. The Spanish bishops, backed by Philip, refused to publish certain papal bulls, for instance, *In Coena Domini,* for which royal permission was withheld. There was immediate danger of a breach between the Catholic King and the Pope; the former being in a state of righteous excitement, the latter entirely adamant on the side of the Church. "Although it was only right," says Pastor, "that a prince should have knowledge of the things being done in his territories, the Pope nevertheless could not approve of the high-handed way in which the royal authorities acted in this respect, not only preventing the execution of salutary Apostolic bulls, but not even vouchsafing to give their reasons." [1]

[1] Pastor, *op. cit.,* vol. xviii, p. 41.

But the dispute almost settled itself when the Pope heard of gigantic preparations going forward by the Turks, who were determined that a European invasion was their best defense against the Christians. Without Philip's help there could be little hope for Catholic success, and Philip was busily engaged in his own private wars, fighting against the Moriscos in southern Spain and against the Calvinists in Flanders. Finally the King did send his brother, Don Juan, gaily off to the war, and at Lepanto on October 7, 1571, there came that glorious Catholic victory which has since been sung the world over. The Pope attributed the victory as much to the power of Mary's rosary as to the abilities of Don Juan in whose honor he cited the words of Scripture: *Fuit homo missus a Deo, cui nomen erat Ioannes.*

At the same time as the Turkish threat there was the problem of heretical England which must concern both the Pope and the King. The Pope at first had some hope of Elizabeth's conversion but he ended by calling her a crowned criminal, the supposed ruler of England. He supported the claims of Mary Stuart and tried to get the Kings of France and Spain to invade England, marry off a likely noble to Mary and set both of them on the throne. Mary herself in 1568 believed that if Philip II would help her she should be Queen within three months. Another potent reason for an Anglo-Spanish war was the terrific toll being taken of Spanish shipping in all parts of the world by the deviltry of English freebooters and buccaneers. But again His Majesty had his hands full with other conflicts and did not yet dare to send his armada northward.

The rebels in the low countries were as much a worry to the Pope as to Philip, but it took the latter some time to incline to the view of Pius. He pretended that he would make a personal appearance with the troops to quell the heretical disturbances, said that Alba was merely to prepare the way, even had public prayers offered for his safety on the expedition. The truth is that

he had no more idea of setting out for Flanders than he had of
following the papal advice to deal gently with the Dutch. His
cynical son, Don Carlos, frequently in hot water with his royal
father, knew he would not leave Spain and sat down to produce
his first and only book. It was titled: *The Great and Admirable
Voyages of King Philip,* and all its pages were blank except the
first one which read: "From Madrid to the Pardo, from the Pardo
to the Escorial, from the Escorial to Aranjuez, from Aranjuez to
Segovia, from Segovia to Madrid." His father did not like the
Prince's literary effort.[2]

Carlos was a royal rascal but, unlike so many other mischief-
makers of his age, he was not a lovable one. The report of his
Protestant leanings moved Pius to exclaim: "My God! My God!
There is but too good reason to believe it, for We knew that this
prince had no love for priests or monks, and had shown no
respect for any ecclesiastical dignity." [3] For once the boy's esca-
pades had gone too far. Various rumors said that he had plotted
the death of the King, was in league with the Morisco rebels and
the French heretics, tried to interest his cousin, Don Juan, in a
plan to divide the empire with him. The blow fell in January,
1568, when the King ordered his arrest "for the service of God,
and for the safeguarding of religion, his realm, and his subjects."
Six months later the boy died in prison, but not until he had
been fortified by the last Sacraments so that the Pope himself
could attend his funeral obsequies in Rome.

Worries crowded Philip from every side. The new outbreak
of the Moors in Andalusia, where the Suarez family holdings
were located, were occasioned by his own mishandling. The
presence of an enormous number of these Moors was a constant
threat to Spain's internal peace even though for many years
there had been no marked outbreaks. It had been the firm conviction of intelligent men living in the danger spots, among whom

[2] Loth, *op. cit.,* p. 176.   [3] Pastor, *op. cit.,* vol. xviii, p. 43.

were Suarez' father and his maternal uncles, that the best way out of the problem was education. Missionaries should be sent to evangelize these Spanish Moors just as they were being sent to the Indies to convert the natives. As long as religious differences remained, they argued, there would be disaffection and a threat of wholesale rebellion. Besides that, the Protestant preachers were coming down into the very backyard of the Catholic King; they were brewing hazards in the melting pot of Southern Spain.

Investigations were made by lawyer Suarez at Granada, compared with hundreds of similar studies made in other parts of the country, and then sent to Philip. The king asked for an estimate of the cost of educating the Moriscos and of bringing them into the fold of the Church. When he received it he declared that it was prohibitive, that there were more pressing needs for such sums of money, that while the apostolic method had much to recommend it he would use a quicker and more modern way. He thought it would be easier to take away their Mohammedanism by force than to give them Christianity by gentle persuasion. In 1566 he published an edict which forbade even the most harmless Moorish customs, and levied heavy fines on those who spoke Arabic, practiced a foreign religion, or wore Moorish dress.

He had acted against the advice of those who knew the situation intimately, especially of Ruy Gomez, Spain's most astute diplomat who had gathered reams of information and who foretold that a Moorish rebellion would follow the edict. Gomez warned that the Moors had been the terror of Spain and that a warlike race does not lose its characteristics in less than three generations. The soldiers, as well as the civilians, who lived among them in Andalusia believed that they could be moved eventually by persuasion but never by direct compulsion. The new Inquisitor General, Cardinal Espinosa, more smooth and crafty than any of the politicians surrounding the king, argued against them. He was determined to show his abilities in this new office. By strong-arm methods he would accomplish the conversion of the Moors.

The revolt that followed was a nightmare to the Andalusians. Moorish arms and warriors appeared out of nowhere, and Moorish atrocities were recounted in many a Spanish patio behind barricaded doors. From the walls of the city of Granada the Suarez' family saw their estates go up in flames. Even within the city, their property, like that of thousands of other Christians, was frequently attacked and seriously damaged. Before the rebellion had passed the family income had dwindled to a pitiable percentage of its former amount. They were not left destitute, but the horrors, worries and sufferings they underwent were at least the indirect cause of death to both parents, Antonia and Gaspar.

Doña Antonia died in the beginning of October, 1567, fortified for the future life by the presence of her priestly brothers. She received the sacrament of the dying, and passed away in much the same manner as she had lived, piously, cheerfully, calmly. Salamanca was not far from Granada, as modern means of travel go, but at that time it was too great a distance for Francis Suarez. The body of his mother could not be kept until his arrival; at any event both mother and son understood the meaning of death too well. He would like to be there, and she would like to have him before her last hour. Suarez stayed at the university to continue his studies.

His father was growing old before his time. It was delightful to have his large family around him, but the death of his wife was a serious loss, especially now that he was overburdened with financial and domestic troubles. As the war burden subsided his legal burdens increased, for his services as counsellor were required to settle the claims and disputes resulting from the rebellion. It was more than he could stand, and within three years he too collapsed. He died on March 5, 1570, and was entombed in the vault of his ancestors at the Franciscan monastery of Granada. Again his son, Francis, could not return for the funeral services. The handling of family affairs devolved to the oldest brother John.

Twice in 1569, and four times in 1570, Father Placa, the rector at Granada, wrote to the Jesuit general at Rome concerning Suarez and his family. It is evident that he kept Borgia informed about the young theologian in the hope that Suarez could obtain permission to come home for a short time. Because of the inconveniences of travel, and the length of time consumed in going from one place to another, religious persons were loath to move about much at that period. Suarez himself felt that he could do more by his prayers than by his presence among his brothers and sisters. But things came to such pass that he finally had to lend the weight of his thought and experience to clearing them up.

Travel-wearied but full of hope that he could disentangle the difficulties, Suarez arrived in Granada at the end of September, about six months after the death of Gaspar, his father. There he remained for about a month and a half, arranging for the dowry and the entrance of his three sisters into the religious congregation of the Hieronymites, at the convent of St. Paul, Granada. He decided to bring his youngest brother, Gaspar, a lad of about twelve, back to Salamanca and to put him in college there. His oldest sister was betrothed. John, too, who was now the head of the family, was married. Thus the children were pretty well settled in their states of life, but there was a further and more complicated problem in the lack of money and income.

Gaspar Suarez had been a wealthy man. Through his own abilities he had vastly increased the inheritances that came to him, had provided a more than comfortable environment for his large family, and had given huge sums toward charitable and religious enterprises. Compared to his former surroundings his condition at death was that of a relatively poor man, and the Suarez fortune never again reached the height it had attained during his lifetime. It was the duty of Francis and John to distribute equitably among the children what was left of that wealth. John was given possession of the residence at Granada, as well as all the rights and heritances from both father and mother, and the patronage of chaplaincies and benefices. Gaspar's portion was kept in trust for him by his uncles. The sisters were taken care of by dowries. For the Society Francis took only four hundred ducats of his own portion and turned over the rest to John. Some of the necessary documents for these transactions were not signed and witnessed for several years, but all the preliminary arrangements were made during Suarez's sojourn in his native city.

Not all inheritances were so easily settled by the religious members of Spain's wealthy families. Some religious orders themselves were gaining a reputation for cupidity through their insistence that the full share should be turned over to them. The Jesuits, however, were always careful to avoid any move that would even seem to indicate that they had preferences in the way in which bequests were divided. The rector at Granada wrote to Borgia about this time telling him how glad he was that Suarez had handled his own problem so successfully and that "it is indispensable that we show ourselves very disinterested" in affairs of this kind.

Suarez himself was to write clearly on this matter later on. When treating of the obligations of religious persons to renounce their possession, he remarked that "in theory, we must observe the counsel of Our Lord to distribute one's goods to the poor and not to one's parents and relations. Sometimes, however, it is better not to follow it. This is true in two cases. The first reason, one which follows from the very nature of things, is when the relatives are in need of help; the second reason, which is only a secondary and accidental consideration, is when there appears a necessity to prevent scandal, contentions, enmities, etc., which are the usual fruits of monetary affairs." [4] These principles justify the disposal Suarez made of his own family inheritances. Both he and his superiors thought it best and wise to compensate John in some way for the reverses that had been suffered. He was, after all, to sustain and carry on the family position, and whatever financial help he could receive would be put to good advantage.

His uncle's pride in his intellectual accomplishments was another occasion for a public display on the part of Suarez. Father Pedro Vasquez was his mother's brother, vicar-general of the archdioceses of Granada and Toledo, visitor-general in that of Santiago, treasurer of the Inquisition, canon of Granada, and rector of the University. As a proud uncle and a prominent man he wished to show off the abilities of Francis, and to prove to the doubting citizens that a theological giant had come back to town in place of the dull little school-boy who had left for Salamanca eight years before. He arranged with Francis and with the rector of the Jesuit College that the young man should make a public defense of a number of special theses. He invited the Archbishop Pedro Guerrero to preside at the function.

This prelate, who was a close friend of the Suarez family, had known some of the early Jesuit fathers at the Council of Trent and had founded their college at Granada. Naturally he was deeply interested in Francis' progress. The news of his success at Salamanca had been almost too good to be true, and by accepting the invitation the archbishop could verify those reports at first hand. Again Suarez charmed his audience with his clipped and terse diction, his ability to solve in a moment the objections of adversaries, but most of all by the gentle modesty with which he went through the whole ordeal. When it was over the archbishop embraced him in the manner of the Spaniards and "ex-

[4] *Tractatus de Religione Societatis Jesu,* V, 4, 4.

horted him to consecrate generously to the glory of God, to the honor of his order and his country, the talents he had received." [5]

With his intellectual prowess satisfactorily proven and his business troubles gratifyingly settled Suarez was able to set off with young Gaspar on the return trip to Salamanca. In the ordinary course of a seminarian's life at the present time, ordination to the priesthood follows immediately upon the completion of the course in theology. Suarez was considered too young to be ordained and too far advanced to continue in the regular course of studies. He was therefore set to the task of directing his fellow Jesuits in their repetition of philosophy.

In his constitutions for the Jesuit Order Loyola had written that "the study of theology should last six years. The first four years will include an explanation of all the matter of the course; the last two will be passed in the review of studies, and those who are to be promoted to the doctorate will undergo the required examinations." [6] Suarez was one of the exceptionally bright students who could be appointed to supervise the studies of others at this period. The Jesuit visitor had reported to Borgia that he was one of those "for whom it would be well to continue in their studies with the prospect of teaching philosophy later on." Sanchez, too, had reported that "he had talent, virtue and good health"; while his rector, Father Gutierrez, declared that he was "a good subject, with talent, medium health, and ability for teaching."

After this year of intense work with his own religious brothers, Suarez received the unexpected honor of a chair in philosophy at the college in Segovia. Ordinarily a young Jesuit's first teaching assignment takes him to some of the lower classes, perhaps of rhetoric or grammar. But his high reputation was already

[5] De Scorraille, *op. cit.*, pp. 121–122. He does not vouch for the authenticity of this event.

[6] *Constitutions of the Society of Jesus*, IV, 15, 3.

earned, and superiors thought it a shameful waste of excellent talent that he should be used in any but the highest branches of study. With him he took his brother Gaspar, who is supposed to have attended the lectures of Francis there. The boy stayed there for his elder brother's ordination and first Mass, and then returned to Salamanca in 1573, where he entered the novitiate of the Society of Jesus. Written in the margin next the record of his entry is an unverified notation that Suarez "was his professor of philosophy at Segovia."

Now Segovia was one of the most important cities of Castile, with a large population, flourishing industries, great commercial activities. It is still a place where tourists stand to gaze at the old Roman viaduct, the beautiful Gothic cathedral, and the remains of the Moorish Alcazar. But all of this was of only passing interest to Suarez at the moment. He wanted to get on to ordination. But he could not because there was now another difficulty besides that of youthfulness; one which was holding back the young Jesuits in all parts of the Society. It was Pope Pius' recent decree that only those who were solemnly professed could be ordained in a religious Order.

In the Society, according to the will of Loyola and the early Jesuits, the solemn vows could be pronounced only after a long period of trial, usually about sixteen years. In the meanwhile the Scholastics had simple vows which are distinguished from solemn by the fact that the latter are practically indissoluble. Pope Pius believed that the obligations between the Order and its members should be equally binding, and ordered in 1568 that solemn vows would now be a necessary condition for sacerdotal ordination of religious. His ruling was not a burden to other religious Orders where the novice was professed solemnly as soon as he has finished his novitiate, but it struck at one of the fundamental principles of the Jesuit Order.

The Society of Jesus, according to the plan that Ignatius had conceived for it, was bound to disappear within a few years if this decree were fully enforced. The founder's principle had been one of strict and careful selection after the Scholastic had been ordained and passed through more trials as a priest. After much consultation Borgia had recourse to the expedient of making all Jesuits take the solemn vows of religion before ordination, but reserving the right of participation in the General Congregation to those who would subsequently be admitted to the fourth solemn vow of obedience to the Pope. In this way there could be no danger that those who were less well trained could change the strict requirements of the Order by vote in the Congregations. There was such danger at that time.

In 1573 Gregory XIII revoked his predecessor's order of 1568, but Suarez was caught in the regulations of these short five years and had to make the solemn profession in December, 1571. He was now as closely bound to his religious family as it was bound to him. All ties with his former life and with the world had been severed in spirit at least when he entered the novitiate at Medina del Campo. But now the actuality had occurred. Property, family, worldly longings, all of these were definitely flung aside in the indelible impression which his vows of poverty, chastity and obedience burned into his soul. He felt humbly ready, if a human being can ever be said to be ready, for the honor which would come with ordination.

Within the next few months—the date is not certain—Suarez was ordained sub-deacon, deacon, and priest at Segovia. There was a Jesuit need for men like Suarez; the canonical age of twenty-five was passed; superiors were more than satisfied with both his intellectual and his spiritual powers; he himself was only too happy to make the step to the altar. He celebrated his first Mass on the feast of the Annunciation, March 25th, which fell on the Tuesday of Passion Week in the year 1572.

The choice of this date was a deliberate one. It marks the most glorious moment in the life of Suarez' most devoted friend, Mary the Mother of God. All through the later years this feast day was sacred to him. He prayed, meditated, wrote on the mystery of the Incarnation of God which took place on that day, and after almost twenty years placed before the public his first finished book: *De Verbo Incarnato*. To people of little understanding and less prayer, this choice of a special day may seem but simple fancy. To others who realize that the Incarnation is the pivotal event of all world history, it is deeply significant as a key to the character of Suarez.

CHAPTER IX

Apostolate of Activity

WHEN A MAN brutally forces his way to power at the age of twenty-five, subjects have but little choice except to obey his direction. But the history of the world shows very few such cases. Likewise it seldom happens that men voluntarily choose so youthful a person to direct them in either their spiritual or their material destiny. Still more exceptional, then, is the case of Francis Suarez, who was given the unheard-of privilege of being spiritual director for the whole Jesuit community at the College of Segovia.

He who was being trained yesterday is the trainer to-day. Only eight years in the religious life, a priest for less than a month, the youngest of all the priests in the community, Suarez was appointed to guide the spiritual steps of his fellows. There were about a dozen older priests there, some of them grown gray in the service of the Society, but they were placed by the Provincial under the care of this young man. It was an appointment which argues the possession of mature virtue as well as solid wisdom.

This unexpected rôle of Suarez cannot be lightly passed over. Ordinarily the place of spiritual adviser is filled by men of advanced age, whose experience has taught them how to handle the problems of their volatile confrères. Loyola, in his Constitutions for the Order, had given specific instructions for the choice of directors. They were to be of tried virtue and, as far as possible, outstanding in studies as well as in holiness. Suarez certainly had not been tried over a long period of time. His mental acumen was well known by this time, but the extraordinary devotion he had shown in spiritual matters might well have been the customary fervor of any young religious.

Nor did the superiors simply gamble on the possibility of his doing the job properly. Jesuit provincials cannot afford to make costly mistakes in such appointments. They must be sure that the man of their choice is the best man available, for the damage that can be done by a fuddled director is incalculable and often enough irreparable. There were seventeen Scholastics among the religious at the Segovian college, and the careful training of youthful Scholastics has always been the first consideration of superiors.

Some of them were of the same age as Suarez. With others he had only recently been going to the same classes and listening to the same professors. What he had to do for them even at that time fitted exactly the instruction of the Sacred Congregation: "Superiors will likewise see to it that the spiritual directors, to whose special care these young religious are assigned during the entire course of studies, fashion their souls to the religious and clerical life by timely admonitions, by instructions and exhortations; in this way and in no other, they will at length excel in sound doctrine joined with a most holy life." [1]

Of course it is not impossible that a man know thoroughly the theory of the spiritual life without himself putting that theory into practice. There have been theological masters, who were perfectly acquainted with all the subtleties and nuances of complicated treatises, but who led personal lives of an unedifying kind. It is quite improbable, however, that a spiritual father can successfully "fashion the souls" of religious and clerics unless he is himself an exemplary religious.

[1] *Instruction of the Sacred Congregation of Religious,* December, 1931; quoted by Creusen, Garesché, Ellis: *Religious Men and Women in Church Law,* Milwaukee, 1934, Bruce, pp. 270–271.

In his personal conduct Suarez formed a pattern for that most serious advice which the Council of Trent had only recently given regarding religious students. These clerics "ought by all means so to regulate their whole life and habits that in their dress, deportment, gait, conversation, and in all other things they may ever show themselves to be grave, well-regulated, and religiously mature." [2] That he was this model was attested by one of the young Scholastics who was then at Segovia under Suarez, and who later wrote that "both in his words and actions he was the support of our spiritual life. . . . In his own life he afforded us a perfect model of that holiness to which we should all aspire."

It was only to be expected that a man so young would be put in the spotlight of attention by others. There may have been a twinge of jealousy because of his quick appointment to an important position; there may have been a feeling of astonishment that so youthful a priest should be preferred to older men; certainly there was intent interest on the part of all. Father Diego de Ocampo, one of the men who was with him at Segovia, was observant enough to write down his impressions. "I watched him with great attention," he said, "because of the good I drew therefrom, and I was struck by the control he had of himself always and everywhere, at recreation, in argumentations, at any time. It seemed as though he were always just coming from prayer or rather that he never left it."

This is the very power and secret of the directive art: that a man practices what he teaches. Perfect mastery over oneself was taught by every religious founder in the history of the Church, and it perhaps reached its summit in the admonitions which Loyola laid down for his own followers. Suarez was already a master in the doctrines of philosophy and theology; he was here stepping into an ineffably higher kind of doctrine and mastery. At a time when holy men abounded in the religious

[2] Session xxii, c.I., *De Reformatione.*

Orders of Spain this same De Ocampo could honestly declare that he had never met anyone, either inside the Society or out of it "who edified me more or excited me more powerfully to the practice of virtue than Father Francis Suarez; and that by the harmony of his entire conduct and by the perfection of all his acts."

Jerome Ballester was another young Scholastic who had a critical eye cocked for defective chinks in Suarez' spiritual armor. He watched him all the while he was at the college at Segovia, and finally came to the conclusion that he would have made as good a master of novices as he was a master of philosophy. For the young men he was both professor and father, satisfying their difficulties of intellect and soul by his explanations and counsels. His was the perfect approach: both scientific and spiritual, the one complementing and improving the other.

But the offices of professor and spiritual adviser at the college were not the only occupations of a young and zealous Suarez. The point that is most often missed in discussing his life and work—and indeed the life and work of most scholarly men—is the fact that he was tremendously social minded. The scope of a Jesuit's field of activity can never be confined to his students and immediate confrères. He is first, last and always a priest of God—and a priest of God always has the welfare of God's children at heart. That welfare is inseparably spiritual *and* material.

Social and religious reform was in the air. During the pontificate of St. Pius, which had just ended, these things were brought to the fore, and the Jesuits were keen to take a hand in them just as Ignatius himself had done. As Fülöp-Miller states: "The evils which the Jesuits took up the task of combating were in many ways similar to the social evils which exist at the present time: begging, unemployment, child-neglect, and prostitution." [3] Unfortunately these problems have not been fully solved even

[3] Fülöp-Miller, René: *The Power and Secret of the Jesuits,* New York, 1930, Garden City Publishing Company, p. 70.

after Catholic teaching and practice has for several centuries developed a high feeling of social responsibility.

Unfortunately, too, Suarez' attack on local social problems was too brisk for his own good. For two years he spent every spare moment, Sundays and feast days, travelling around to the near-by villages as well as working in Segovia itself, helping people who were being woefully neglected by both spiritual and temporal administrators. As a matter of fact he almost killed himself doing it, and his superiors had to order him off the work. Coleridge remarks that "his delicate health and frail constitution were so much injured by his exertions, that his superiors thought it best to withdraw him altogether from such employment." [4]

He never forgot this experience. During the long years of his professorate his prime interest was always to teach others his social theory, the need for improvement, and the basic laws which must always be followed. In these two brief years, however, he learned an enormous amount, and taught others a great deal more, about life as it should be lived. Confraternities which the great Pius had instituted were apt tools in his hands. The papal influence either founded or promoted the Confraternity of the Rosary, for condemned criminals, for the settling of feuds, for travellers, for poor girls, but most important of all, the Confraternity of the Christian Doctrine. At the present time in America this latter Confraternity is in a flourishing condition; but Suarez in his own way put it to great effect for the simple people of Castile.

One of the promises which a Jesuit makes to his religious superiors is that he will teach Christian doctrine to the young and the ignorant. At the time of Suarez this was being done by means of the famous catechism of Canisius, which its author was using to good purpose in Germany, and which has since been called "a bulwark against all the enemies of the papacy."

[4] *Op. cit.,* p. 61.

But instruction was being sorely neglected among the people, and young Jesuits took time out from their classes and studies to make up the deficiency.

In Spain the catechism is neatly named *la Doctrina,* expressing beautifully the fact that it is the science of sciences, the highest study. The Spanish peasants took to it as doctrine-starved people everywhere take to the word of salvation. In the mountain hamlets around Segovia, Suarez had his greatest success with these semi-literate natives. He would talk to them carefully and precisely of the things they wished to know and, strangely enough for a learned college professor, he was able to clarify his teaching to such extent that even they could grasp its meaning. Not fruitless now was the memory of those youthful years when he himself had the utmost difficulty in his studies.

In the lecture hall before brilliant students and professors, and in the rude huts of poor uneducated people Suarez made stroke after master stroke as a teacher. But in one method of conveying knowledge he was a failure. That was in pulpit preaching. He lacked some acting genius, some vital flame, which distinguished his old friend Father Ramirez and the numerous other Jesuit preachers of Spain.

Perhaps there was some special flamboyancy needed in that day by the man who could sway the populace. At any rate, Suarez did not possess it. He himself realized that he lacked the essential spark for popular preaching, but on one occasion he was assigned to give a sermon, an assignment he accepted under obedience. It was a Holy Week sermon treating the Gospel text: *Quis ex vobis arguet me de peccato?* "Because of his inexperience in the pulpit," remarks De Scorraille, "and in his professorial style he spoke at great length, following all the rules of the Scholastic method, and establishing the thesis of the impeccability of Jesus Christ." [5]

One of his students wished to compliment him afterwards

[5] De Scorraille, *op. cit.,* p. 138.

but found it difficult to express his praise. With an inspiration
that was more ingenuous than complimentary he said: "I believe
that your Reverence has not received from God the vocation of a
preacher but that of a professor." Suarez humbly admitted that
he agreed with the boy and that this initial attempt would not be
duplicated unless superiors so ordered. Evidently they did not
order it for there is no record of his preaching in public again
for the rest of his life. That was one of the reasons why the
years that followed were confined to teaching, writing and con-
ferences for his fellow Jesuits.

The other reason was the matter of his health, which was not
at any time robust. His visits to the poor and sick and ignorant
were suddenly cut short one night when he became almost fa-
tally ill. He had been instructing people in a well-heated house
several miles from the city. Covered with perspiration he walked
back through the icy mountain winds, and by the time he arrived
at the college he was reeling with pain. The long-term result of
this was that he suffered a constant irritation in his chest; the
immediate result was that his superiors forbade any further public ministry of this kind.

In a sense it was undoubtedly providential that Suarez was
now forced to concentrate the full strength of his ability on
intellectual considerations. Later on he himself humbly attributed most of his success to the unbroken length of time he could
thus give to bookish occupations. Among the Jesuits, he would
say, there are many other men more gifted and capable than he;
but most of them do not reach complete knowledge and the full
development of their talent for the special work to which grace
and nature destine them. The reason for this is that they are
forced to busy themselves about a multitude of duties, first one
thing and then another, and they never become fully proficient
in the field where their best abilities lie.

But there are other avenues to public acclaim besides that of the pulpit. The dissipation of one's energies into various fields of active contact with the people is not always the surest way to reach the ears of those people. For a while Suarez was the vogue at Segovia. In yet another little while his reputation expanded over the whole province of Castile so that the notes taken by his students were in active demand at the other colleges, notably at Salamanca and Valladolid. These notes were feverishly re-copied—as was customary of a time when text-books were few and expensive—and soon found their way around to most of the philosophy and theology students of Spain.

Youthful vogue is a dangerous thing. Suarez was too young to be famous, just as the Society of Jesus was too young to merit all the heap of praise it was then receiving all over Europe. There was jealousy among the older Orders when the Jesuit theologians began to gain the notice of the world, for as Orders go, the Jesuits had hardly passed through the noviceship of the religious life when they were giving their opinions at the Council of Trent. Similarly there was envy, both interior and ex-terior, when a young priest who had himself scarcely left the school benches began to give his own opinions on ancient and controverted theses.

Novelty of doctrine was the all-embracing charge made against Suarez by some of his own religious brothers in Castile. Novelty of method had been the charge against Ignatius Loyola only a few decades before; and I suppose it is novelty of doctrine and method that critics everywhere grumble about when they first begin to take notice of a rising genius. At any rate, substance and style are the two most convenient points of approach for the critic, and Suarez was accused on both scores. The attack at Segovia was merely the first. There was another and more serious one a few years later when he was teaching theology at Valladolid.

The truth is that Suarez was not an eccentric. He was not one of your modern breed of popularizers who must descend to startling singularities to win a reputation. He was indeed subtle in his argumentation and fertile in finding clear and sound ways of putting over the arguments. As Coleridge remarks, "he was too thoughtful and industrious to hand on and repeat by rote just what he had read or been taught. He did not belong to the school of epitomizers, the set of men who compile *cursus* or *compendia,* who have done so much to destroy deep and accurate learning. Where there is a truly theological mind, there will always be profound and therefore independent thought; and where there is independent thought, there will also be, to some extent, originality of expression or of method—obsolete opinions and invalid arguments will be discarded, and unchangeable truths set forth in a new light." [6]

The Segovian charges against Suarez were investigated by Father John Suarez, the provincial who had admitted Francis to the noviceship, and who had recently been reappointed to that office. He came over from his headquarters at Valladolid to find out what this brilliant professor, whom he had at first considered so stupid a boy, had done to cause all this commotion. He liked the young priest immensely but his impartiality in the case had to be above reproach.

All the notes of the different courses were brought out for the provincial's scrutiny. He questioned those who had made the charges, studied the evidence, and finally called Francis himself to learn what he had to say in his own defense. In the face of adverse criticism given by some of the fathers who had been commissioned to examine the matter, the provincial gave him permission to continue as he had been teaching. He was impressed as much by the soundness of the explanation as by the humility and straightforwardness with which it was presented.

Frequently thereafter the doctrines of Suarez were challenged,

[6] Coleridge, *op. cit.,* p. 63.

sometimes by his co-religionists, but mainly, toward the end, by
the heretics when many English Catholics would be brought before the judges to swear whether or not they held with his teachings. Ogilvie, for example, before the hangman swung with him
from the scaffold to make sure his neck was broken, was asked:
"Do you maintain the teachings of Suarez?" And the martyr answered: "I have not read his book. If anyone wants to refute
him let them write a better book on the subject." [7]

But other things of more immediate concern were on the mind
of Suarez before another concentrated attack on his doctrines
persuaded the Jesuit general to bring him to Rome. From Segovia, near the end of 1573, Francis himself wrote to Father
Everard Mercurian, the successor of Borgia. He requested that
he should be allowed to come to Rome for three or four years
so that he could acquire some of "the virtue, science, theoretical
and practical knowledge of the spirit of our institute." Instead
of having his request granted Suarez was sent to the important
city of Valladolid, in the old kingdom of Leon.

At Valladolid the Jesuits had established the College of St.
Ambrose, connected with the university, and having its own
faculty of philosophy and theology. Besides teaching the latter
subject Suarez was for a year a sort of *factotum*, prefect of studies for the Scholastics, presiding at their disputations, and working on a treatise which he would afterwards publish as *De opere
sex dierum*. In all of his work he again gave complete satisfaction to his superiors, even though there appeared an occasional
glimpse of disagreement on the part of some.

It seems as though a whirlwind of change hit Suarez about
this time. Within eighteen months he was removed three times,
going from Valladolid to Segovia, and then to Avila, and back
again to Valladolid. That such rapid shifting of personnel is
ruinous both to the college and to its professors is a common-

[7] Brown, W. E.: *John Ogilvie*, New York, 1925, Benziger, p. 186.

place of educational theory. Sometimes, however, the changes
cannot be avoided, and so it was in the case of Suarez. It was no
fault of his own nor was it a situation which the Father Provincial particularly desired. The Jesuit professors had to follow
the Jesuit Scholastics, and these young students were at the time
rather impermanently placed.

The main trouble was that there were no fixed Scholasticates
exclusively for Jesuit training as we have them at the present
time. In our own day the general secular standards for philosophical and theological studies are woefully inadequate for the
purpose of training professors. Therefore, the Scholastics cannot receive their education in the ordinary colleges and universities; special schools must be set up for them in each province.
At the end of the sixteenth century, however, practically all of
the colleges taught philosophy and theology in such fashion that
clerics could mingle with lay students to the positive advantage
of both.

The Spanish Scholastics, then, were distributed in different
colleges and in varying numbers, depending upon financial considerations, agreements made with the college founders, conditions of health and other circumstances. Sometimes a group,
with its own professor, would change to another college for a
while and then return to the original place. Sometimes they
went to the faculties of universities taught by the Dominicans,
at other times to those taught by their fellow religious.

It is for these reasons that Suarez' ramblings during that year
and a half seem to us somewhat chaotic. Ignatius Loyola had
realized fully the necessity of having his young religious carefully trained. He insisted that some provision be made in the
foundation of colleges which would take care of this training.
When it was not forthcoming he refused to approve the foundation or to send Jesuit teachers. When William IV, Duke of
Bavaria, asked Ignatius for a college at Ingolstadt he agreed that

it would be for Jesuit students as well as for laics. But William's successor, Albert V, wished to exclude Jesuits from the endowment, and for that sole reason Loyola would not approve the foundation.

Dr. Farrell explains the Jesuit stand on this question and thus allows us to have an inkling of the difficulties under which Suarez and his Jesuit predecessors labored. "The colleges Ignatius had in mind," he writes, "were for two types of students, lay and Jesuit; and since the endowment afforded a free education to the lay students, he thought it should do the same for his own subjects. *Otherwise there seemed no means of providing the knowledge of doctrine and skill in teaching it which was needed by members of the Order.* For it must be remembered that at that time the Society had no training colleges for its younger members and the gratuitous nature of its teaching yielded no revenue for their support. Thus circumstances forced Ignatius to insist that each of the endowed colleges should provide for the training of a few of the Order's future teachers." [8]

In 1575 the Jesuit province of Castile found itself in the unique situation of having more professors of theology than it had places for them in the colleges. More unique still was the fact that they were all outstanding men. Writing to the General Everard Mercurian in August of that year, Jeronimo de Avila lists his best theologians as follows: Gutierrez, Suarez, Perez, Galarza, Siguenza, Ojeda, Ribera, Vega "and others who do not at the moment come to mind."

[8] Farrell, *op. cit.*, pp. 134–135.

Chapter X

The Road to Rome

THE NEXT FOUR YEARS were steps on the road to Rome. Suarez spent them (1576–1580) at Valladolid in his favorite work of teaching the *Summa* of St. Thomas. With mounting enthusiasm he started his courses, and with even greater enthusiasm he completed them. But in the meanwhile he experienced what was probably the most painful personal attack upon his pedagogical ability. The result of it was that he was called to Rome by the Jesuit general and given the high position of theology professor there.

On the staff at Valladolid, besides Suarez, were Andres Martinez, formerly his philosophy teacher, and Bartholomew Perez. They divided the whole *Summa* into three parts, and then each divided his own section into four additional sections corresponding with the four years in which the work would be covered. In this way their students benefited by the logical sequence of the Angelic Doctor's masterpiece and were able to digest intellectually every part of it. The *Summa Theologica* lends itself to such division even more than does Thomas' *Summa Contra Gentiles*, considered by most critics a masterstroke of coordination.

In any event it was the *Summa* which these Jesuit professors used. The Council of Trent had recommended that it should be the official text-book of the schools, and that Council was completed only eleven years before Suarez began his teaching of theology at Valladolid. Thomas was all the rage. His work was

to be the bible of philosophers and theologians, accredited sometimes with a divine inspiration which it certainly did not have,
thus opening the path to a possibly deadening formalism.

Suarez got into trouble by sidestepping this formalism. He
"was faithful in his citations and loyal in his attempts at interpretation of Thomas;" says Mahowald, "and his works breathe
a feeling of love and reverence for him." [1] But he refused to be
rigid in either his teaching or writing. Attackers were close at
hand to attempt to force him back to the exact and literal trans-
mission of the Thomistic classic.

The subject matter which the young priest taught in his classes
is contained for the most part in the first tome of the *Summa*.
There was included much of what is now treated in natural theology: how God is known and His existence proved, the divine
attributes and the question of creation. Other treatises were
strictly theological: the divine unity and trinity, the divine relations, the Holy Spirit. Still others left wide room for interesting
speculation and discussion, such as those regarding the angels,
where Thomas asks whether one angel can move the will of another, can talk to another or to God, whether the angels grieve
over the sins committed by men whom they guard.[2]

Suarez went along happily for a while although there was an
occasional rumble of local opposition. Again he was over-
whelmingly popular with his students; and to some of his hide-
bound confrères, student popularity meant only one thing: the
man was teaching either novelties or nonsense. In either case
he bore watching; and they watched him. Complaints came to
the Father Rector, who was satisfied with Suarez; they came to
the Father Provincial, who from previous experience at Segovia
was sure of him. Finally they came to the Father General who

[1] Mahowald, George: "Suarez, De Anima," in *Jesuit Educational Association Proceedings*, Chicago, 1931, Loyola University, pp. 170–171.

[2] *Summa Theol., Pars Prima, q. cvi–cxiii.* This portion is only one sample
of Thomas' attractive handling of fascinating problems.

promised they would be investigated when next he sent an official
visitor into the province of Castile.

But Diego de Avellaneda was a poor choice as Jesuit investi-
gator of a Jesuit problem. Despite his high recommendations
and tried background he seems to have botched badly his job in
Spain. As a secular priest he had been hailed for talent and
performance. As a thirty-three-year-old Jesuit he was known
as religious and virtuous, the confidant of Philip II and of
his ambassador to Vienna, whilom confessor to the Queen
of France, and professor in the Roman College. His birthplace was Granada, where he undoubtedly knew the Suarez
family.

Avellaneda's reputation preceded him to Valladolid and
Suarez breathed a sigh of relief that he should be allowed to present his case to so capable and distinguished a judge. On the
score of his doctrine he confidently believed that he had nothing to fear; regarding his manner of teaching, he was sure that
this great man would fully approve. What he did not know
was that the visitor was an aloof and haughty person as well as
a severely critical arbitrator.

The General's visitor arrived, made his survey, and departed
during the first three months of 1579. The kind of trail he left
can be picked up immediately in a letter which John de Atienza,
rector of the college in Valladolid, sent to Father Mercurian on
the fourth of April. "It has been reported," wrote the rector,
"that Father John Suarez is going to be sent to Madrid and that
Father Avellaneda will take his place as our provincial. Father
Suarez' departure would be an evil, but his replacement by
Father Avellaneda a still greater evil. I say nothing of his
severity, for, to religious men of good will, it is of little importance; but he has shown himself so artful and cunning that he
has alienated all and pleased none. He has left such discontent

in his wake that even if he worked miracles he could not remove it." [3]

The thing that most stuck in Avellaneda's craw was an incident which occurred at the University of Salamanca. He went over for a public disputation in which some students of Jesuit professors were taking part. A certain Jesuit Scholastic, in answering an objection regarding the extrinsic denomination of the soul, had gone contrary to accepted and ancient teachings. Bartholomew de Medina, Dominican professor in the principal chair of philosophy and a really worthy man, had branded the assertion novel, chimerical and heretical, "and he gained a triumph at our expense." In searching for the source of these opinions which were putting the Society of Jesus in a bad light Avellaneda pointed the finger at Francis Suarez and wrote to the general that he had talked to the young priest who had promised to mend his ways.

But Suarez was not keen about mending his ways in this particular regard for he was convinced of their rectitude. He was called to the visitor's room for an interview. Avellaneda sat there in the rôle of judge, critic and adviser, and in his most pontifical manner read the whole list of charges made against Suarez. Treatise after treatise, purported to have been found in his lectures, now appeared before him under a most heretical aspect. Was he not teaching things which could not be found in the *Summa*? Was he not following Duns Scotus' doctrine regarding the immaculate conception of the mother of God, rather than the opposing view held by Thomas? Anyway, had not the late saintly Pope Pius forbidden heated and public controversy on that very point? One must be very careful, especially

[3] De Scorraille, *op. cit.*, p. 158. He quotes also Domingo de Alcola's opinion of Avellaneda: "Es un Padre que tiene unas palabras muy doradas y açucaradas; pero debajo de ellas pone la pildora y la purga con que a desgustado el gusto de muchos."

when one is so young; the reputation of the Society must be safe-guarded; and all the rest.

Humbly the young professor heard him through, promised that he would correct all these things if Father Visitor gave him a copy of the list of charges. This Avellaneda did, and therein gave Suarez the opportunity he wanted. As the latter put out his hand for the document he asked whether all of the accusations were completely listed. They were; including severe criticisms on his method of teaching.

Suarez wanted nothing better than this complete and written exposé of his supposedly heretical doctrines. He knew that this was the opportune time for his stand against the pedagogues of ancient vintage, and that his rebuttal would either vindicate him entirely or remove him forever from the lecture hall. Either course would satisfy him, but he could not go on in this way, never knowing where he stood, what he could teach, whom he could trust. He owed it to himself and to his intellectual descendants that his name be cleared and his doctrine approved.

These may seem high and mighty thoughts for a young teacher of thirty-two. Would it not be more politic to bend to the weight of criticism? His position was assured for many years if he would simply conform to the demands made upon him. But even here he was not sure what was meant by "conforming." He sat down with the visitor's list before him, and alongside it wrote out another of his own, matching each individual charge with a clear explanation of his own views on the controverted points. In his calm and careful way he completed this and appended to it a letter to Father Mercurian.

"Father Visitor," he wrote to the Jesuit general, "on his recent visit informed me that my manner of teaching is not satisfactory, that it is considered singular, and that it is spotted with opinions contrary to St. Thomas. There were [in his criticism] a few other particulars about which I keep silent, my purpose being not

to complain, but to render an account of what I have done and to
ask what I should do. As a matter of fact, I am somewhat per-
plexed and do not exactly know what is expected of me, and
whether dissatisfaction has really been shown with what I have
done up to now. If there is anything in the following explanations which seems to be self-praise, please do not understand it
in that way. I do not at all wish to praise myself, but to say the
things that must be said."

This opening paragraph of Suarez' letter is of capital importance since it strikes the keynote of the relations existing between
himself and his superiors, while it also gives his own intense
attitude toward the work he was trying to do. Characteristically
he points out the charges one by one. His teaching is not satisfactory to the men commissioned to investigate it. He suspects
that fact to be to its praise rather than its condemnation. It is
singular, unique, different; perhaps such technic is what the lecture halls of the time needed. It seems in spots different from
that of St. Thomas; and that indicates that Thomas' theology was
alive and growing, capable of development.

There is neither false pride nor false humility in Suarez' belief
in himself. "First of all," he continues in his letter, "I am convinced that I hold the surest and most common opinions in all
my theological teaching, especially in questions of importance;
and I am supported in all of it by the doctrine of St. Thomas,
except on one or two points. The best way to verify this statement is to examine the matter I have given in my courses. This
examination will require time, and while waiting for it to be
made, I am sending to Your Paternity a document which Father
Visitor has given me. It contains all the assertions that are novel
or contrary to St. Thomas, and which, according to the man who
gathered them, are found in my lectures."

Actually, these assertions were not the teachings of Suarez.
Some of them were pure fabrications, others garbled almost be-

yond recognition, still others only slightly varying from his
original remarks. Most of them seem to have come by way of
students' notes scribbled in class, notes which every college boy
knows are notoriously liable to be wrong. To offset all this
Suarez says: "I add to this in another document, an exposé of
my real opinions and the foundations upon which I base them.
I do not pretend to defend them, but wish to show clearly what
they really are."

In the light of historical reflection the main reason for opposition to Suarez is found in the somewhat original and vital manner in which he rattled the dry bones of theological speculation
in his lectures. "In the second place," he continues, "of the
several clearly visible circumstances that could have created this
bad reputation for me one should be especially noted: It is the
method I use in my teaching, a method different from that of
most others. The custom in this country is to teach by dictation
from copy books, to hand down the doctrine almost exactly as it
has been received. This is done instead of studying it profoundly at its sources, divine or human authority and reason,
each one according to its proper value."

Suarez' mention of dictation and copy books brings out a point
which was a real abuse in the colleges of his day. Diego Carillo,
the previous provincial of Castile, had complained about the same
thing in a letter to the Jesuit general in 1567. He noted that the
students seemed to have an enthralling desire to make their col-
lection of treatises very complete, rivaling each other in the practice, and considering it an evidence of real ability. They wished
to carry these notes with them because of the scarcity of textbooks.
"They have gotten to the point where they possess and carry
about with them whole libraries of manuscripts which are very
expensive. For the cost of having one copy book transcribed is
forty or fifty ducats, and soon there were so many of them
that the students could not possibly carry away with them

all they had, and asked that they be shipped to them afterwards." [4]

The insatiable mania for transcribing endless theological
treatises was thus ended at the Jesuit college of Salamanca. The
provincial put a stop to all this traffic in note-books and in the
same action removed the threat to religious poverty which went
with it. Loyola had written in the Jesuit Constitutions that no
member of the Order was to have books without permission, nor
write in them, nor carry them away when moving to a new place
of residence. All of this must have been in the mind of Suarez
when he too objected to the practice; but there was an objection
which touched him more intimately than this.

The fact is that he objected to parrot-like repetition of the
words and formulae of theological thought without sufficient
reflection over the thought itself. Superiors checked the breach
of religious poverty and regularity. Suarez was intent on check-
ing the stultification of intelligence. To copy down avidly all
that others have written is detrimental to intellectual progress,
to the faculty of critical thought, and to the formation of personal
opinions. Often enough the best stenographer writes words
without reflecting on their meaning, and these students at Valladolid, too, may have been satisfied that they knew theology
simply because they had it all down in their copy books. They
are great scholars, as someone has said, who lose their knowledge when they lose their luggage.

In his *apologia* to the general, Suarez was personally aware
of all these defects when he wrote: "It has been my endeavor to
depart from this method and to search for truth at its very roots.
The result is that my lectures are always presented with a certain
air of novelty which comes from the scheme I follow, my manner of explanation, the type of proofs I use, my manner of solving
difficulties, the problems I raise at points where others do not

[4] *Ibid.,* pp. 90–91.

raise them, or finally from any other circumstances that may chance to arise. Thus my doctrine is not novel; but it becomes novel in its presentation and in its departure from the routine of the copy books. This is all I have to say to Your Paternity regarding my doctrine and my type of teaching."

These remarks were pertinent to the Jesuit mode of educating the Scholastics, and the young priest did not wish them to be glanced over hurriedly by some busy or incapable person at Rome. He was confident that an examination of his doctrine and method would exonerate him, but he wanted this examination conducted "carefully and by men who were capable of investigation and comprehension, of which there are—thanks be to God!—many in our Society."

Furthermore, Suarez wanted no more time-wasting complaints and charges on the part of his associates. If he was in error he wished to have it stated clearly so that he could amend; but if he was not in error he wished that, too, to be fully understood by all so that he would have done with all these petty annoyances. As he wrote: "If this examination proves that there are any serious incongruities and embarrassing errors in my doctrine or method let it be told to me clearly, for my only desire is to conform in everything to the will of Our Lord. I will try to change whatever needs changing; and if I do not succeed in this I would prefer some other employment where I would not cause complaints instead of this one in which I seem to give rise to them."

His next paragraph is a request that the general call off the critics, and leave him in peace. "If you recognize that the affair is not worth all the trouble it is making, I beg Your Paternity to order that I be allowed to do my work in peace and consolation. Since these duties cost me the labor they do—an enormous labor—and since I myself desire only to perform them as well as I can to the satisfaction and benefit of all, it is unjust that I am constantly troubled, annoyed and suspected in a matter as delicate as dogma. Nothing is more liable—not to speak of other effects—to bring about the loss of all authority."

Finally, Suarez concludes his letter by repeating a plea which he had previously made to the Jesuit general. He is still desirous of travelling to Rome and studying there at the central headquarters of the Society of Jesus. He wishes to be known personally to Father Mercurian, and not merely by hearsay. At Rome Suarez "would find great help in living contentedly and in enduring trials such as these which are certain to be met in this type of work. If the opportunity is some day offered to me it will be a great consolation and joy. But as long as the will of Our Lord is otherwise I will resign myself to patience, convinced that the charity of Your Paternity will uphold me wherever I am, will put up with my faults and will aid me by prayer to correct myself. May Our Lord console us by preserving Your Paternity for many long years and grant you according to your desires an increase of his blessings." [5]

The result of this straightforward explanation of Suarez to the general worked all in the favor of the young priest. Mercurian's answer is not known, nor is it known whether he answered this letter directly. He was, however, fully satisfied with the sincere and quietly determined answer to the attacks on Suarez' doctrine, for in the following year he sent for him to come to Rome.

The final year of Suarez' professorate at the University of Valladolid was smoothly lived. Domestic difficulties had ceased, perhaps through the interposition of the provincial's authority, and he was permitted to work in the peace and quiet which he so much desired. He did not learn until the following June that he was to go to Rome but he was definitely aware of a changed

[5] De Scorraille, *op. cit.*, pp. 161–163. He reproduces here a facsimile of Suarez' original letter to Father Everard Mercurian, from Valladolid, July 2, 1579.

attitude among those who surrounded him. Perhaps the news had drifted to Valladolid that he was being particularly observed for a higher post, that he was to be given an opportunity to demonstrate his well-known pedagogical method at the Roman College.

Those who watched could well have emulated Suarez' methods. He was the forerunner of an entirely different type of professor in the halls of theological and philosophical learning. The trend he started was a significant one. No longer would it be the end and all of a teacher's endeavor to startle his students with erudition, with Ciceronian phrases tumbling in beautiful cadences, with syllogism built upon intricate syllogism. That was not the method of Socrates and Aristotle, nor of the Schoolmen when they first flourished in Europe. The objective was—as it must be with every successful teacher—to put the teaching into the minds of the students. In large assemblies, and in more recent times, the tendency of simple lecturing has again appeared; but here in Suarez and in the most famous of the Jesuit professors there was always an attempt to make sure that the student was really learning.

In that respect Suarez was a model of good teaching. Although it may have appeared novel, unique, quaint, undignified, his method attained the prime objective of its use. And that is always the acid test of any method.

CHAPTER XI

Center of the World

THE HIGH SPOT of Suarez' five years at the Roman College was the unusual honor paid him by Pope Gregory XIII, who attended one of his early lectures. The presence of the Holy Father was as unexpected as it was unusual, for the young professor still had, fresh in his memory, the difficulties he had undergone regarding his doctrine and method at the College of Valladolid. There was likewise the memory of other years when he had been considered too dim-witted even to finish the ordinary studies of his vocation. "Suarez was received at Rome," says Coleridge, "not as a teacher who was suspect of novelties, but as a theologian of the highest character and fairest promise." [1]

That the Pope should appear in the classroom of a young Jesuit theologian at the Roman College is not so phenomenal as it would at first seem. This Jesuit institution was important—Harvey calls it "the mother of many of the colleges throughout the world." [2] It was the fulfillment of the idea which Ignatius Loyola had inaugurated thirty years before: the idea of a central college not only for Rome but for the entire Catholic world. Gregory helped it to such an extent that he was called its second founder, and to it was given the name which it still bears: *Gregorianum*.

Francis Borgia had given the original grant for the foundation of the college in 1550, and classes were opened for the first

[1] Coleridge, *op. cit.,* p. 64.
[2] Harvey, Robert: *Ignatius Loyola,* Milwaukee, 1936, Bruce, p. 155.

time during the following year. The enrollment grew so rapidly that Borgia's money was not sufficient for its maintenance. Loyola begged in France and Italy, sent Nadal to Spain to raise money, and still, for years, the financial condition remained distressing. Lainez and Borgia and Mercurian in their generalates of the Society, tried to fix a permanent income for the school but they were not more than temporarily successful. Finally, Cardinal Matteo Cantarelli is supposed to have called Gregory's attention to the situation by likening the college to feet of clay.

"The feet," said the Cardinal to the Pope, "I see in the Roman College, which, being the establishment for training and instruction common to all, surpasses them all. But at present it is in a dwelling place so confined and ruinous, and is moreover so insufficiently endowed and so deeply in debt, that it cannot last long." [3]

Moved by the Cardinal's words, Gregory XIII made an annual grant in 1581 which amounted to a perpetual foundation. Further than that, he ordered the erection of a large new building which he himself blessed in 1584. When the cornerstone of this immense structure was put in place, a studiously academic session was held in which twenty-five theses were presented in twenty-five different languages: an indication that the college was to teach philosophy and theology to students from all nations of the world.

Suarez was himself present in Rome during these momentous beginnings of the Gregorian University. About half the time he taught at the old college, and in the latter part of his stay conducted his lectures in the new building. He witnessed also another mark of favor which the Pope gave the Jesuits and their work. This was his approval of the Sodality of the Roman College to which, in 1580, were added many privileges and blessings.

"In 1584," writes Dr. Farrell, "the same Pope made the Sodal-

[3] Pastor, *op. cit.*, vol. xix, p. 250.

ity of the Roman College the head and mother of all present and future Sodalities of Jesuit colleges throughout the world. . . . The tremendous stimulus it [the Sodality] gave to the entire student body arose from the fact that in practice no boy could gain admission to the Sodality who was not both pious and studious." [4] This was indeed an organization dear to the heart of Francis Suarez for it embodied all that he believed most essential in a student's life. It brought clearly to the fore the very combination of sanctity and application of prayer and work, which he had himself so carefully followed.

The love which the Holy Father had for the Blessed Virgin was one of the bonds which brought Suarez closer to him. Gregory, as is attested by the annals of the college, was a frequent visitor at the Jesuit residence, and his conversation was always directed personally to the men who were making the college a famous institution of learning. Besides Suarez, there were, during Gregory's pontificate, other renowned scholars, like the great Robert Bellarmine, who had already fought strenuously against the heretics, the celebrated mathematician, Christopher Clavius, and the distinguished humanists, Torsellini and Orlandini. Thus, the order which had Mary for its secondary patron, was highly and frequently honored by the Pope who loved Mary in the highest degree.

Despite the honor paid Suarez by Gregory it must not be imagined that the two were on terms of intimate friendship. Some of the biographers of Suarez, in the ancient biographical strain, would like to make a case for such intimacy. They even suggest that the Pope had heard of the theologian's Spanish reputation and had asked him to come to Rome. Descamps, Sartolo, Massei, and others give the impression that Gregory could hardly await his arrival to hasten immediately to his first class. According to the critical analysis of De Scorraille, it is more probable that the

[4] Farrell, *op. cit.*, p. 246.

"first lectures" which the Pope attended was Suarez' first dissertation or lecture which he gave at the opening of the new university.[5]

The truth remains, however, that these two great men knew
and respected each other. Gregory was of the opinion that the
Jesuits were responsible for much of the needed renovation then
going on within the Church. He was their generous protector to
such a degree that his secretary of state, Cardinal Galli, remarked
that they were one of the religious Orders best loved by the Pope.

In another person, too, Suarez found the example and pleasure he had anticipated before coming to Rome. That was the
new Jesuit general, Claudius Aquaviva, who had been elected
about a month before the Spaniard arrived in the Eternal City,
and who was only thirty-seven years old when he took up that
important office. When Aquaviva was presented at the Vatican
after his election, Pope Gregory was astonished at his youthfulness and remembered him as one of the private chamberlains of
Pope Pius V only thirteen years before. There was only five
years difference in age between Suarez and Aquaviva and they
were much of the same cloth: vigorously intellectual and com-
pellingly modern in their outlook.

Aquaviva and Suarez were both in the tradition of active
Jesuits who were withdrawn from public work. The former
had every ability essential to those who make a large mark before
the world, but his prime ability was that of governing. The internal direction of the Society of Jesus during the longest and most
crucial generalate of its early history was capably performed by
him. If for nothing else he deserves ranking honors for the
part he played in forming the *Ratio Studiorum,* the Jesuits' historical contribution to education. Suarez, for the most part, led
a similarly retired life in that he was continuously concerned
with teaching and writing. During five years at Rome he was

[5] Cf. De Scorraille, *op. cit.,* pp. 171–172.

frequently consulted by Aquaviva, and he contributed much weight and initiative to programs which appeared only after his departure for Spain.

Aquaviva had been a fellow novice of St. Stanislaus Kostka and, with Suarez, was now coming into daily contact with other saints. Pius V, his friend and patron, has since been canonized. Loyola, Borgia, and Xavier, all saints, were only recently dead. But other men who were to be later raised to the altars of the Church, were in or near Rome at that time: Bellarmine, Borromeo, Canisius, Gonzaga, Neri, Camillus de Lellis. Contemporaries, too, were the six greatest Spanish Jesuit theologians whom Astrain ranks as the three Andalusians and the three Castilians in this order: Toletus, future cardinal, and predecessor of Suarez at both Salamanca and Rome, Suarez himself, and Sanchez. From Castile were Molina, Gregory of Valencia, and Gabriel Vasquez, all of whom will repeatedly cross the path of Suarez' history.[6]

Rome offered excellent opportunities for a professional teacher such as Suarez. Back in Spain he had guessed wisely when he thought that this Roman experience would put the needed finishing touches to his plans and ideals for the propagation of truth. At the College of Valladolid he had taught the young manhood of the Society of Jesus and had profited immensely in the work. At Rome, as the college annals succinctly remark, "he taught for five years with singular success." Here there were more than a hundred Scholastics, chosen for their abilities from several countries of Europe and sent on for the express purpose of getting the best of Jesuit teaching. About half of these attended the lectures of Suarez, and all of them enjoyed his brisk and trenchant style.

Reputedly among these students was Aloysius Gonzaga; but actually he could not have been in the classes taught by Suarez,

[6] Cf. Astrain, Antonio: *op. cit.*, vol. iv, p. 56,

Early chroniclers, always ambitious for the prestige of Suarez, gathered in all the great names of the period and linked them with that of Suarez. They wished to give Suarez the honor of having St. Aloysius as a student, and to Aloysius the honor of having Suarez as a master. Definitely that error is sent to the historical limbo by the records of the Roman College for 1587, which relate that the year was fortunate for those at the college by the acquisition of a new guest, Aloysius Gonzaga, who studied metaphysics under Father Paolo Vallo, and who gave a public dissertation on the whole of philosophy. Suarez left Rome at the end of the school year, 1584–1585. Gonzaga came there for the opening of the school year, 1586–1587.[7]

There were, however, three men of future importance among the theological students following Suarez' courses at this time. Mutius Vitelleschi was there. He would follow Aquaviva as the sixth general of the Society. There was also Henry Garnet, who later entered the thick of the Catholic struggle in England as superior of the Jesuits, and ended his life as a martyr. The last of the trio was Leonard Lessius, prominent as the author of learned and pious books on theology and asceticism.

The relations existing between the student, Lessius, and the master, Suarez, are particularly indicative of the latter's influence. Lessius was an original mind, keen, penetrating, and to a large degree self-contained. He taught philosophy for seven years at Douay and studied theology privately before coming to the Roman College. His system of study was distinctly his own. He would read over a thesis in St. Thomas, then close the book, darken his room, shut his eyes, and think over carefully point

---

[7] De Scorraille, *op. cit.,* footnote on p. 175. Wishful thinking of biographers in this case is similar to that in which Suarez is linked with St. Theresa of Avila. Suarez was a close friend of Balthazar Alvarez, Theresa's spiritual director, and was at Avila for a while in 1575; but flimsy evidence of this kind does not establish a historical fact. The same might be noted of the supposed connection between Suarez and St. John of the Cross. (Cf. *infra* pp. 282-3.)

by point the content of the treatise. His logic was perfect, and with the help of a remarkable memory he was able to pick flaws in the arguments he thus pondered. Satisfying himself on all angles of the question he would then rewrite the thesis as he thought it should be.

Following this method Lessius naturally found himself in disagreement with the cut and dried doctrines of more ancient writers, and when he came to Rome he told Suarez of his scruples on this point. Of course, such original technique of thought was immediately welcomed by Suarez, who had himself energetically battled the blind following of accepted doctrines. He told Lessius that in matters of faith and moral he could not deviate from dogmatic precepts, but in other things it was reasonable and beneficial to dissent sometimes from the opinions of even great authorities. Lessius followed the advice of Suarez, and his later writings, especially those on predestination, prove that he put it to good use.

So thoroughly, indeed, did Suarez encourage Lessius to cultivate independence of thought that in after years the latter was sometimes to disagree even with Suarezian teachings. He wrote to Robert Bellarmine that he "frequently differed from Father Suarez," but he always gave carefully reasoned arguments to fortify his own views. All of this was the very life blood of Suarez' educational theories; and in Rome he was able to work out those theories without hindrance of destructive criticism. The men working on the faculty with him were themselves original thinkers; their private controversies were many but their respectful attention was always paid to the man who could intelligently defend his own opinions.

All things seemed to point to Suarez' indefinite stay as one of the theological luminaries of the Roman College. The enthusiasm of his students surpassed even that displayed by his former students in the schools of Spain. His reputation both within and without the Society was increasing tremendously. His superiors were more than satisfied with him, and his fellow professors found him a stimulating and agreeable co-worker. But the low geographical position of Italy was no place for a man with ailing lungs, and the Roman climate finally forced Suarez back to the higher and drier climate of Spain.

The official register at Rome for 1584 points out Francis Suarez as a man of mediocre health; *laborat dolore pectoris,* he was suffering from that pain in the chest which he had contracted in his apostolic work at Segovia. But the record continues by showing that if his physique was impaired, his mind was of an extraordinarily brilliant nature. "He is of sound judgement, excellently qualified in theology, capable in all things but especially fit for teaching in the Scholasticate." His quiet and reserved manner, also noted in this document, was undoubtedly due to the physical sufferings he was undergoing. He was by nature and temperament of an external modesty which fits the pictures usually drawn of saintly men. But remaining at Rome would have been his death sentence.

Ill health visited another member of his personal family. To Suarez himself it brought a cessation of his labors at Rome; to his brother, Gaspar, it brought an unexpected and premature death. This young brother was hardly eight years in the Society, still a theological student when he offered his services for the mission of the Philippines.

Philip II had recently gained control of the Philippines for Spain and had, with his usual high regard for the natives, appointed the Dominican, Dominic de Salazar, to the post of bishop. Salazar asked for several Jesuits to help him on the mission. They were to go by way of Mexico, but twelve of the twenty-two selected died on the voyage. Gaspar Suarez survived the crossing of the south Atlantic and was among those who left from the beautiful Mexican port of Acapulco on March 29, 1581 sailing out to the isles of the Pacific. He died in the passage without having set foot on the soil of the new mission which he had hoped to make his permanent home.

Some years later, when the second generation of Suarez was coming of age, this youth's place was taken by his nephew, also named Gaspar. He was one of the seven children of Francis Suarez' elder brother, John, who had inherited the family estates at Granada and who was carrying on the Suarez name. This nephew was sixteen years old when he entered the Society of Jesus at Salamanca in 1589. He lived to the advanced age of seventy-nine, and was occupied mainly in pastoral functions, preaching, hearing confessions, taking care of parish duties.

It is quite probable that the combination of bad climate and weak health was the main reason for Suarez' departure from Rome. It is suggested also that his boundless energy for work and his constant application to teaching had some part in bringing on his condition of ill-health. The fact is that he never ceased his industry, whether here at Rome or in his later assignments in Spain and Portugal. In those places he was able to carry the burden of constant writing and lecturing with only occasionally serious detriment to his physical well-being. The work he performed at the Roman College is nothing more than a pattern, from which can be cut a sample of almost any other period of Suarez' life.

During the first year he lectured on the end of man, *de fine hominum,* using as his authority not only St. Thomas but also the doctrines of numerous other Scholastics, going back even to the patristic writings and the ancient pagan philosophers. In the second year of his teaching he followed St. Thomas quite closely, in the two separate courses he presented: *de voluntario et involuntario* and *de vitiis et peccatis.* These were strictly moral questions and comprised most of the study which is now made in seminaries under the title of Moral Theology.

In the school year, 1582–1583, Suarez taught the important subject of Grace, which would be published only after his death as a treatise *De Gratia,* and with which he was to be greatly concerned during the controversy between the Dominicans and the Jesuits. During the latter part of this year, and all during the next, he conducted courses in the theological virtues of Faith, Hope and Charity. In these classes also he was preparing notes and outlines for the large work which would be published some years after his death: *De Fide, Spe, Charitate.*

The final year of his professorate at Rome enabled Suarez to return to the favorite subject of all his teaching and study: the Divine Incarnation. It was this topic which kept him busily engaged for many years while at the same time it gave him steady food for spiritual meditation. It is significant to note that Suarez left Rome without having touched the problem which would eventually keep his name immortal. I mean that his famous theories regarding law, popular sovereignty, and the other accompanying ideas, had not yet made any prominent appearance in his work. He was thus far preëminently the theologian, and the tracts on Grace and on the Incarnation represented the summit of his achievement.

For their intrinsic worth, these treatises are far superior to those which he developed in the fight against James I. But in their benefit to humankind in general, and in their attractiveness to the twentieth-century commentator, they are far overshadowed by his political theories.

All in all, the time spent at Rome by Suarez gave the finishing touches to his perfection as a theologian. Not many of the best known theologians, either then or now, spent all of their lives away from the eternal city. Practically all of them, however, at some time or other, profited by the ecclesiastical atmosphere of the place and, by being close to the root and source of Church life, were able also to maintain scientific orthodoxy.

Coleridge declares that a stay at Rome is important "among the thousand influences, natural and supernatural, which must combine to produce a consummate and faultless theologian. Suarez might have been very great without it, as others have been: with it, he became the *Doctor Eximius*; a theologian surpassed by no one since the days of St. Thomas Aquinas." [8]

[8] Coleridge, *op. cit.*, p. 67.

CHAPTER XII

The Jesuit Code of Education

IT WOULD BE PATENT NONSENSE to claim that Suarez, or any other individual Jesuit for that matter, was chiefly responsible for the famous *Ratio Studiorum*. This practical code of education was in the making for more than fifteen years, dating from the time of Suarez' stay at Rome till 1599, when it received its third and final form. Into the making of that final edition, says Farrell, "went the best efforts of a group of brilliant administrators and teachers, the manifold influence of Renaissance theory and practice, particularly the influence of the University of Paris, and the practical wisdom gained from severe and prolonged tests in a hundred colleges in many countries." [1]

All of this was necessary for the stupendous task which the Jesuits had set before themselves when, as Belloc puts it, "they thought out and made of one piece, solid and permanent, a whole new system of education which became the model for Europe, which remains to-day the basis of all the best instruction in the traditional schools of the Continent." [2] They were doing the thing which would, in the eyes of commentators, set them apart from all the other religious orders of the Church, and which would give their own Order the reputation of educational leader of the Catholic world.

Yet the part played by Suarez cannot be submerged in the

[1] Farrell, *op. cit.*, p. xi.
[2] Belloc, Hilaire: *How the Reformation Happened*, McBride, 1928, New York, p. 224.

132

whole. The result, after all, was the result of many human individuals, each of whom gave his little portion, measured it
with the others, modified, improved, and made new suggestions.
Suarez was asked at various times to take part in the work,
first at Rome and then at Alcalá. His part was secondary in that
he had no appointment except on the critical committees, but
it was essential in that he was asked for his practical criticisms
upon the conclusions of the other priests.

Almost immediately upon his election, Aquaviva had named
a committee of twelve Jesuits, representing six nationalities, five
of whom were Spaniards. This group spent almost four years
in assembling, sorting, and discussing the vast amount of
pedagogical material which had been drifting into Rome ever
since the very beginnings of the first colleges. In 1584 these
were replaced by a committee of six summoned to Rome by the
general and representing the countries where the Society had
its main colleges: Spain, France, Italy, Portugal, Austria, Germany. On December 8, 1584, they began intensive work on
the plan, holding daily discussions of three hours, and sub-
mitting periodically their findings to six of the principal professors at the Roman college. This board of critics was comprised
of three Italians: Sardi, Bellarmine and Justiniani, and three
Spaniards: Parra, Suarez and Pereira.

There is still preserved in the Jesuit archives at Rome a thick
bundle of manuscripts containing the criticisms of these eminent
Roman professors.[3] There, too, is to be found the wise advice
which Suarez gave in the numerous particulars of Jesuit peda-
gogy. He insisted, for example, that the course in theology
should be taught for four years with a minimum of three profes-

---

[3] These manuscripts were given the title, *Documenta de Ratione Studiorum,
1581–1613. Censura Patrum Collegi Romani circa ea quae a Patribus Deputatis
de ordine ac ratione studiorum praescripta sunt.* (De Scorraille, *op. cit.*, p.
187.) Farrell, *op. cit.*, p. 455, who has had access to them describes their contents.

sors. If there were only two professors the course should be extended to five years. Suarez' demand for long and careful theological study had been foreshadowed in his own practice of developing fully whatever topics he taught. He believed that too much time could not be given to the study of the divine science, either by teacher or student.

When it came to a discussion of the technical points of teaching Suarez was strictly in his element, for he was again in the old battle for freedom and initiative on the part of the professor. He was a past master in methods of arousing the interest of students, an expert in the direction of argumentation and the handling of objections. His contention was again an attack on the method of dictation, though he concedes that the professors should lecture at a pace that would allow a brief taking of notes in class. He admits that the prefect of studies in the college might reject certain doubtful opinions from class matter, but only after consultation with the professor in charge.

These intimate opinions of Suarez, given in the privacy of committee meetings, show the master theologian in his best light. They demonstrate his attitude regarding the subject of individual thinking and personal responsibility, two of the qualities upon which he repeatedly insisted in his controversy with James I of England. They forecast, too, the theory he formulated anent popular sovereignty by stressing his objections to rigorous regimentation of the human intellect and will. Of course, he did not go the way of the complete libertine, who understands neither liberty nor restriction. His opinions were always founded upon the bedrock of reality, upon the status of a human person as he lives in decidedly human and frail society.

The *Ratio*, formed at this time, was divided into two parts, the first giving the regulation for discussing speculative theses in theology, and the second dealing with the practical conduct and organization of classes in theology, philosophy and the humanities. The whole was meant for nothing more than a temporary tryout in the colleges of the Jesuits. Thus it was that Suarez, who was removed to the college at Alcalá just before the publication of the *Ratio* in 1586, was able to put into practice its norms and to observe the reaction they produced in the teaching of his fellow faculty members.

The first edition was limited in number and was sent out with a letter explaining its use and purpose. The plan here suggested —the appended letter noted—was not in the nature of a law. It was merely a pliable scheme which Jesuits in various provinces of the Order were to study at their leisure; some of its suggestions they might wish to put to the test in their own classes. Furthermore, there should be appointed a committee of fathers in each province, who would read the *Ratio*, examine and discuss it thoroughly, and then send in their written opinions of it to Rome within five or six months.

At Alcalá this second examination of the educational plan was undertaken by the rector of the college, Alonso de Sandoval, and three of the professors, Francis Suarez, Juan de Florencia, and Cyprian Suarez.[4] They made the examination, as ordered, and then drew up their criticism on two separate reports, the first signed by all four of the examiners, the other by Suarez and Florencia. The extant papers dealing with these meetings and discussions demonstrate the freedom of thought which was allowed in handling the project of Aquaviva's special committee of six at Rome.

These provincial discussions show, too, the wisdom and prudence practiced by the Jesuit superiors before authoritatively sending out a uniform plan for the whole Society. They were wise in asking the judgements of almost innumerable competent

---

[4] Not related to the Suarez family of Toledo and Granada.

men, and they were prudent in measuring the findings of one group against those of another. It must be kept in mind, however, that there was in general a greater uniformity of studies in those days, and less complexity of subjects treated than in our own times. Men who were then masters came out of a Christian educational tradition where certain things were considered legitimate fields of study and others merely esoteric and private investigations.

While the *Ratio* was being quietly studied by Suarez and the other Jesuits all over Spain, there were other individuals who took an immediate dislike to the scheme, particularly to the first part which treated of rules for orthodoxy of opinions and of the catalogues of propositions which were to be imposed or forbidden. While the best Jesuit thinkers wished to allow a latitude of judgement on matters open to question, they believed that certain false and dangerous doctrines should be suppressed from the outset. They were insistent, however, that the doctrines of St. Thomas need not be slavishly followed in every detail by Jesuit professors.

Furthermore, all of these plans were for the private and sole discussion of the members of the Order, and were not meant for publication until a definitive *Ratio* could be compiled. The opposition of a certain Father Enriquez aroused a veritable tumult in Spain. He attacked the plan on the grounds that it was in direct contradiction to the teachings of St. Thomas, and sent his attack to the Spanish Inquisition instead of to his superiors. Other memorials were written and given wide publicity so that the Inquisition confiscated copies of the *Ratio* for closer scrutiny.

The result of this action on the part of the Spanish Inquisition has been an undying slander against the Jesuits. Even modern writers make the mistake of declaring that the plan of studies had been condemned as heretical because it approved of opinions contrary to Thomas' teaching.[5] Nothing could be further from the truth. As Farrell states, "The Ratio was never suppressed as heretical; it was neither condemned nor reproved by the Inquisition; and it was not revised as a result of criticisms by the Dominicans and the Inquisition."

The fact is that this incident concerning the *Ratio* was merely one item in the general tumult which was then surrounding the Society in Spain. The Jesuits had been accused of practically every sin in the catalogue, from soliciting women for immoral purposes to the teaching of false doctrines. The Spanish Inquisition was high-handed and direct in its dealings not only with accused members of the Order but also with their superiors. Antonio Marcén, provincial of Toledo, was thrown into prison with two professors of the college of Monterey. Soon a fourth Jesuit, Father Ripalda, rector of the college at Villagarcia, was imprisoned with them.[6] The general charges were accusations of heresy and of defection from the Catholic faith. "Out of the trial of the four Jesuits," writes Pastor, "there soon developed a process against the whole Jesuit institute, and as the latter had been approved by the Pope, the private controversy developed into a public one, and a quarrel between the Spanish Inquisition and the Holy See."[7]

Aquaviva complained to the Pope about the incarceration of the four Jesuits, and the Grand Inquisitor Cardinal Quiroga, complained about the Jesuits to the King, Philip II. A royal decree was issued forbidding any Jesuit to leave Spanish territory without written permission of the Inquisition. This permit was given to the vice-provincial of Toledo, Francis de Porres, who forwarded an authentic and witnessed copy to Rome. Aquaviva

[5] Cf. Quick, R. H.: *Essays on Educational Reformers*, 1898, p. 34. Also Smith, Preserved: *A History of Modern Culture*, 1930, p. 234. Other similar charges are listed in Schwickerath, *Jesuit Education*, pp. 112–114.

[6] Astrain, *op. cit.*, vol. iii, pp. 376–380.

[7] Pastor, *op. cit.*, vol. xxi, p. 157.

gave it to the Pope. "Then Sixtus V lost patience. He at once ordered the nuncio in Spain to deliver a warning to Cardinal Quiroga in the Pope's name that he had exceeded his powers in demanding the Papal bulls from the Jesuits. He must return them at once, and in the event of his disobedience the Pope would depose him and take away from him his Cardinal's hat. The acta of the trial of the four Jesuits must be sent to Rome." [8]

The Jesuits were fully acquitted after two years in jail, and are thus forever unique as part of the very few prisoners who came out of the Inquisition's hands unharmed. In the meanwhile Aquaviva was a dynamo of energy. He ordered memorials to be drawn up showing all angles of the struggle, a description of all the secret plots hatched within and without the Order. He pointed out to the Pope that a visitation of the Spanish Jesuit houses by men who were not members of the Society would be more harmful than helpful to the Church's cause, and particularly how Jeronimo Manrique, who was himself illegitimate and had three bastard sons, was not a suitable visitor of the proposed reform of a religious order.[9]

The very existence of the whole Society during these years was in a precarious position. Even Sixtus V wanted to make certain changes in the constitution; then thought better of it, and finally decided that only the name of the Order should be changed. His death occurred in 1590 before he could sign the decree to this effect. But frequent changes of papal attitude toward the Society were no new thing with the Jesuits. Paul IV had altered the first plans of Ignatius Loyola; Pius IV restored them to their original condition; Pius V made several important changes, which were later revoked by Gregory XIII. The final judgement of the Roman Inquisition, however, was favorable to the Society, and even Sixtus V, after an inspection of the constitutions, gave up his planned alterations. He did, however,

[8] *Ibid.,* p. 161. Cf. also Astrain, pp. 397 ff.   [9] Astrain, *op. cit.,* p. 441.

show himself severe to individual Jesuits, on occasions, and even had one of Bellarmine's controversial works placed on the new index of forbidden books.

Among the documents which Cardinal Quiroga had confiscated there were also those which belonged to the college at Alcalá where Suarez was then teaching. Whether the report made by himself and the other fathers on the first draft of the *Ratio* was included, is not known. But it is certain that Quiroga carefully examined the *Ratio* itself, and declared himself entirely dissatisfied with the first part treating of doctrinal practices and opinions. His general attitude toward the Jesuits in Spain is well known, although in the end he protested to the Pope that he was merely attempting to perform his sacred duty and that he had no personal animus toward individual members of the Order.

Suarez always cocked a prudent eye on such difficulties between prelates and Jesuits, and tried in his own way to smooth things over. Thus, in 1590, he honored the cardinal by dedicating his first and monumental work, *De Incarnatione*, to "The Most Illustrious and Most Reverend Gaspar De Quiroga, Cardinal of the Holy Roman Church, Archibishop of Toledo, Primate of Spain, Supreme Inquisitor of the Faith." Probably with his tongue in his cheek, Suarez wrote in the preface about the cardinal's humanity and his outstanding benevolence to the whole Society. He offers Quiroga these first fruits of study and labor which are probably not worthy of him but are due him because of his rewards and favors to the whole Society.

In the meanwhile at Alcalá, Suarez, Sandoval, Florencia, and the other Suarez, were carefully drafting their own report to be sent to Rome for the perfection of the educational plan. For one thing, they were unanimously opposed to any definitive catalogue of forbidden propositions. They held out also for mutual tolerance on the part of all in matters of free opinion. They remarked sagely that to draw up such a list would be to attempt what no council, university, or religious Order had yet dared to try. To arrogate to themselves such doctrinal authority would give the public impression that the Society was overstepping its rights.

That is precisely the opinion drawn by those who achieved a premature and unintended examination of the first *Ratio*. Thus the men at Alcalá foresaw the immediate danger and ultimate futility of a dogmatic insistence on the approval or disapproval of variable theological opinions. Their report warned that some of the forbidden theses were from St. Thomas, or at least attributed to him, and that their prohibition might provoke a critical episode especially in Spain. The fourth part of the Jesuit Constitutions of Ignatius Loyola declared St. Thomas the official author for Jesuit schools, and the Alcalá report of which Suarez was one of the signators, mentioned that fact.

"Let us beware," said the report, "about lessening the authority of our constitutions in which Father Ignatius duly honors the doctrine of St. Thomas. We would thus be letting down a barrier so that some of our professors might conclude that the Angelic Doctor is not so much a master as simply another author like the others; and that would be a great mistake. For it is of the utmost importance to Christianity that this divine author, who is held in the highest esteem by sovereign pontiffs, by the councils, and by the most celebrated Spanish universities, and who is, on the other hand, so despised by heretics, should be considered of the first rank. When the human mind treats lightly the less important statements of a man, it is liable also to treat lightly the more important ones." [10]

This criticism was backed up by many similar ones from other Jesuit provinces; and the general opinion seemed to be that it would be best to inflict a minimum of prohibitions anent St.

[10] De Scorraille, *op. cit.,* p. 191.

Thomas. Eventually the idea died of its own futility. For a couple of years after its appearance the *Ratio* was answered from all parts of Europe, and most of the comments were pointed at the proposed list of obligatory and optional theses. When the second tentative edition was sent from Rome in 1591 Aquaviva sent word with it that the doctrinal part would some day be completed and sent to all the provinces except those of Spain. The Spaniards, for their part, were to follow their previous custom of teaching St. Thomas almost exclusively.

As for the rest, Bellarmine noted at the end of 1590 that nearly four hundred propositions on the objectionable catalogue had been argued out of existence by Jesuit critics themselves. He was asked to give his judgement regarding the two hundred and seven that survived; and he thought, just as Suarez had, that only a very few propositions should be definitively set up, and these only for the sake of security. "Such lists would prove an intolerable burden to professors," he said; "they would never be drawn up so accurately as to leave no room for cavil; they would afford the Dominicans a legitimate grievance; no other religious order nor learned body, except the University of Paris, had favored them, and the Paris definitions were the laughing-stock of all Europe; finally, they would probably be the seed of much grumbling and quarrelling in the Society of Jesus." [11]

The practice, used then in Spain, soon became the custom all over the Society. The catalogue of propositions was abandoned, though it is worth noting that in the middle of the next century (1651) Piccolomini, then general, published a list of sixty-five prohibited assertions in philosophy and theology. But these were propositions already proscribed for the most part by individual preceding generals.

The hand of Suarez can also be seen in another recommenda-

---

[11] Broderick, James: *The Life and Work of Blessed Robert Francis Cardinal Bellarmine, S. J.,* New York, 1928, Kenedy, vol. i, p. 383.

tion made for the *Ratio* by the Alcalá committee, of which he
was an active member. This had to do with the more penetrating study of Holy Scriptures by young Jesuit students. The committee went on record as admitting that there was too great
ignorance of the dignity and utility of this sacred knowledge.
The young men were throwing themselves wildly into the study
of Scholastic theology while they neglected the charm of biblical
study, its use in their own sanctification, in their future aposto-
late, in helping Christians and confounding heretics.

Suárez in his own writings continuously went to the authority
of the Scriptures, as did Bellarmine, Salmeron, Maldonat, Rivera,
some of the most learned of living men at that time. They were
not foes of straight speculative Scholasticism, but they saw the
fruitlessness of such study unless it were accompanied by a
judicious understanding of the revealed word of God. They
felt that it was a particular duty for religious men to become
thoroughly acquainted with the Scriptures.

There was another important point upon which Suarez and
his fellow committeemen insisted. It was the matter of professor-
training. They thought that the only way expert teachers would
be developed in the Order would be by means of actual classroom work. They should learn to lecture by lecturing. Therefore, even though the theological course would be limited to
four years, there should be at least three, possibly more, professors in each Scholasticate. If necessary, there should be smaller
classes with fewer students under the direction of each professor.
If the Jesuits were to have learned men in the same numbers
as other religious Orders, more men would have to be consecrated to the profession of teaching. We Jesuits, they contended, are satisfied with following strict necessity, and as a
result we form very few competent masters and quickly use up
those we have.

Another point made by the fathers of Alcalá was that the

Jesuit Scholastic should not be given a teaching assignment until he had finished his course in philosophy. Often enough, especially in the early Society, this recommendation could not be followed, but at the present time it is almost the universal custom. It was admitted by the commission that theology would suffer by being put off and separated by several years from the study of philosophy. But, on the other hand, the experience of teaching which the young religious obtains at this period of his life is invaluable. To the great joy and satisfaction of succeeding generations of Scholastics the practice of spending several years in teaching before taking up theology has been fairly consistently maintained.

Finally, besides the report submitted by the whole group, Suarez and Florencia sent in a separate recommendation regarding the practice of dictation in class. Was the teaching to pass from the intellect of the professor directly to the pages of a copy book, or was it to pass first to the mind of the student and then in brief form to the book? Here again, Suarez was battling for a thing which seems perfectly obvious even to the casual observer. Learning was a mind-to-mind process. The pupil should not center his attention on the mechanical and slavish writing of notes; he should focus on the understanding and then jot down brief reminders.

This question of dictation was a very real one among the Jesuit professors and students. There were arguments both for and against the practice. The *Ratio,* as then planned, was entirely against it. Suarez and his confréres at Alcalá were against it only in so far as it hindered the process of learning, but they thought a pupil should be allowed to take some notes. When the system had degenerated into pure dictation, and nothing else, as it had at Alcalá, some of the students profited not at all from their classes. The young prelates and lords who came to lectures brought with them hired secretaries who took down in a kind of shorthand everything the professor said. The note-books came home to the students' desks and were hardly ever referred to.

In the end the *Ratio* made no specifications regarding the practice of dictation, taking it as axiomatic that once the professors knew the objectives to be attained in their classes, they would govern their method accordingly. The misuse of the method was a peculiarly Spanish thing.

Aquaviva sent out a new *Ratio* in 1591, corrected according to the criticisms submitted in the interim. This one was binding on the whole Order but it was not final and unchangeable since it asked that three years' trial be given in the colleges and universities. Thus, when the new judgement was to be passed by the fathers of Alcalá, Suarez was again asked to give his opinions. The much-disputed *Delectus Opinionum* had been omitted and the rules had been made less detailed but the Spanish Jesuits were still dissatisfied with what they considered a too rigid and formalized educational scheme.

Thus there seems to have been among the Jesuits near the end of the sixteenth century a distinctly divergent view on educational practice. The first, coming from Rome, was a tendency to unify and codify, to bring other colleges into line with the successful policies of the Roman College, to forestall a quick expansion that might run to seed. The other was of a more liberal nature and was especially exemplified among the Spaniards. Philosophical and theological learning had flowered in the peninsula and in these two branches the Spaniards wanted to go their own way. Ultimately the two tendencies fused in the perfection of the third *Ratio* of 1599, the first tempered by prudence and the other by obedience. The way in which these views worked out over the course of fifteen years of preparation for the final plan indicates to some degree the source of stability and vitality in the Society.

A little more than two centuries after the death of Francis Suarez, Father General Roothan published (1832) a revised edition of the *Ratio Studiorum*. It was prepared in much the same careful and painstaking manner as the first, and like that of 1599 took into consideration the peculiar exigencies of the times. A remark in Roothan's preface serves to sum up the entire attitude of Suarez in the matter of education: "The adaptation of the *Ratio Studiorum*, therefore, means that we consult the necessities of the age so far as not in the least to sacrifice the solid and correct education of youth." [12]

[12] Cf. Hughes, Thomas: *Loyola and the Educational System of the Jesuits*, New York, 1892, Scribner, p. 293.

CHAPTER XIII

First Publications

WHILE SUAREZ WAS TEACHING at Alcalá, in the heart of Spain, and preparing his first books for publication, the religious and political business of Europe was assuming the figure of a sharp triangle. The Pope had said that England was a fulcrum with France and Spain on either side of the scale. But the fact is that a better comparison is that of a rigid triangle, the three points of which were Pope Sixtus, King Philip and Queen Elizabeth.

These were three giants ever wrangling; continuously changing from trust to distrust of each other. The Pope was striving for the good of Christianity, the King for the benefit of both Spain and the Church, the Queen for the progress of England. The "New Jezebel" was the fortress of heresy, a protector of buccaneers, a weak woman hostile to the two most powerful men in Christendom. Coyly and ruthlessly, through her ministers, she took in both men at almost every turn of the diplomatic game. Although both men saw that there was nothing left but an intervention by armed force, they guilelessly maintained to the end their hope that Elizabeth would be converted to the true Faith.

As far as Spain itself was concerned, says Walsh, King Philip was well pleased with it. "It was one country in the world where people could sleep soundly at night, certain of protection by the King's justice and safe from civil war, witch-hunting and heretical preaching. But there was still one place in the world

146

that gave him much uneasiness. England was incorrigible. He was fully convinced of that now. The first astounding news of Drake's raid on the coasts of Spain had come during his sickness in Aragon. Now all was confirmed, and more than confirmed. There was no longer the slightest doubt that Queen Elizabeth was openly supporting the enterprises of a corsair and slave trader against the unarmed subjects of a friendly nation." [1]

In his quiet study at the University of Alcalá, Suarez was even then excogitating the philosophy of national and international law according to which such disputes could be solved. At Rome he had lectured on the reasons for war and on its just and unjust conduct. He had with him his notes and the outline of this course, which strangely enough was called *De Fide, Spe, Charitate*, and in those notes he could find arguments justifying the actions of Philip and Sixtus.

If men argued, as they did, that Philip could justly carry war to England because of Elizabeth's refusal to accept the true religion, Suarez would promptly answer that this is a fallacious basis for war. If they justified the proposed invasion, as they did, on the grounds "that God may be avenged for injuries done to Him through sins against nature, and through idolatry," Suarez would answer that such reasoning is false. "For God did not give to all men the power to avenge injuries done Him by them." These two arguments, therefore, must be rejected in the search for proper motivation.

But this scholarly founder of the philosophy of international law could, on two points of his teaching, show that Philip had a moral basis for sending the Armada to England. The first is a highly theological one, demonstrating that the prevention of the acceptance of the true faith is a real evil, and intimating that a Christian Prince like Philip, could interfere with the

---

[1] Walsh, William Thomas: *Philip II*, New York, 1937, Sheed and Ward, p. 627.

unchristian policies of a Queen like Elizabeth. The other was
the commonly accepted principle that a sovereign was bound
to protect the rights of his subjects. There can be no disputing
the latter, although the former argument would be assailed on
all sides in our modern jumbled process of international
thinking.

Obediently then Suarez could be on the side of Philip for
more than mere patriotic motives. "This butchery of unarmed
civilians without even a declaration of war was indefensible,
cold, deliberate, inexcusable malice. Like a sinister torch it
seemed to light up for the first time before the gaze of the
Spanish King the immense darkness that was spreading over
the north, and in it the true lineaments of the royal bird which
he himself had incubated and which Cecil had hatched behind
the wide skirts of Queen Elizabeth's spangled fotheringay." [2]
It had taken King Philip thirty years to learn that his sister-in-law
could not be trusted. "But now he pronounced her doom; and
he smiled to watch the misguided woman still negotiating for
a universal peace, as his Armada sailed into the Channel." [3]

It is not difficult for moderns, who have passed through crisis
after threatened national crisis, to estimate the tense anxiety
gripping Madrid, Toledo, Salamanca, Alcalá, Barcelona, and all
those great Spanish cities. The people at home used the weapon
they best knew. Prayers for the Armada's victory were sent to
heaven; at Alcalá there were public processions on feast days
and exposition of the Blessed Sacrament every day. In Madrid's
forty churches the Forty Hours was held forty times. But, as
every schoolboy knows, the Armada of 1588 failed miserably.
It had sailed away in May, and at the end of October the first
half-wrecked ships and half-starved men of the expedition strag-

[2] *Ibid.,* p. 629.
[3] Strachey, Lytton: *Elizabeth and Essex,* New York, 1928, Harcourt, Brace,
pp. 15–16.

gled back to Spain. But—as Walsh remarks—"it was not the English, but the elements that broke the morale of the Invincible Armada and scattered over a thousand miles of sea the timbers of the best ships and the bones of the bravest men of Spain." [4]

It is no wonder that conditions such as these were not conducive to the publication of theological works. Suarez was having technical difficulties. Printing materials were hard to obtain, and capable printers were even harder to find. Men were fully engrossed in the affairs of their country. After the collapse of the Armada, money was scarce, although Philip's agents were going about collecting for a new expedition before the end of the year. This alone was responsible for a delay of many months.

But there were other delays, particularly that of the official censorship. It is a delay which has moved more than one author to tear his hair in despair, especially in religious Orders where competent men are not always free from other duties for an immediate perusal of the manuscript. The Jesuit constitutions state that books must not be published without the approbation of the general, but the task of approving or rejecting prospective publications is usually delegated to the provincial, who in turn delegates it to two or more fathers. In the case of Suarez' first work, *De Verbo Incarnato*, or *De Incarnatione*, Aquaviva wished the censorship to take place at Rome.

Finally, on December 27, 1588, the general wrote to Gonzales de Avila, provincial of Toledo, expressing the opinion that Suarez' knowledge would do a great amount of good and that his writings would not be inferior to the reputation of his lectures; and the manuscript was sent on its way back to Spain. There, at Alcalá, the printing of the work got under way, and the finished copies came off the press only in 1590.

There is no incongruity in the appearance of an involved theological work at a time of national disturbance. In the first

[4] Walsh, *op. cit.*, p. 664.

place, the people of Spain considered their recent set-back a merely temporary affair; there could be no threat to their safety and national prestige. In the second place, they were thorough-going Christians to whom theological questions were of even greater importance than military questions. For students and professors—and these were the people who read any book then published—theological problems were a common subject of conversation. Arguments over controverted points went on outside the lecture halls with greater freedom and more heated discussion than inside those halls. There is nothing really startling in all this. Knowledge of God and His works should be equally as important as knowledge of the most recent athletic contest or military achievement.

Suarez was forty-two years old when this first work appeared, and had been teaching for a long time. He explains in the preface his seeming dilatoriness in bringing out his books. "I have seriously hesitated for a long time, *studiose lector,* whether I should publish these disputations in which I have expounded to my listeners the sacred mysteries of the Incarnate Word, or whether I should suppress them and keep them for personal use. The magnitude and sublimity of the subject surpassed my poor abilities, and then it seemed to me that the depth and erudition with which learned men have spoken and written about it would make my own work appear weak and faulty. Finally I am aware of the danger of writing for a public which is offended by even the smallest faults and imperfections. For these reasons I had decided to withhold this work."

These expressions are very much along the line which Suarez followed in his own personal dealings with other theologians, hesitating to offer his criticisms and his considered opinions until persuaded to do so. The reasons for publishing outweighed those against publishing, and Suarez continues by saying that "certain learned friends, endowed with prudent and sincere judgement, who read the work at my request, liked it and said that it would be very useful for theological students. . . . For a small sum of money a student can save the time so uselessly and laboriously required in transcribing lectures, and can use all that time in studying and thoroughly investigating truth and in reflecting upon each of these disputations. My friends were further afraid that these discussions which are outlined by me in class and sometimes carelessly taken down by students would be published in a shortened form as my own work." But, continues Suarez, neither these arguments nor the requests of his friends could convince him that he should publish. It took the moving power of obedience to bring him to the conviction that his class notes and outlines were worth expanding and publishing. This dispelled his doubts and hesitations and made him take up the arduous work of an author.

These explanatory utterances must not be misconstrued as the pious babblings of an over-humble religious. Suarez was not baiting his hook for the readers by showing them a false humility. He was genuinely concerned about the advisability of letting loose this distinctive commentary of St. Thomas in a land where Dominican theologians and controversialists had always considered the Angelic Doctor their own private property. Nor was he apprehensive in the sense that a literary tyro is fearful of severe criticism on first attempts. Actually, he stated the case simply and clearly when he inferred that the public would pounce upon the work and ferret out weak spots.

Men of an intellectual stamp, with the Suarezian temperament, feel a quiet confidence in their own prowess while at the same time they feel neither need nor inclination to boast about it. The belief that no one is a good judge of his own potentialities is a belief that applies rather to men of middling abilities, and it is most likely to be false in the case of superior intelligences. These men are the first and most thorough critics of their own achievements, and they are severe in their self-analysis because they humbly know better than strangers their own shortcomings.

When unwarranted meddling had interfered with Suarez' work at Valladolid he did not hesitate to protest vigorously; he stood unafraid in the face of criticism and maintained the truth as he saw it. Years of teaching in Spain and a successful period in the brilliant Scholastic assemblies at Rome could only have strengthened this resolute self-confidence. But the world is not a lecture hall, and readers are not adoring students. Every author, on the publication of his first book, must be a bit shaken at the prospect of dissipating prejudices which make readers arrogantly critical, ignorance which makes them superbly exacting, traditional ways of thinking which make them indifferent to new concepts.

Suarez never again prefaced his books with similar apprehensions regarding their reception. Immediately after his *De Incarnatione* came out and before he published its complement, *De Mysteriis Vitae Christi*, he was thrown into a tornado of controversial opinions. A second edition was needed to fill the popular demand, but neither the author nor his readers were satisfied with it. Some considered the treatment too jejune; others thought it too fickle in its commentaries on St. Thomas. Suarez himself got out a third edition at Salamanca in 1595, rearranged, corrected, and lengthened by about a hundred pages. In this preface he remarks: "When I first published my treatise on this subject I was afraid that it was too long and detailed; but since that time my learned friends have persuaded me that it was too scanty in places where the importance of the question required more detailed treatment. Furthermore, other works have since come out attacking my doctrine so that I recalled it to explain it more fully. Thus both my friends and my foes have obliged me to lengthen my work. There is not a single treatise which has not been enriched and elaborated so that this really ought to be considered another work. God grant that its usefulness and worth may have increased with its bulk." [5]

How he found the necessary time to put out the work on the *Mysteries of the Life of Christ* (1592) is a question only in the minds of those who do not realize his immense capacity for labor. Like the book of 1590, this volume of twelve hundred pages was composed entirely in his spare time, after his regular duties in the class room were over. It is true that he was for the most part freed from parochial tasks but even these would have required at the most only a few hours on Sundays. The fact is that he had learned the secret of utilizing time to its utmost span. A spare hour in the day meant the production of several pages of manuscript, and if spare hours are thus measured by concrete pages of writing it is amazing to note how rapidly a book can grow. In later life Suarez was given the help of secretaries. Walking up and down the room with a sheaf of notes in his hands, but relying for the most part on a remarkable memory, he would dictate to them, keeping three of them busy at a time.

When writing on Christ's life, Suarez was treading familiar ground. Years of meditation and study made it easy for him to discourse on the Savior's earthly and heavenly existence, temporal and eternal, on the lowliness of His first coming and the glory of His second, on the splendors of His never-ending reign. From the philosophical and theological points of view this Spaniard treated the central subject of Christianity more fully than had ever been done before. Heart and intellect combine to bring out completeness of thought; intellectual piety and pious intellectualism produced a refreshing vigor in his treatment of certain points, especially those regarding the Virgin Mother of God.

[5] Suarez' treatises *De Incarnatione* comprise volumes 17, 18 and 19 (approximately two thousand pages) of the *Opera Omnia*, edited by Charles Berton, Paris, 1872, Vives. All quotations from Suarez' writings refer to that edition.

Suarez is reminiscent of St. Bernard when there is question of Mary. He devotes about a third of this work to her participation in Christ's life and mission. In his preface this seeming disproportion is explained thus: "When it is a matter of considering the sublime dignity, the unequalled virtues, the wonderful life and glories of the Blessed Virgin, who could be so sterile of thought and weak in style as to write briefly and dryly? For myself I have always found—if you will allow me this complaint —that theology is too somber and niggardly about this beautiful and expansive subject. It is a matter dulcid and useful, abounding in truth and worthy to be treated with all honor by theologians. And if this is true in the case of the Mother, how much more is it so in that of the Son, Our Lord? How then can we give only a hasty glance at this life and death from which all benefits flow?"

Like every author who wishes his writings to reach a large audience he offers other reasons for the perusal of this book on the Mysteries. The subject is so significant that in the very title Suarez proposes two reasons for the present treatises: *ut et Scholasticae Doctrinae studiosis, et Divini Verbi concionatoribus usui esse possit.* Thus he expected his thoughtful arguments and conclusions to be useful not only for Scholastic scholars but also for preachers of the Divine Word. Perhaps as a result of this study, he thought, those who preach in the churches and expound the sacred mysteries to the faithful will be more successful. Knowing the facts thoroughly they could tremendously induce piety, and piety itself would be a motive for further study.[6]

As a matter of tested fact this book still remains a mine of material for modern preaching. In its depth and breadth there is an almost inexhaustible amount of carefully cogent argument and well-turned explanations regarding the most absorbing doctrines of Christianity. Through them all runs the traditional Christian

[6] *De Mysteriis Vitae Christi*, Preface: *Ad Lectorem.*

spirit of a man who has drunk deeply from the very source of knowledge. The Latin is not difficult for even a middling student of the language, indeed, in spots it is positively eloquent.

A fundamental study of this kind is too frequently swamped by the torrent of descriptive books dealing with the externals of Christ's life. Of course, these are necessary, for nothing that touches the activities of the Divine Master is useless, whether it be the description of historic Judean ruins, of places sanctified by His presence, of the political, economic and social atmosphere in which He physically breathed. All of this is ornamental and, if handled properly, can be beautifully persuasive. Geography, history, culture, and the rest, made up the surroundings of the God-Man's passage through earthly time; they can assist theology in giving us a knowledge of God—but they cannot replace it. Theology alone, as Suarez and the other straight-thinking Catholics wrote it, can learn intimately the causes of things and put them in their proper order according to the divine plan. It protects your curiosity against the pitfalls of adventuresome piety, restrains you from falsely interpreting the truths of the Gospels.

Gabriel Vasquez, who was Suarez' rival at Alcalá and his sometimes acidulous critic, was thoroughly impressed with the treatment of the Blessed Virgin in the *De Mysteriis*. "Suarez has rendered an outstanding service to the sacred science," he remarked, "when he used the Scholastic method and submitted to strict theological criticism all questions relating to the life and glory of the most pure virgin Mary, Our Lady." [7] De Scorraille maintains that this praise was nothing more than Suarez' due in his treatises of the Blessed Virgin, but that there should be no stinting when one comments on the other works. They all offer the same plenitude of treatment and the same solidity of doctrine.

[7] Nieremberg: *Varones Illustres,* quoted by De Scorraille, *op. cit.,* p. 257.

But all of the writer's contemporaries were not similarly in accord with his teaching as expressed in the *De Mysteriis*. He was singled out for attack by a fellow Jesuit, Father Enriquez, the same dissenter who caused such inopportune disturbance over the first draft of the Order's *Ratio Studiorum*. He denounced some of Suarez' statements to the Spanish Inquisition. A belligerent Dominican, Father Alonso de Avendaño, likewise complained of the Suarezian doctrines and of the whole Jesuit Order in general. These charges dragged through the years and were not settled until the first decade of the seventeenth century.

On the other side of the ledger there is an overwhelming counterbalance in favor of Suarez. The two attacks made upon him, involved though they were, can be entirely discounted in the avalanche of praise which greeted the theologian's first publications. If we can talk of the "smash hits" and best sellers of that period we must undoubtedly number these works among them. The author enjoyed the suasive qualities of popularity and authority throughout the entire Spanish peninsula, qualities which would ensure the success of almost everything he wrote. He was well-known and respected in Rome as a former lecturer at Christendom's central source of learning, the Gregorian University. To France and the low countries, and even to England his name and fame had penetrated.

The acid test of an author's success is his publisher's attitude toward his book. If the sales are large enough the work will be widely advertised, and though advertising in those times did not take the form of current dynamic blurbs, it was sufficiently strenuous to bring further business. Suarez' first two books were reprinted numerous times. They came out in folio, in enormous editions, which no one would have agreed to undertake unless there was definite hope of a steady demand. To-day his work would probably have to be subsidized by his friends or his Order, but in the sixteenth century theology and theological discussions were a very part of the atmosphere people breathed.

All of this was very consoling, and would be for any author. But the professor of Alcalá wanted to know how the thing went with the general at Rome. In the middle of 1590, when the first book was almost ready to be issued, Aquaviva showed his intense interest by writing to Lucero, the rector of the college at Alcalá. "Since the book of Father Suarez is almost entirely printed and will be completed when the procurators of the provinces come to Rome, tell them to bring me a copy. The good work of this father would be very useful and profitable to us here." [8]

The Jesuit general must have been very well pleased with the *De Verbo Incarnato* for he frequently encouraged the scholarly author to further literary work. Occasionally during the passing years he would ask Suarez or his provincial about forthcoming books, what they would treat of, when they would be published, and so on. This does not mean that he was simply seeking more books for the sake of quantitative production on the part of Jesuits. As a matter of fact he was not in favor of a too rapid increase of Jesuit books and authors. About this time he wrote: "I am taking care not to allow the number of authors to grow." In 1592 he cautioned that "the publications of our Fathers are multiplying to such extent that we must moderate their zeal, laudable as it is, and we must be less easy about giving permissions [for new works]." About three years later he wrote again to the provincial of Toledo, saying that "we have considered limiting these permissions, since we see our appetite for publicity increasing these last few years. It would be wiser not to grant, at least for the moment, the authorization that Father John de Salas asks, especially since Father Vasquez, Suarez and Molina are writing on the same subject." [9]

[8] De Scorraille, *op. cit.*, p. 257.   [9] *Ibid.*, p. 258.

Thus was Suarez approvingly launched upon his career as one of the century's most prolific authors. Thus likewise was he given the acclaim he most desired in his humble fashion, that of the highest superior of the Order. He had undertaken the arduous task of writing at the behest of obedience, and he found it most pleasant to know that his efforts were achieving appreciation from the general—and friend—to whom he owed that obedience.

Chapter XIV

Internal Discord

The most cutting criticism that can be endured by any self-respecting Scholastic theologian or philosopher is that he be called "one of the moderns." The term connotes that the man has abandoned the teachings of the ancient masters, from Aristotle through Thomas, or that he has mutilated them beyond recognition. Gabriel Vasquez, the brilliant Jesuit rival of Francis Suarez, called him one of the moderns and thus precipitated a discussion that seems at first blush incongruous with the lives of pious and learned men.

Vasquez was fiercely Spanish and truculently Scholastic in everything he wrote, said or did. His path crossed and recrossed that of Suarez, and the opposition of the Belmontane probably caused the Granadine more anguish than any other thing in his long life. They were at the same time compatible and incompatible; they were fellow travellers in the same period of time, the same religious Order, the same country, profession, talents and work. They consecrated their energies to the same studious employments; both wrote commentaries on the *Summa* of St. Thomas, and both filled the same chair of theology at Rome and at Alcalá.

In the shifting scenes of historical Scholasticism there is a constant interplay between these two names. One recalls the other; one never quite cancels the other. The works they left do not always clash—they do not irrationally disagree on fundamentals—but they seem to rival each other in extent of knowledge, depth of penetration, power of clear expression, weight of authority.

De Scorraille enthusiastically describes these two great men in this way: "More eager to love God than to know Him, both of them realized in themselves an admirable union of passionate study and ardent piety, of extraordinary learning and very high virtue. But there is another thing—and it is because of this that they have remained eminent—they knew how to place their rewards and successes under the safeguard of humility and obedience. The life of Suarez has offered and will continue to offer many proofs of this; that of Vasquez is also rich in actions worthy of great saints." [1] If the lines are somewhat overdrawn in favor of Vasquez it is only because the reputation that great thinker left has refused to fade from the memories of men.

Vasquez himself had no thought of future immortality among the theological greats, nor, I think, had Suarez. It was not that they had greatness thrust upon them; they worked tremendously to deserve it but neither of them had a thought of it at the time. Vasquez was told one day that he would within a century be considered one of the great masters and he replied characteristically that such prophecies did not interest him. At another time someone tried to persuade him to accept a teaching position where he could guarantee himself success and honor. He contemptuously declared that this was a mere semblance of glory and was not worth the fatigue it entailed.

Human beings are strangely constituted, and this ancient truth is nowhere more clearly exemplified than in the intimate interrelations of a religious Order where personal idiosyncrasies are immediately dubbed singular. One man will meticulously follow every jot and tittle of regulative ordinances but miss woefully the larger aspects of his vocation. Another will mistakenly pursue the "larger things" of life, the great sweep of human

[1] De Scorraille, *op. cit.*, pp. 283–284.

activities which must not be hampered by the minutiæ of the
Rule, and will neglect the essential daily and hourly self-disci-
pline which leads truly to sanctity. Where to put Vasquez in
these two categories is something of a problem. From appearances it would seem that he belongs in the first. His contemporaries would put him in between the two, along the line of
the golden medium where all outstanding religious men and
women are placed by their biographers.[2]

Gabriel Vasquez was born from one to three years after
Suarez[3] at Villaescusa de Haro, near the prominent town of
Belmonte in the province of Cuenca. In his works he frequently
used the subtitle, *Belmontanus,* proud of the fact that he was
associated with that beautiful and ancient site. He entered the
Society of Jesus at Alcalá in 1569, later taught theology at the
College of Ocana, then at Madrid, Alcalá, Rome, and again
at Alcalá. He became known personally to Suarez only in 1591,
when he returned from Rome to find the latter occupying his
former position as the principal theologian of the college. From
that time until his death in 1604 he was the intellectual thorn
in the side of Francis Suarez.

Perhaps it is a prick to the traditional dignity of these two
great men to talk of some of the inconsequential things over
which they differed. They are appallingly trivial and petty at
times, especially on the part of Vasquez, but they help to bring
into sharp relief the personalities of men who are usually far
removed from mortal haunts by the pens of arid historians.
Popes and kings had their personal foibles. Saints too have
involved themselves in puzzling details, and their characters
are not fully known unless there is a relation of these details.
Petty jealousy seems to have motivated Vasquez in belittling

[2] Cf. Astrain's estimate of Gabriel Vasquez; *op. cit.,* vol. iv, pp. 68–73.
[3] Vasquez' birth is variously placed in the years 1549 and 1551. There appears no genuine record showing the exact date.

Suarez. Something of a persecution complex seems to have held Suarez to a resentment of such treatment.

In general there are two principal charges hurled against Vasquez by the commentators on his theological treatises. The first is a fairly serious one: his doggedly independent spirit in holding to his own opinions. The second is a decided tendency to speculate on useless questions, a habit more in vogue at that time than in our present day. There is something more than mere derogation in the formulation of these two censures.

Over a course of two years Vasquez found it extremely difficult to unbend and make pliable some of the opinions in his first publication, *De Adoratione Imaginum*. For that length of time the Jesuit general held back the book, while its author was trying to make up his mind about changing some of its contents. Aquaviva demanded considerable revision and was quite pleased when the provincial of Toledo told him: "I have sent for Father Gabriel Vasquez to talk over the printing of his book, and have found him so humble and docile about omitting or adding whatever is suggested, that I beg you to leave the whole affair in our hands."

This indicates that Vasquez finally listened to reason, but he did not come to this conclusion without a fight. In a long letter to Aquaviva he defended vigorously everything the book contained, giving every conceivable argument in defense of his theses, and showing in no uncertain terms that even in the face of censorship he firmly believed in the validity of his own position. The religious overcame the scholar and wisely ended by bowing to superior judgement. "Your Paternity demands," he finally wrote to the general, "that to get this book printed I must conform to the common terminology of the doctors. To obtain this conformity Father Provincial has told me that I must seek the judgement of competent men, a thing which will be done immediately according to your will and his. In all these matters

I adopt the attitude of Gamaliel: if this work comes from God it would not perish; rather superiors would change their opinions or disappear; but if it does not come from God, I would be more happy than anyone else to lay it aside." [4]

A fair example of the type of questions investigated by Vasquez is one in which he discusses the whereabouts of God: whether God could be outside of heaven, or in a vacuum inside of heaven, or any place at all before the creation of the world.[5] There are many other similar futile discussions, which had been in fashion in most of the mediæval schools and which give some point to the way in which modern commentators exaggerate the futility of their educational system. The example of the number of angels dancing on the point of a needle has been so badly overworked that it scarcely needs recall.

Both of these Vasquezian habits earned him the name of a casuist, a title scathingly and unjustly applied to men of his type. Above everything else he could always make a good case for his side of any question, and that is in itself an achievement. He was astute in taking over from the Dominicans the doctrine of Probabilism, and his arguments were so influential that the Jesuits more and more defended it while its previous defenders turned to the more rigid doctrine of Probabiliorism. "Thus it ultimately came about," says Fülop-Miller, "that the Dominicans became violent opponents of the principle they had originated, while the Jesuits, on the other hand, became its most ardent defenders." [6]

Somewhere along the route between Italy and Spain in 1585 the returning Suarez passed the Rome-bound Vasquez. It was probably on the Mediterranean Sea, for travelers at that time most frequently embarked at Barcelona. Suarez reached

---

[4] Cf. De Scorraille, op. cit., p. 285.

[5] An Deus extra coelum, vel in vacuo intra coelum esse possit, aut ante mundi creationem alicubi fuerit.

[6] Fülop-Miller, op. cit., p. 188.

Alcalá in good time to take up his lectures when the school year began, but Vasquez came down in Florence with a fever and was detained there several months before he could begin his classes at the Gregorian. Neither had met the other personally even though they had not been separated by many miles during years of work on the peninsula.

But they knew each other's reputation and worth; each went out of his way to make recommendations for the other. Thus, Suarez wrote to a friend at the English College in May of the following year, when Vasquez was still convalescing: "The good news received from Father Vasquez has caused me great joy. I recall that illness kept him a long time at Florence. But when he arrives at Rome he will undoubtedly be appreciated by everyone, and will more than satisfy those who seem to miss me. I know particularly that he has determined to take my place as your affectionate friend. It also gives me extreme pleasure to know from your letter that you expect to treat him as you did me, and to make him in every respect my successor. However, I propose one condition: that I be not entirely forgotten. No matter what the distance is I am not less close to you in memory and affection than on the day when we had the happiness of working together in the English vineyard." [7]

Each kept an eye on the other, as is natural for any professor who has the progress of his former students in mind. At Alcalá Suarez took over a class which Vasquez had already started in the study of the Incarnation, and he rapidly reviewed what the other had taught, to make sure of the foundation of his own lectures. Vasquez later resented this, complaining to Aquaviva that the new teacher taught those lessons "over again without the least necessity, but only to introduce his own private opin-

[7] The English vineyard refers to the English College at Rome where the Jesuits were preparing priests for the Catholic revival in Queen Elizabeth's persecuted country. Suarez often lectured there, as did Bellarmine, Vasquez, and the rest, and had as students many of the future martyrs for the faith.

ions." This letter was sent from Toledo fifteen years later, indicating that the occurrence rankled for a long time in the heart of Vasquez.

Whether Vasquez had opportunity of doing the same thing at Rome is not quite clear, but we may be certain that he held no brief for previous teaching which ran counter to his own doctrine. His success there was immediate. There was a genial sparkle and polish to his public personality which Suarez could never emulate. Lively, likable Vasquez was the man of the hour among the students. They strutted in imitation of him, mimicked his facial contortions, mouthed his dynamic phraseology, tried out his arguments on each other, and often remarked, *Si Vasquez abit, tota schola perit.* He was an oracle to these young men but he was just another professor to his fellows on the theological faculty; and that was hard to take. After five years he asked to be removed from Rome, and in the following year, 1591, obtained his request. The school did not perish, as the students thought; in fact there was scarcely a ripple in the even flow of Roman activities.

Vasquez asked for another appointment for reasons which he said were known only to himself; but a man of his volatile temperament cannot long keep such reasons within himself. A letter to Aquaviva makes crystal clear that this fiery patriot could not get along with professors of other nationalities, especially the Italians, who were supposed to have belittled Spanish prowess.

"I think I should tell Your Paternity," he wrote in 1593, "how important it is that you remove from yourself certain restless men who are nourishing a natural aversion to the Spaniards. These Spaniards are entirely devoted to Your Paternity and came to Rome with the intention of preserving between the two nations that union established by our early fathers. Anything that will be done to remove the dissidents will be done

in the cause of this peace and understanding. . . . It is necessary either that there be no longer any Spanish professors at
Rome or that they should not be looked down upon by the
Italians. . . . If I should chance to come to Rome I shall not
fail to point out the rôle played by certain men prejudiced
against our nation, and this despite the fact that they were
educated by Spaniards." [8]

Vasquez' grievance undoubtedly had some foundation, but
an identical letter from some Italian father complaining of
Vasquez would likewise have had the same foundation in fact.
Nationalism was a growing novelty in those times, so much so,
that Ignatius had to write a warning into the Rule, advising
that men of different nations should strive to get along amicably.
Further than that Suarez himself had found even provincial
jealousies a difficult obstacle, first at Valladolid and later at
Alcalá; and the origin of the latter could be found almost entirely in the personality of Gabriel Vasquez.

Perhaps it is too much to expect of human nature that Vasquez should quietly take a back seat when he returned to Alcalá
in 1591 and found Suarez reigning in his former place, the
principal chair of theology. Both enjoyed tremendous repute;
as De Scorraille remarks, they were "two great men beneath
the same roof; it was one too many." Aquaviva himself perceived this disturbing situation when he wrote to the Father
Provincial, Gil Gonzalez, in 1592: "I would have preferred
that you had not left Vasquez at Alcalá; for it could easily be
seen that with Suarez there peace and union could only be lost." [9]

Suarez could not hope to dislodge Vasquez in the affections
of the Alcaláns. In his quiet, studious and reflective way he
used solid intellectual conviction rather than dramatic appeal as
a means of making progress for his pupils. He always remained
something of a stranger at Alcalá; by his early studies and

[8] De Scorraille, *op. cit.*, pp. 286–287.   [9] *Ibid.*, p. 287.

former reputation he belonged to the rival college town of Salamanca. He did not depend upon bizarre methods to startle and capture his audience and to arouse the enthusiasm of the youths; and thus it took a much longer time for his worth to be discerned. Pure, cold merit was his greatest appeal and the reappearance of his predecessor cancelled this to a great extent.

The return of Vasquez, on the other hand, was like that of a conquering hero. Laughing, boisterous crowds of young men greeted him wherever he appeared, asking him when he was going to take up his courses again. Hundreds of friendly and admiring students remembered him from the old days when they used to say: "Let's go hear the 'green cincture' lecture." And Vasquez loved it. He still affected the worn and sunfaded cincture which had earned him the sobriquet. In the town itself, people everywhere recognized him by his thirty-year-old coat and a still older hat which he wore with the jaunty air of one who knows himself to be a trade-marked figure in the locality. Only the archbishop could make him discard them for more decent clothes, and then only on the occasion of a large public discussion.

People knew him even better for his genuine intellectual sagacity. When they learned he was to appear at any public disputation the students would flock to it as though they were going to a Spanish bull-fight, and while the first speakers were going through their arguments the audience would be rudely inattentive, impatiently and loudly calling now and then for the appearance of Vasquez. To obtain quiet the presiding officer would wave the priest to the rostrum before his regular turn in the argument. The audience would be absorbed in every word and gesture, and greet the end of the talk with prolonged shouting and stamping of feet, and then rush out of the hall without waiting to hear the arguments of those who followed Vasquez. Many a disputation was practically disrupted in this

way and it was difficult to find anyone hardy enough to appear
on the same program with him.

Both townspeople and students demanded that Vasquez be
given his old position which Suarez now held. They saw it as
a humiliation that their popular hero should be forbidden his
public while a relative stranger took his place. Pressure was
brought to bear so that confréres on the faculties also asked for
Vasquez, and even the rector, Father Lucero, whom Aquaviva
chided for his apparent partiality, was in favor of his return to
teaching and eventually to his former position in the principal
chair of theology.

Vasquez had good reason to be quiet in the midst of all this
discussion. The Jesuit general had ordered him to write instead
of teach, and to be very careful about his doctrines when he did
write. "As for Vasquez, I think—and I made him understand
so himself—" wrote Aquaviva to the provincial, "that as long
as he is not more supple in the matter of opinions, it would be
better not to put him back teaching. As for Suarez, let him remain in charge of the course at Alcalá; it is for the best since he
acquits himself of it with success, profit and sureness of doctrine."

About a year after this letter, the provincial wrote to Aquaviva,
telling him that internal affairs at Alcalá had come to a disgraceful pass. He said: "Someone who has to suffer a great deal here
is Father Francis Suarez. I would wish, of course, that he were
a little less sensitive, but patience that has been deceived ends up
by being irritated. Strangely enough, these fathers who are so
very patriotic desire that the professor who has returned from
Rome to Alcalá should again take up his courses. I am very
annoyed over this because cooperation is being in great part lost,
and because from this arise those cliques which are the pest of
common charity. I see that the evil is only increasing." [10]

[10] *Ibid.*, pp. 289–290.

In the meanwhile Suarez tried to hold himself constantly under control. He was burning up a tremendous amount of energy in performing regular lecture duties and at the same time preparing his books for publication. Bodily strength was giving way under the load of work, and his patience was being exhausted under the constant strain of criticism. He was completely fed up with his position and was more than willing that the local men should have their way. "If you release me from this work," he told Aquaviva, "you will please those who are now the patriarchs of this province, and who take so much to heart the advantage and honor of its members. If Your Paternity grants them him whom they desire, their happiness will be very great. As a matter of fact, considering the condition in which affairs are now, it would be only just to give the province this satisfaction. There remains, however, the real need and also the urgent duty of watching carefully over the doctrine."

Before Aquaviva could make another move to settle the matter Suarez' health broke down, and on the insistence of a medical man he was forced to give up teaching. Even during his relatively healthy years Suarez was accorded the simple attentions which careful superiors always arrange for their delicate subjects, and these attentions form the gist of an amusing and childish letter of complaint which Vasquez wrote to the general.

The rector blames me, said Vasquez in effect, for being a source of disunion in regard to Father Suarez. How could I be a source of disunion? In clothing, food, and all the rest I respect the equality of common life; I help the lay brothers in their ordinary hard work; I preach and hear confessions regularly. Does Suarez do all this? Why, he has a suite of two rooms such as has never been seen in this province. He has a lay brother to clean it for him and to take care of the fancy drapes and comfortable bed that adorn it. He gets four-course luncheons and even keeps a supply of food in his room where he holds little

parties for the Scholastics. He has even had an ex-Jesuit there. I
have never seen him serve table in the refectory nor assist at
litanies. Behold his abstemiousness! With all of these comforts
I would willingly pass all the days of my life.

These physical advantages were undoubtedly given to Suarez,
but they were little enough for a man who was constantly suffering a purgatory of pain. The records show that Vasquez was a
robust giant of a man hardly ever experiencing an inconvenient
illness. The comparison he made between himself and Suarez
was really too puerile to merit emphasis, and he himself probably
regretted the petty outburst in later years. He admitted that this
was the only occasion on which he had allowed his feelings so to
betray him.

The outcome of the rivalry over the chair of theology at Alcalá
was that Aquaviva told the provincial to appoint anyone he
wished after the resignation of Suarez. Of course, Vasquez was
the unanimous choice. But just as he was preparing his lectures
for the opening of the school year in 1593, orders came from His
Holiness, Clement VIII, expressly forbidding him to teach.

Vasquez had been denounced to the Pope for teaching—even
while he was still in Rome—the proposition that contrition, by
its very nature and without habitual grace, produces sanctification
in man and takes away sin.[11] Actually, however, Vasquez never
taught this opinion in the lecture hall or in any public manner
although he was personally convinced of its truth. At the University of Alcalá he had gone about to all the professors and
obtained their approval of it. Two of them were Dominicans;
one the consultor of the supreme council of the Inquisition, and
they signed a statement in approval of the particular thesis which
neither the Pope nor the general would permit Vasquez to teach.

Clement VIII was angry at this seeming insubordination. As

[11] *Contritio natura sua, sine gratia habituali, constituit hominem sanctum
et peccatum delet.*

Aquaviva wrote to Vasquez in August, 1593: ". . . a week ago the Holy Father, learning that you had your proposition signed by some doctors, called me and ordered me to tell you not to send those signatures here. His Holiness acts in this wise because, as he definitely informed me, he wishes blind obedience in these matters. We ought, therefore, to obey, I in giving you this order, you in conforming to it. We have since then tried to get permission for you to resume teaching, and thanks to good intercession we have succeeded. The Holy Father consents to you being a professor but always on the condition that I should order you not to teach this opinion of yours when you have to lecture on these matters, but the opinion which others maintain, namely, that man is justified by habitual grace; *justificatio fit per gratiam habitualem.* Otherwise you are no longer allowed to teach. I therefore order you to do this in virtue of your vow of obedience. . . ."[12]

Father Vasquez submitted to the Pope's orders as relayed to him by the Jesuit general, and took up his theological teaching when the school year opened. In that same autumn Suarez took his departure for the University of Salamanca where he spent several years almost exclusively in writing. The internal conflict was over but external controversies were already taking definite shape and he would be called to take a most active part in them.

[12] De Scorraille, *op. cit.,* p. 293. Superiors of religious Orders very seldom command their subjects by invoking their vow of obedience. As in this case it is done only when the matter in question is a very serious one, or when there is a probability that the subject will not obey.

CHAPTER XV

External Strife

IN THE PERSON of Gabriel Vasquez, Suarez had a critical opponent worthy of his mettle, a man who would come right to the
point at issue, a religious who had the decency to keep family
differences within the family. But now there appeared three
others who were annoying pests rather than worthy foes to
the great scholar. One was a Jesuit, Enriquez, the two others
Dominicans, Mondragon and Avendaño, whose persistent buzz-
ing about the ears of Suarez brought him finally to the notice of
the Spanish Inquisition.

Enriquez was a dissaffected Spaniard who pried into everything Jesuitical, whether it concerned him or not, and then, after
putting an evil interpretation upon it, thought that he was bound
in conscience to denounce it to the Inquisition. He had caused
his Order a great deal of unnecessary anguish by sending to
Cardinal Quiroga a copy of the confidential first draft of the
Ratio Studiorum. Two or three volumes of his own writings had
been held up by the censors pending important and necessary
changes. This was particularly humiliating for him because, as
he asserted, the first two publications of Francis Suarez, his former pupil, contained the very same propositions for which he
himself had been censured.

He had been mixed up in the notorious clique of Spanish
Jesuits who had been causing trouble for over a decade by their
demands for a change in the Order's constitutions. When
Clement VIII succeeded Sixtus V in 1592, Enriquez joined in

the general rejoicing of the Spanish rebels, for they believed that the new Pope personally disliked Aquaviva. Philip II was on their side, and they thought they could also win over the great Toletus to favor their innovations. The Spanish rebel took the oath of allegiance which was demanded by the general congregation held in 1593, and was therefore not included among the twenty-seven conspirators expelled by that congregation.

It was found that twenty-five of these men were of Hebrew or Saracenic origin, and from this fact there came the famous fifty-second decree of the congregation which ruled that such applicants were not to be received into the Society in the future. Enriquez was not officially denounced at that time but he was certainly closely connected with those men who were dubbed: "false sons, disturbers of the peace, and revolutionists whose punishment had been asked for by many provinces. The congregation, therefore, while grievously bewailing the loss of its spiritual sons," writes Campbell, "was nevertheless compelled in the interests of domestic union, religious obedience, and the perpetuation of the Society, to employ a severe remedy in the premises. . . . If for one reason or another, they cannot be immediately dismissed they were declared incapable of any office or dignity and denied all active or passive voice. . . . Those suspected of being parties to such machinations shall make a solemn oath to support the Constitution as approved by the Popes, and to do nothing against it. If they refuse to take the oath, or having taken it, fail to keep it, they are to be expelled, even if old and professed." [1]

Enriquez was not among those ejected from the Society, but the story has it that he voluntarily left its ranks after he had been publicly discountenanced. Then he joined the Dominican Order wherein he was also dissatisfied, and finally toward the end of his life was readmitted to die among the Jesuits.

[1] Campbell, *op. cit.*, p. 212.

Accusing Suarez directly or indirectly he posted one letter to the Inquisition in 1593, and ten in 1594, thus establishing himself, as De Scorraille puts it, "in the rôle of a kind of doctrinal policeman and delator of his brethren." [2] He wished to point out the reprehensible assertions contained in many writings, especially those novel doctrines which had come to be called Suarezianisms. Using his constant formula: "to ease my conscience," he first denounced a dozen propositions of Suarez, and three months later sent the Inquisition a new list of forty-seven.

From among these later denunciations Suarez' biographers pick out a few which they repeat with relish, demonstrating the absurdity of Enriquez' critical faculty. The twenty-eighth accusation was only one instance of them. It said that Suarez did not regard as certain the marvellous things which the Fathers recount concerning the birth and infancy of Our Lord, for example, that the idols of Egypt fell to the ground at the approach of the infant Jesus and that the trees themselves bowed down before Him. The fortieth accusation was that Suarez claimed the lance pierced the left side and not the right side of Christ on the cross.

In the end, Enriquez' constant attack upon his former pupil had as little success as it had foundation for its existence. But it gained for him a certain notoriety that did not remain a merely local affair. The Inquisition in Spain did not act upon the charges but the Jesuit superiors took the matter in hand and informed Aquaviva of all its angles. The latter ordered Enriquez to come to Rome and place his charges before the fathers of the congregation then in session there. Enriquez demurred on the pretense that the Inquisition refused to allow him to leave Spain. Thus no official action was taken against Suarez and nothing serious came of it all except that it supplied further ammunition for the attacks of the two Dominicans.

For twenty years Alonso de Avendaño constituted himself a

[2] De Scorraille, *op. cit.*, p. 262.

one-man crusade against the adolescent Jesuit Order. During those two decades (1575-1595) he measured his eloquent and sometimes vulgar wit by numerous condemnations of every Jesuitical thought and thing and person in Salamanca, Medina del Campo, Valladolid, Burgos, Madrid, Alcalá, Guadalajara and Saragossa. Reputed as a theologian and philosopher he was most of all a demagogue whom Pastor called "infatuated," and whom his own fellow Dominicans thought a madman.

Ribadeneira, a novice under Ignatius Loyola, first historian of the Jesuits and a contemporary of all these sixteenth century occurrences, reported in his *Glories and Triumphs of the Society of Jesus* the opinion Avendaño held of the Company. According to him, he writes, "we Jesuits are heretics, anti-Christs, ministers of the devil, false prophets. . . . The Society is everything that the Devil has best invented to ruin the Church of God; it is not an Order nor its members religious; we reveal the sins of penitents, teach confession by letter, lead a luxurious life, abolish penance; that we are hypocrites, simulators, misers, avaricious, liars, pharisees, ambitious and so on; that by sorcery we win over the women who come to confession; that to preach in public and to teach Christian Doctrine to the children of the streets by calling them with a hand-bell is as ridiculous as beating a drum; that prayer is not fitting to married people or even to the laity and that to teach them is to prepare a nest where heresy will breed; that to put aside St. Thomas on an important point is a mortal sin; that his Order possesses the key of knowledge and the Society has only the false keys, his is the living fountain of truth and ours a muddy pool." [3]

The Jesuits thought that the case of Avendaño was helpless. He was so blinded by his prejudice that neither they nor his fellow religious could convince him otherwise. They tried, how-

[3] Ribadeneira, Peter: *Glorias y Triunfos de la Compañia de Jesus en sus Persecuciones,* quoted by De Scorraille, *op. cit.,* pp. 264–265.

ever, to reason with Garcia de Mondragon, professor of theology at the College of St. Gregory in the University of Valladolid, who had made denunciations of Suarez and the Society, but in a less violent strain than those of his confrére. The Jesuits, Martinez and De Acosta, visited him at the Dominican rectory and discussed the whole affair for more than two hours. With Suarez' book open before them they argued the points of departure in a scholarly and unruffled way, but Mondragon's only reply was that he was impelled to fight these opinions, as in the past, for the honor of Our Lord.

The superiors of both Orders were heartily sick of the disturbances and recriminations which were thus disrupting their professional and ministerial duties. The greater number of both Dominicans and Jesuits in Spain wished peace and mutual coöperation between the Orders. When Father Lucero complained to Father De Guzman, Dominican provincial then at Alcalá, regarding the activities of his two subjects he promised to reprimand them and impose silence.

The apostolic nuncio, Camillo Gaetani, also wrote to the provincial of the Dominicans demanding in severe terms that he punish his recalcitrant subjects who were speaking evil of the Society. But Avendaño and Mondragon would accept neither the blame nor these threats without a struggle. In the summer of 1593 they put their heads together for the justification of their own actions, drawing up a list of their charges against Suarez and the Jesuits and sending it to their superior.

Suarez was still at Alcalá in August, 1593, when Avendaño climbed into the pulpit at Valladolid on the feast of St. Dominic to take a parting shot at him. He had been forbidden to attack either the Society or any of its members, so he simply went into an eloquent denunciation of a certain religious Order and a certain professor—without ever once mentioning any names. Of course, the target of his remarks was immediately recognized by his audience. His fellow Dominicans, seated in the choir, were amazed when he cried, "They are writing against Jesus Christ!" and he turned to them saying that though they disapproved he must speak since God was sustaining his voice. To the audience he dramatically shouted: "But, these are saints! Who says they are saints? An old woman and two pious little girls!" Less than a year later the storm broke upon him when the nuncio ordered a process against him which ended in his condemnation.

The antagonism of Avendaño and Mondragon toward Suarez was much more than a superficial difference of opinion, or even of deep personal hatred between men. As is clear in the whole controversy about Grace, which immediately followed this relatively local dispute, there was a more deeply significant cause for the attack upon the Society. It was much more a matter of prestige than of doctrine.

"The reason why they were being thus persecuted," writes Pastor, "could not be found in the doctrines which they had taught, since others had taught the same things without their having provoked any attack. The historian certainly cannot describe this complaint as unfounded; the passion displayed by some of the Dominicans against the new Order is too manifest to allow of any such thing. On the other hand the bitterness is easy to explain. The young and rising Society of Jesus had in several cases entered the lists against the older Order, which was already covered with renown, and had won brilliant successes, especially in the field of pastoral work and teaching. How then could it have failed to seem unjust to certain Dominicans, who for centuries had borne the heat and burden of the day, that they should be left behind by these newcomers at the eleventh hour? The Order of Preachers had jealously looked upon theological science as its privileged field. . . ." But Molina and Suarez had published important works in that field and "it seemed as though the younger Order was preparing to storm the last fortress of the older. The Dominicans would not have been a body of men, if there had not been among them some of choleric temperament, who from the first looked with suspicion and jealousy upon the works of their special rivals, and who in their mistrust did not fail to find in their writings things which in reality were not there." [4]

The brunt of the doctrinal attack by Mondragon and Avendaño was borne by both Molina's *Concordia,* which appeared in 1589, and by the works which Suarez published in 1590 and 1592. In the letter written by the two Dominicans, in which they attempted to justify themselves before their provincial, the very first thrust was made at Suarez. They expected this missive to remain confidentially in the hands of De Guzman, but the latter thought it so well done that he handed it over for the inspection of the apostolic nuncio. He also gave a copy to Father De Porres, the rector of the Jesuit Professed House of Madrid.

Suarez was replaced by Vasquez at the University of Alcalá in the Fall of 1593, and on his way to take up his new position at Salamanca he passed through Madrid. There he was acquainted with the contents of the Dominican letter by the Jesuit fathers and was also given the occasion to pay a visit to the nuncio, Camillo Gaetani, then in the city. He went over the case with the latter prelate and decided that the charges were too serious to ignore. Returning to Salamanca he worked intermittently on his celebrated response, and on January 15, 1594, sent it to the nuncio. [5]

[4] Pastor, *op. cit.,* vol. xxiv, pp. 300–301.

[5] Astrain, *op. cit.,* p. 169, says that this letter was addressed to Cardinal Quiroga. De Scorraille, *op. cit.,* p. 267, says it was sent to the nuncio, but in 1595. The correct date is 1594, and it is quite probable that a copy was sent to Quiroga though the original is headed thus: *Data Camillo Gaetani, Nuntio Apostolico. Scripta Salmanticae, die 15 Ianuarii 1594.* For the complete text of this interesting document cf. Stegmüller, Friedrich, "Eine Ungedruckte Denkschrift des P. Franz Suarez, S. I.," in *Archivum Historicum Societatis Iesu,* Rome, vol. vi, pp. 58–82.

The first question he took up was that of the charges made against his own book on the Incarnation, in which he was supposed to have written slightingly of the sufferings of Our Lord. He had misinterpreted entirely, his adversaries said, the teaching of St. Thomas regarding the austerities contained in the life of Christ. They claimed that he was paving the way toward an indulgent way of life for Christians by teaching that Our Lord did not observe the same strict penances which John the Baptist practiced. Suarez countered with the assertion that the Baptist's life was austere and ascetic in the extreme while that of Our Lord was like the common and ordinary life of the people around Him in food, clothes, and the treatment of his physical needs.

Avendaño had claimed that all of this was merely a Jesuitical trick to lessen the esteem which people had for the ancient, strict and rigorous religious Orders, and that Suarez was attempting to show the advantages of the Jesuits' more active but less ascetical conduct. The latter responded that the charge was entirely gratuitous. The doctrine and practice of the Church regarding corporal austerities and on the necessity for penance in general were admirable. Each Order, according to its end and vocation should harmonize spiritual and corporal austerities; each should find what is best suited for the special type of work it is pursuing. None of this could be found to be contrary to the doctrine of St. Thomas.[6]

The second and third questions answered by Suarez treated matters which had been ascribed to the Jesuits almost since the beginning of the Order. The Jesuits did not teach that the sacrament of confession can be administered by the exchange of letters between the penitent and the priest. None of us, remarks Suarez, holds this as a regular doctrine. If a Jesuit professor in his lectures treats the question as probably correct he is in a numerous and good company of ancient doctors, most of them

[6] Cf. Astrain, *op. cit.*, pp. 170 ff.

of the Order of St. Dominic. This put the matter aside for the moment but it was to cause still more trouble in the years to come.

Again the Jesuits, neither individually nor as a group, neither theoretically nor practically, demanded the names of accomplices in their penitents' confessions. The old monster which had been rampant at Granada in Suarez' childhood and which had attracted his boyish mind to the Jesuits, was again rearing its head. The Society taught the doctrine of the great theologians, particularly of St. Thomas, that certain circumstances of a person's evil habits must be known to the confessor if he is to give sound, careful direction. Suarez seriously considers the charge and then dismisses it for the ancient calumny that it was.[7]

The next point was directed against Molina's work for it charged that the Jesuit doctrine on grace therein contained really deserved the Pelagian label. Avendaño declared that Molina was teaching with too great a freedom, was condemning as erroneous the doctrine of St. Thomas, and was greatly scandalizing the Scholastic masters. Suarez does not go deeply into this question, for he was to have more to say regarding it later, but satisfies himself with showing that it is possible also to go to the other extreme in depending upon grace so that one finds himself in the company of Luther and Calvin. He includes also the oft-quoted fourth canon of the Council of Trent's sixth session, regarding the coöperation of the human will with divine grace.

Finally there was the doctrine, still important at the end of a century of Spanish colonial expansion, and of European religious wars, which declared that people could be forced at the point of a sword to accept the Gospel. Suarez replied that Christianity could not be imposed on people by force and that neither he nor his confréres had ever taught that it was right to do so. They did teach, however, that the liberty of preaching the Gospel

[7] Stegmüller, *op. cit.*, pp. 76–78.

could be defended by the force of arms—and that is an entirely different matter.

Suarez concluded his letter to Gaetani by remarking the impossibility of answering Avendaño's vague charges about the intolerable and innumerable doctrines with which the Jesuits were supposed to be disturbing the peace of the Church and the influence of the Dominicans. The nuncio sent this *apologia* to the detractors of Suarez through their superiors. But it did not end the attacks; if anything they became more violent.

Avendaño preached the Lent at Valladolid and, with the help of another enemy of the Society, Diego Nuño, who was teaching there, alternated between buffoonery and dramatic explosions in a new series of attacks. Whenever he met a Jesuit on the street, he would pretend to cringe and make the sign of the cross saying, *Judica illos Deus ut decidant a cogitationibus suis.* Nuño would tell his students that the doctrine of Molina was against the faith and that Molina himself was an ignorant presumptuous blasphemer. After that the mention of the Jesuit's name would bring a tremendous stamping of feet from the students.

Of course, Cardinal Quiroga, the Supreme Inquisitor, heard of these happenings and he was getting tired of all the complaints pouring into his office. The nuncio decided to bring Avendaño to his tribunal and he ordered the Dominican to appear at once in Madrid to defend himself. It was not difficult to establish his guilt during the process of investigation but his fellow religious interceded for him, and King Philip himself intervened. The King sent his confessor to the nuncio and to the superior of the Jesuits with a proposal which the latter considered unacceptable. Avendaño was finally condemned and silenced on January 5, 1595.

The battle of mutual recriminations was by no means over with the disposal of Suarez' calumniator. It was in fact only beginning, for the controversy *De Auxiliis,* which shook the whole learned world for many decades, was only then entering its more serious phase.

It is most interesting to note, however, that some contemporaries considered the doctrinal difficulty a mere surface thing. Father Gil Gonzales Davila, the visitor to the Jesuit province of Castile, declared that the supposed difference of opinion regarding St. Thomas' doctrine was merely a pretext for the Dominican attacks. The real reason was that the Jesuits had surpassed the Dominicans at Toledo, Soria and Salamanca, and that in the latter place the Jesuits had associated themselves with the Augustinians.[8] The charges and counter-charges had merely served to pour oil on the fire of jealousy raging in the hearts of a few disaffected and misguided men.

[8] Astrain, *op. cit.*, pp. 174–175.

CHAPTER XVI

The Metaphysics

THE FRATERNAL squabbling, so undignified and yet so human, that led to Suarez' removal to his alma mater, the University of Salamanca, was somewhat alleviated by the royal reception he received upon his arrival. His entrance into town was greeted like the return of a long-absent son. Siegfried says that "The entire University went forth to receive him at the gates of the city and brought him in in triumph. His learning, piety and gentle modesty inspired with reverence the youth who crowded to his lectures; breathless silence reigned in the hall that no word falling from his lips might be lost." [1]

But Suarez had not come back with the intention of teaching. The sorry state of his health demanded release from that burden, and his superiors had promised it. As the crowds of enthusiastic friends escorted him to the university, held banquets and other public functions in his honor, he sighed with relief that now at last he could give undivided attention to the compilation of his books.

Here, he thought, there would be no students to take him from the engrossing task of writing. Here there would be no bothersome Vasquez always ready with a clever quip, asking the students *Quid dixit vetulus mane?* "What did the old man have to say this morning?" Vasquez could do that with impunity at Alcalá; could gather the students around him and give them all

[1] Siegfried, F. P.: "Francisco Suarez," *The Ecclesiastical Review,* vol. xxix, p. 264.

the arguments against Suarez' doctrine; could force the master to reteach the entire lesson next morning. But here at Salamanca Suarez was among his friends and well-wishers who would be considerate enough to allow him the time and opportunity required for composing books.

All was well with the retired professor; and almost immediately after his arrival he settled to a steady grind of work. For a month he kept secretaries busy transcribing notes, taking dictation, correcting manuscripts. Then at the beginning of November his routine was shattered, and he was forced to return to the lecture hall to take the place of Father Miguel Marcos who had been elected to the general congregation of the Society and who was soon departing for Rome.

The subject of the course in theology which was thus unexpectedly thrust upon Suarez, was for the most part on the sacrament of penance. Marcos had started the school year and had given some of the necessary preliminary notions to his students. As on another occasion, when he replaced Vasquez, the new professor repeated the matter already seen by the class. But unlike the previous experience, Suarez here had to correct several variations taught by his predecessor. The result of this procedure was almost another domestic quarrel such as he had experienced at Alcalá, for Marcos, upon his return from Rome several months later, jealously objected to these corrections of his teaching.

The whole doctrine of penance was a troublesome and difficult thing to handle at that time, and it seems that Suarez himself was not certain regarding it. The question of confession by letter was one of the most important in the whole treatise, and was constantly the subject of rather violent dispute in university circles. Marcos and Suarez disagreed on its interpretation. The Dominicans, too, grasped it as a lever against the Jesuit professor, and less than a decade later a stormy controversy would rage over it. Suarez' teaching on "Confession in Absence" would be censured by papal authority, and would leave on his reputation the same stigma which was Bellarmine's when the Controversies were prohibited.

After the general congregation had ended in Rome, Marcos expected to receive his old post at the college in Spain. But instead of voicing this expectation, he pretended to be horrified at the novelty of doctrine introduced by Suarez and refused to take up where the other would have left off. He disclaimed any intention of disturbing the peace by constant quarreling. He wrote to Aquaviva to tell him that "Father Francis Suarez is here again in this province, and is one of the principal inventors and exponents of novel teaching. He is at Salamanca, where I am, and since there is evident opposition of ideas between us, there has naturally followed division and factions among the students." [2] For the sake of peace, then, he asked the general to allow him to go to the mission of Galicia; but for the sake of the college and the Society he asked that Suarez be retired from teaching.

Marcos did not obtain his request to leave for the missions. He remained as prefect of studies, tried to get on amicably with Suarez, with whom he had studied for six years in his youth, and finally replaced him in the chair of theology in the autumn of the following year, 1594. There were other unpleasantries centering about Suarez, some of them founded in human jealousy, others in a bona fide fear that the Spanish Inquisition would at any time swoop down upon all the Jesuits in condemnation of certain doctrines that had come to be called Suarezianisms.

Suarez bore it all with a remarkable degree of patience. Objections of this kind, given as they were by some of the most learned men of the peninsula, indicate that the man was already set apart as an original thinker. Thus they were not all to be accounted damaging blows. They meant that Suarez was considered the

[2] De Scorraille, op. cit., p. 321.

head of a group, or school of theologians, which did not hesitate to throw overboard anciently revered opinions when they were untenable. The slings of criticism in this particular case redounded ultimately to the great reputation of the theologian.

Relieved again of his professorship he went back to uninterrupted writing. As in all the storms that beat around his head during his life, he was a passive rather than an active participant. Never a man to seek the public eye, Suarez was happiest when in the quiet of his own study, listening to the raucous scratching of his own pen on foolscap, or dictating pleasantly in his distinct voice to a secretary. For a whole year he withdrew entirely from arguments and disagreements. The result of this withdrawal was the appearance, first of a new and revised edition of his *De Incarnatione,* and then of his first work on the Sacraments.

This fresh opus came from the printer in 1595 and contained a complete treatment of the Sacraments of Baptism, Confirmation, and Holy Eucharist. As a logical sequence to the two former works it was an expanded commentary on the rest of the Third Part of St. Thomas' *Summa Theologiæ.* It was the first of a trilogy he proposed to publish, not in the accepted order, but in the order of an analogy to which the matter lent itself. In this first volume, as he explained in the preface, these three sacraments treat of the acceptance and development of the supernatural life in man. The second volume would explain Penance and Extreme Unction by which the sickness of the soul and the effects of personal sins are alleviated. The final volume would treat of Holy Orders and Matrimony which were instituted by Christ for the formation and sanctification of Christian society.

In the ensuing years the rush of other duties prevented the publication of the complete work on the Sacraments as Suarez had planned it. The second volume appeared more or less on schedule five years later, but its author died before the third part of the plan could be followed out. In the meanwhile he spent laborious hours on a work of a far different nature: the Metaphysical Disputations.

This work in metaphysics was not simply another of those books which are tossed off in an author's idle moments, nor was it written simply for the sake of the writing. Astrain explains it thus: "Observing from his experience of teaching that many of his students were not well founded in philosophy and that they needed first to be instructed well in metaphysical principles in order to penetrate deeply the questions of sacred science, he decided to interrupt the publication of theological works in order to produce a solid treatise in metaphysics. Collecting his old notes and consulting all the particular works of this kind, he published a vast treatise divided into fifty-four disputations, which is commonly called the Metaphysics of Suarez. At Salamanca in 1597 he brought to light these disputations which are without a doubt one of the most colossal works the genius of philosophy has ever produced." [3]

One has merely to glance through the two enormous volumes containing these disputations to agree readily with Astrain that they are a colossal work. The laborious erudition that went into their composition staggers the imagination, especially when one realizes that this author was a man of weak health. With precise and telling logic, question after question of the most abstract nature is brought up, carefully discussed, and then neatly disposed of in characteristic Suarezian fashion. It is a work which has held the attention of scholars right up to the present time; and even now there still remain a great number of philosophers who tenaciously hold to the Metaphysics of Suarez.

Fundamentally the modern divergence of thought among non-Scholastic philosophers and theologians is due precisely to their ignorance of a solid and trustworthy metaphysics. "No one can be a good theologian," wrote Suarez in his preface, "unless he

[3] Astrain, *op. cit.*, p. 62.

first possesses a firm foundation of metaphysics. Thus I always realized that before writing my theological commentaries it would have been more useful to finish this book which I now offer my readers, and let it have first place. But, for good reasons, it was impossible for me to defer the publication of my commentaries on the third part of St. Thomas. However, as time went on, I realized more and more how that divine and supernatural theology needs and requires this human and natural science. So I did not hesitate to interrupt for a while my theological works in order to give, or rather to restore, to metaphysics the place and prestige it deserves." If evidence be required, it is evident from this statement that Suarez himself knew this work should have preceded all the others, and it shows again that philosophy and theology are intimately connected and that Suarez knew how to put first things first.

To achieve the purpose he had in mind the author actually devised a work that might be termed a complete philosophical system. Without hesitation he attributes to metaphysics the immense scope of investigation that the word implies. Metaphysics is the science which treats of the most general and fundamental principles underlying all reality and all knowledge.[4] It includes all that vast field of knowledge that eludes the direct grasp of the human senses.

Suarez' metaphysic goes above the merely sensible into the realm of spiritual substances, of God, and the soul, a realm which theology then takes over from metaphysics in order to enrich and increase it by the light of divine revelation. It goes beyond the sensible into the study of abstract and universal ideas that can be

---

[4] "Taking the term now in its widest sense, so as to include both general and special metaphysics, when we say that metaphysics is the science of the immaterial, we mean that whatever exists, whether it is an immaterial being or a material being, so long as it offers to our consideration immaterial concepts, such as substance or cause, is the object of metaphysical investigation." Cf. *Catholic Encyclopedia*, article on Metaphysics, for the explanation of various definitions.

grasped only by the intellect, to the study of being with its properties, causes, divisions, categories. It handles ultimate realities,
the very foundations of all things, and shows how a clear appre-
hension of these leads logically and inevitably to a knowledge
of all substances and perfections in both the natural and the
supernatural order.

The metaphysic is "a science as extensive as the world itself
with all that it is or can be, from the atom to the infinite, but
which is developed by Suarez in the work with gleamings of
greatness and conscientious erudition. Therefore it is a book
that could replace many others. He was impelled to brush no
question aside without debating it, no opinion without discussing
it. The student possessing the doctrine of this book is already a
good philosopher and is on the way to becoming a proficient
theologian, undaunted by the obscurities of the abstract world,
wherein so many halt or go astray." [5]

The *Disputationes Metaphysicæ* came at a time when they were
badly needed. There was then beginning the flux of philosophical thought that has continued unabated till now; there were
stress and strain in theological quarrels which had to be eased
by some such basic treatment. This work of Suarez, remarks
Siegfried, "transcends the limitations of its time and takes its
place on the border line between mediæval scholasticism and
modern philosophy, though constructed substantially on the
traditions of the former. It was truly a timely work." [6] But it did
present an innovation in more than one way, as the author himself pointed out, and as critics of his system during almost three
and a half centuries have continued to point out.

The tradition of the Schoolmen had it that the metaphysics of
Aristotle must be taught, but Suarez disabused tradition of the
trappings it had gathered over the centuries. Thus he explains
in his preface that he always prefers to use the most rational

[5] De Scorraille, *op. cit.*, p. 331.   [6] Siegfried, *op. cit.*, p. 264.

method possible in systematizing a science and in searching for truth. "Now, it would have been impossible to do this if I had followed the example of most commentators in treating the questions evoked by the text of Aristotle. I thought it easier and more useful to investigate and consider everything that touches upon the whole scope of this subject."

The innovation in methodology, then, was a happy one. Professors previously had taken the twelve books of Aristotle, presumably as their basic text. But they invariably left the text to give in their lectures the *Quæstiones,* dissertations or commentaries upon the philosophical problems omitted by the Stagirite or merely indicated by him. These questions became the subject matter of class work because the teacher could wander to his heart's content over all the lush fields of speculation, free and unhampered. The results for the student were sometimes disastrous. The tendency was to multiply novel questions without limit, and the student frequently imbibed sophistical froth instead of solid doctrine. The *Ratio Studiorum* called a halt to this practice among the Jesuit professors at least, and demanded that the teaching of metaphysics should be an explanation of Aristotle's doctrine and not a pleasant flight in fanciful speculation. Suarez went even further than that. He took the doctrine of Aristotle as a whole and then rearranged the text and plan in a more orderly manner.

.. There will undoubtedly be some, says Suarez, who would wish to compare his teaching with that of Aristotle, or wish to learn both of them in order to understand the whole science more fully. Therefore he compiled what he calls a table of references, but which is practically a book in itself, the *Index Locupletissimus in Metaphysicam Aristotelis.* It is a highly valuable pointer to the work of the Greek philosopher and shows at a glance where each problem is to be found in both the Suarezian and the Aristotelian text. By this concordance he presents a guide from

Aristotle through St. Thomas, a synthesis of all human wisdom and an introduction to the divine science. He offers it for its prime purpose: that in its philosophical entirety it might be the humble hand-maiden of theological study.

With typical Latin enthusiasm the biographer Sartolo exclaimed a century afterward that "for philosophers who wrote later, not excepting the most erudite and profound, this work has been what the sea is to rivers, whose waters come back ceaselessly to nourish and replenish without ever exhausting themselves." This is exaggeration with a vengeance; but the clear-headed estimation of a book's usefulness may be deduced from the number of times it is reprinted. Within a few years the Metaphysics of Suarez was reprinted a dozen times in France, Italy, Germany and Belgium; and the masters have made undoubted use of it. They borrowed from it, amended it, criticized it—but they could not ignore it.

Papal approval of the work came too, not only during the author's lifetime but many decades later when Alexander VII asserted that he had always been a disciple of Suarez. His Holiness considered the Metaphysics the prime discovery of his youth, and became so absorbed in it that he could read or study nothing else for a period of over four months. As he declared: *"Omni mihi praeceptoris voce destituta unus praesto fuit suis in lucem editis libris Franciscus Suarez, theologorum hujus aetatis facile princeps: quem cum philosophiæ operam darem, scriptorem novi acutissimum amavique, ideo in ipsa Theologia Doctorem sane perspicuum optimumque sum expertus."* [7]

The circulation of the edition printed in Spain was a large and immediate one. Immense as was the work and expensive as must have been its printing, it soon began to make money for Suarez, who obtained permission from his superiors to use it in the new

[7] Werner, Karl: *Franz Suarez und die Scholastik der letzten Jahrhunderte,* Ratisbonne, 1861, p. 73.

building program of the college at Salamanca. The sum he fur-
nished was applied to one section of the new building, and this
part has since retained the name: Suarezian Quarter. With the
money which continued to come in from this and other works
Suarez established a library fund, the income of which was to
provide books for the college. It is easy to see in these stipula-
tions that Salamanca was always close to the great scholar's heart.

Regarding the Suarezian system of metaphysics itself there
are numerous points significant enough to merit special consideration. The one that is distinctly his own is the treatment of the
famous Suarezian mode which is the ultimate though real determination of a reality, and which does not add a new entity but
merely modifies a preëxisting entity. The mode is really distinct
from its subject and, as such, approaches the formal distinction
of which Duns Scotus speaks. In the works of St. Thomas there
is no mention of a modal distinction. Therefore, Suarez must
be given the dubious credit of having innovated, or at least incorporated for the first time in a philosophical system, the application of these modes.

The nature of the modes is explained by Suarez through the
use of an analogy. "Light, for example, depends on the sun.
This dependence, however, is something other than the light and
the sun. For we could understand the light and the sun to remain
without the light depending on the sun if God were to deny his
concursus to the sun for producing light while by His own power
He might conserve both the light and the sun in existence. The
mind, however, cannot conceive this dependence of the light on
the sun to be an entity wholly distinct from the light itself because, first, by this dependence as through a medium the cause
exerts its influence on the effect; therefore the dependence cannot be something entirely distinct from the effect; and secondly,
this entity could, otherwise, be separated from its subject, at
least by the absolute power of God, which is unintelligible.

Therefore we conclude this dependence is a Mode of light which has a transcendental relation to its subject." [8]

The difficulty in understanding the modes is one of trying to find their place in the scheme of being. The mode is neither a thing nor an entity, nor is it mere nothing. It is a determination or modification of an entity already existing. Suarez clarifies all this by showing the difference between a modal and a real distinction. The modal distinction is had in the non-mutual separation of two entities, that is, one extreme can remain without the other but not conversely. The real distinction is had if the separation is mutual, that is, both extremes remain after the separation has taken place. [9]

It follows naturally that there are accidental modes and substantial modes, and it is through the latter that Suarez has become celebrated because of his teaching on personality and the modal union between matter and form. For a theologian it has particular application in the question of the hypostatic union existing in Christ. Suarez—as every Catholic does—believed that Christ had a perfect human nature but not a human personality, and that this human nature, hypostatically united to the Word, subsists by divine personality. Suarez explains that the human nature of Christ lacks human personality because of the absence of the mode of personality, and that the union of the humanity to the Word is accounted for by a substantial mode of humanity. [10]

Another metaphysical question requiring special mention in the discussion of the Suarezian system is the author's teaching on the problem of individuation. Technical and involved, it cannot be treated at length here. Krost believes that Suarez' treatment is the clearest of all explanations and the one to which most

[8] *Disp.* vii, I, 17–18.

[9] For a careful analysis of the modes cf. Nolan, Peter: "The Suarezian Modes," *Proceedings of The Jesuit Educational Association*, Chicago, 1931, Loyola University Press, pp. 184–200.

[10] *De Incarnatione, Disp.* viii, I and III.

of the other authors must go back eventually. The fervidly defended theory of St. Thomas was that the principle of individuation is *materia signata.* In the Fifth Disputation of the Metaphysics Suarez comes to the conclusion that "as far as it is anything real, physical, and intrinsic to the being that is individual, the foundation of individual being as individual is identified really with its entity, without any special principle or foundation really distinct therefrom."

For a clear understanding of Suarez' handling of this problem it is necessary to make a careful study of that section of the Metaphysics where it is treated. Krost, who has made such a study, declares that it is "admirable as a consistently progressive whole. . . . His general doctrine seems to possess about it a transcendental character such as the subject demands, so that it fits later with complete harmony into the variegated scheme of spirit and body and matter, and of form whether substantial or accidental. As one of the culminations of his system of metaphysics, his teaching on individuation aligns smoothly with the great fundamental concepts of being and unity, and clicks tightly into groove with the first notions of number, distinction and identity. One single perfect doctrine of individuation must square perfectly not only with this or that more specific application of these concepts to immaterial or material, to substantial or accidental being, but must meet the requirements of application to all being. If Suarez' teaching on individuation approaches close to such perfection in one system for solving the true meaning of the underlying principle of absolute individuation, it does so because of his rigorous clear-sighted subjection of various universal concepts to the transcendental ones that are realized in things that are individual." [11]

[11] Krost, John: "Suarez's Teaching on Individuation," *Proceedings of The Jesuit Educational Association,* Chicago, 1931, Loyola University Press, pp. 210–211.

Finally, there is another question developed in the Metaphysics, one which has been of deep interest to rational psychologists ever since men began to wonder how the human mind knows things outside itself. It is Suarez' theory of cognition in which the philosopher holds that the intellect knows an individual material object by a proper species of it, directly without reflexion. This is one of those points on which Suarez dares to part company with St. Thomas, and is probably the most important of the differences between the Suarezian and Thomist systems. Cardinal Mercier declared that these main departures were three: Suarez "rejects the real distinction between essence and existence, admits the possibility of the separate existence of first matter, and accords to the intellect the power of forming a direct concept of the individual." [12] But of these the last is of most significance at the present time.

Perhaps in no other metaphysical problem have philosophers of all times gone so far afield as in the question of human cognition. The matter is highly speculative, and therefore one can easily understand a divergence of opinion between eminent scholars like Suarez and Thomas. From their starting base, they are, of course, in agreement that the intellect can know universals. All Scholastic philosophers admit that the intellect truly cognizes immaterial objects, such as an angel or God, and practically all teach that the intellect has clear and distinct concepts of material objects, such as a tree or a house.

The question here is whether these singular material objects are known directly or indirectly by the intellect. Suarez holds for the former opinion, that is, that proper *species impressæ* of the objects are impressed on the passive intellect. As he remarks, "it is positively nearer the truth to say that the species, impressed

[12] Mercier, Cardinal: *A Manual of Modern Scholastic Philosophy*, St. Louis, 1917, Herder, vol. ii, p. 427. (Doctor M. de Wulf handled the historical section of this work.)

by the active intellect, does not abstract from the representation of the individual object in the phantasm, but only from the real and entitative materiality of the phantasm itself; without this it can be a representation of the same individual object no matter how material; for to be or to become such by a spiritual form or quality or entity is not an impossibility, as is evident in the case of the angels and God Himself." [13]

In a concise article treating of this question Mahowald summarizes Suarez' stand in favor of direct cognition, or the active intellect's production of a proper species of the individual object: "There is no contradiction in this; no physical reason can be assigned to show that this cannot be done by the active intellect; without reason it must not be denied; it is more in accord with experience, with the natural order of cognition, and with the purpose and natural activity of the active intellect whose function it is, by means of spiritual action, to render the passive intellect as similar as possible to the representation of the phantasm." [14] The contention of Suarez, then, is based on the solid footing of natural experience, omitting as far as possible the speculative sidepaths into which many other philosophers have wandered in their treatment of this problem.

There is one further external quality about the Metaphysics which cannot be passed over even in this brief survey. It is the carefully scientific approach which Suarez used in this and all subsequent works. In the very beginning of the work,[15] he criticizes some of his contemporaries because "a large part of the doctrine is taught by modern dialecticians in a confused manner." As for himself, he would prefer to omit a question entirely rather than insert it at the wrong place in a book or teach it out of order in a class. So important did Suarez consider this matter

[13] *Disputationes,* vol. ii, *Disp.* vi, VI, 7.
[14] Mahowald, *op. cit.,* p. 169.
[15] I, iv, 13–16.

that he went into detail in the Metaphysics to point out a careful division of the sciences.[16]

All of this is, of course, mere methodology, but no one can ever abandon entirely the method for the attainment. It is well enough for abstract and mystical individuals to excogitate in the highest realms of metaphysical speculation without attention to order or method. This is pure self-indulgence, and might at best be called the Platonic approach. But Suarez was a teacher, and had thus always to keep in mind the fact that he was passing on the fruit of his knowledge to others. The orderly presentation is the most effectual, and Suarez was aiming to clarify rather than mystify.

This propensity for clear and careful analysis is one of the reasons why Suarez' Metaphysics were scrupulously studied by the founders of modern philosophy. His influence was felt by Descartes who chose, out of the vast library of previous philosophical works, the *Metaphysical Disputations* of Suarez and the *Summa* of St. Thomas, and kept them with him in all his travels. Leibniz claims that he read Suarez like a novel; and Spinoza, too, seems to have been well acquainted with his metaphysical doctrines. Schopenhauer thought the work of Suarez a "true compendium of Scholastic wisdom." [17]

Like everything else that Suarez produced, this perennial work must be considered against the background of the late sixteenth century in which it was written. Too often the mistake of shallow critics is that they lift a man's actions and works out of the scene in which he moved, and thus distort them completely. What could be done and said in the fifth century was considered foolish in the fifteenth. What was known of experimental science in

[16] *Suarez and the Organization of Learning* is a competent and scholarly study of this particular question by Clare C. Riedl. Cf. *Jesuit Thinkers of The Renaissance,* ed. by Gerard Smith, Milwaukee, 1939, Marquette University Press, pp. 1–62.

[17] *Ibid.,* p. 5.

the twelfth century is thought outmoded in the twentieth. There is a frequent failure to recognize that Suarez had a penetrating knowledge of the high things with which the Scholastics busied themselves and that the modern widespread knowledge of minutiæ is the accumulation of many thoughts over many centuries.

Thus the *Metaphysical Disputations* will continue to be judged variously according to the way in which the critic looks at them. They were written for a generation of astute thinkers, and the modern disregard of them may for that reason contain some unflattering implications.

CHAPTER XVII

The King Again

PHILIP II, ruler of the greatest empire on earth, was approaching the end of his magnificent career just when Francis Suarez was starting on the long crest of his intellectual meridian. But a great king would use a great subject for the achievement of high things. During his last months Philip prevailed upon Suarez to accept the principal chair of theology at the University of Coimbra, in Portugal.

The Spanish monarch was five years a-dying. "He looked like a dying man," writes Walsh, "when he entered Madrid on the last day of 1592. The people who filled the streets to see him pass in his open coach were shocked to see how old and feeble he was. Every one was saying that His Majesty's journey to Aragon had all but finished him. The physicians, greatly disturbed, warned him that if he wished to live longer he must curtail his activities and adopt a new regimen of diet, rising and retiring, and work. This he did; but he was under no illusion that many years remained. After the death of his confessor, Fray Diego de Chaves, he began to prepare more earnestly for his own leave-taking." [1]

No one has ever called Philip II a saint, but he was by all odds the leading Spanish Catholic of his time, and he was the most powerful ruler of the century. As he put himself and his affairs in readiness for the end he could look back upon a long life which, if it was not saintly, was certainly nothing to be ashamed of. He walked side by side with Sister Death, for she came

[1] Walsh, *op. cit.*, p. 697.

close to him many times and he was not afraid of her. One after the other, his illegitimate brother and sister, Don Juan and Margaret, and his true sister, Juana, were taken by death. He had outlived four wives, Maria of Portugal, Mary Tudor, Isabella of France, Anne of Austria, and six of his children, Don Carlos, Catherine, Ferdinand, Carlos, Diego, Maria. Now there was left the young lad who would become Philip III, and who was being carefully groomed for the throne.

Philip in his last years could look back, too, upon a long list of creditable performances in protection of the Holy Roman Faith, the least-known of which, but not the least of which, were his services to Christian education. Philip, the politician, the Spider of the Escorial, the Emperor, the devout Catholic, was also Philip, the promoter of universities and colleges in the Spanish domains. He had had a hand in founding or subsidizing practically all of the colleges to which Irish seminarians came for the study of philosophy and theology during the English persecutions. They were established all over the continent, Rome, Salamanca, Seville, Compostella, Madrid, Alcalá, Lisbon, Douay, Louvain, Antwerp, Paris, Bordeaux, Rouen. The English Jesuit, Persons, came to Spain for Philip's financial aid just after the loss of the Armada. He not only received enough for the English students at Douay, but was encouraged by the King to bring some of his students to Valladolid. Philip was called the founder of this latter college in Clement VIII's bull of confirmation of November 3, 1592. He contributed an annual revenue of sixteen hundred crowns, "and on the occasion of a visit to the seminary was profoundly moved at the sight of these youths who had left their country for the sake of the faith, in order to face a life of suffering and persecution; he thereupon increased his annual contribution, and took all the debts of the seminary upon his own shoulders." [2]

[2] Pastor, *op. cit.*, vol. xxiv, pp. 7–8.

All of this points to the reasons Philip had in wishing to obtain the services of the best-known theologian in his country for the University of Coimbra. But there is a whole concatenation of events leading up to Suarez' departure for the new position in Portugal.

For over a century there had been intermittent wars between Portugal and Spain. The monarchs had endeavored in various ways to annex the little kingdom in order to spread Spanish rule over the whole peninsula, but the thing was not accomplished till Philip's time. In 1578 his impetuous nephew, Don Sebastian, King of Portugal, flung himself and seventeen thousand troops against thirty thousand Moors, and was killed in the uneven battle. Philip was dejected at the news but did not hesitate to take over the Portuguese addition to his realm. There were others who claimed the throne, but the best legal claim undoubtedly belonged to His Catholic Majesty of Spain, whose mother, Isabella, had been the eldest daughter of Emanuel of Portugal.

Thus Philip came into possession of Portugal. Though he was prepared to invade the little country and to make good his claim at the point of the sword he soon found that such extreme measures were unnecessary. There were a few malcontents, especially the illegitimate Don Antonio, who had himself crowned at Lisbon and then fled at the approach of Alba by land and of the Marquis of Santa Cruz by sea.

Whenever new territory fell under his sway Philip immediately went to work on its integration and reorganization so that it would fit well into the body of his large empire. The citizenry, of course, was of most importance, and the spiritual welfare of his subjects was of greater concern to Philip than their temporal welfare. Everything that went with the Portuguese people in their maintenance of the true faith had to be protected and fostered, and among the things which engaged most of the royal attention were the affairs of the Church and its religious Orders.

The Spanish King had been at odds with Pope Sixtus V at various intervals and he was not over sorry to hear of the Pontiff's death. The next Pope, Urban VII, of Castagna, was very popular in Spain and seemed about to coöperate handsomely for the progress of both Christian Church and Christian empire. But he reigned only a few days. His successor, Gregory XIV, had hardly started his pontifical duties when he too died in the same year. A third short-lived Pope was Innocent IX, who likewise had no opportunity of demonstrating his attitude toward the Spanish desires.

In the important papal election at the beginning of 1592 the Cardinals at Rome practically flouted the wishes of the Catholic King by turning down six of the men he nominated and accepting the last and least desirable, Cardinal Aldobrandini, Pope Clement VIII. "The Holy Ghost had once more asserted His independence of Spanish political desires and interests. . . . Pope Clement VIII proved to be one of the holiest Popes of the sixteenth century. His long reign (he outlived Philip by seven years) was one of the most glorious in the history of the Church. He confessed every day, fasted twice a week, wore a hair shirt, and presented a serene and humble exterior that made a memorable contrast to the titanic presence of Sixtus V. Any politician who looked for timidity under the soft speech of Clement or for any self-seeking behind his mild and steady gaze, was destined to an uncomfortable surprise." [3]

But it must not be thought that Philip was of small enough spiritual stature to be always in conflict with the Pope any more than he was forever opposed to the Jesuits. The man was interested in both Church and kingdom, and though his personal desires were frequently thwarted by Popes and Jesuits he saw spiritual values too clearly to allow constant belligerence. Toward the Jesuits he had an attitude something similar to that of

[3] Walsh, *op. cit.*, p. 682.

Sixtus V, who had grumbled, "Why should we have to bow our heads every time we mention them?" Not only did the monarch send Jesuits to his foreign possessions, but at different times he employed them to visit and reform other Orders in Spain itself, and at all times wanted them to apply their vigorous methods in university teaching and administration.

From the time when Portugal became an integral part of the Spanish kingdom Philip had been desirous of placing some Jesuits on the faculty of theology in the capital city of Coimbra. The principal chair of theology had been held by a Dominican, Antonio de Santo Domingo, even before the Portuguese King, Sebastian, died in battle. This thoroughly capable and learned professor lectured there for twenty-two years, from 1574 till 1596. At his honorable retirement, the Dominicans showed no willingness to relinquish a post which their members had held for over thirty-five years and which they looked upon as a kind of religious inheritance. De Scorraille notes that they wanted to keep a kind of Dominican dynasty at Coimbra just as they had at Salamanca, but the intervention of the King gave matters a different complexion.

So the Jesuits were assured of the professorship, but there was a further question regarding which Jesuit would fill the chair, and again the King had to settle the matter. The prime favorite, the famous local light in the Society at Coimbra, was the scholarly and controversial Molina. Though a Spaniard, and born in Cuena (1535), the much maligned Luis Molina spent most of his years in Portugal, making his novitiate and studies there and teaching at the colleges of Coimbra and Evora. The Jesuits had a college at Coimbra as early as 1555 [4] and Molina made his theological studies there between the years 1559 and 1562. During the next four years he lectured in philosophy there, and then, from 1567 to 1583, he taught theology at Evora. Here he de-

[4] Farrell, *op. cit.*, pp. 109 ff.

veloped the famous ideas on divine prescience and predestination which made him the focal point of that tremendous Dominican-Jesuit controversy, and which now made it inadvisable for him to accept the chair of theology at Coimbra.

Siegfried writes that "the votes of the faculty were divided between Molina, who was then at the zenith of his fame, and Suarez. In view of the fact that the teaching of Molina was at the time under examination, it was deemed prudent to appoint the latter." [5] Historically, the affair was not quite so simple as that. It is not at all clear whether the faculty had only to elect Suarez, or whether the royal injunction was absolutely necessary to bring him to Portugal. The evidence at hand seems to favor the latter view. In the actual event of Suarez' glorious success, the university always claimed the initiative in the movement to bring him to Coimbra, and maintained that Philip had merely and indefinitely demanded any great master they could put their hands on.

At any rate it adds immeasurably to the prestige of Suarez that he should be chosen over Molina, who was then the most fiercely burning firebrand among the Portuguese theologians. Philip knew him and respected him for his undoubted theological prowess, but he also feared to have him placed in so prominent a position. Actually, however, he knew Suarez more intimately, respected him even more fully, and trusted him to be always on the side of orthodoxy. From time to time he had consulted the great Spanish theologian indirectly through his royal representatives and found that the sagacious mind had always the correct answer to offer. A century ago the Suarezian ancestors had advised Ferdinand and Isabella on military and administrative matters at the conquest of Andalusia; now the theologian was giving advice of an eminently higher nature.

In May of 1596, Suarez, who was then at Salamanca, received

[5] Siegfried, *op. cit.*, p. 264.

a copy of the King's letter demanding him for the office in Portugal. Philip had written to the visitor of the Jesuit colleges, Garcia de Alarcon, that "the principal chair of the faculty of theology at the University of Coimbra is vacant, and at that place no man can be found who has the necessary knowledge and qualifications for the post. Now I am of the opinion that Francis Suarez, a religious of the Society, could ably fill it. I therefore give you this express commission of ordering him to go and teach in this chair for a few years. He will have no other duty than that of giving his course, and he will receive no salary, since your constitutions do not permit it. But I will order the university to give him, out of its income, as an alms, everything he will require. In doing what I ask you will give me great pleasure and will serve me well." [6]

Now Suarez was undoubtedly *the* man of theology among all of Philip's Spanish subjects, and his acceptance of this royal offer would have lent immediate impetus to the King's cause for higher learning in Portugal. The relations between Salamanca and Coimbra were of the best, and there would be no difficulty in obtaining the necessary permission from Jesuit superiors to make the change of college and province. But Suarez was not of the same mind as the King. In coming to Salamanca his one whole desire had been to write. He had been forced to fill in at a teaching position for a while, but now he wished with all his heart to relinquish the platform for the solitude of the study.

Definitely, in the mind of Suarez, the career of teaching was over for him, and even a king's order would not change that opinion. Never a robust man, he needed to conserve his strength for the composition of a complete work in theology. Others agreed that the works he proposed to publish, and had already outlined, would be of invaluable service in the advancement of knowledge and in the defense of the Church. The rest of his life

[6] De Scorraille, *op. cit.,* pp. 335–336.

must be distracted by no arduous and time-consuming duties like lecturing. The wrench would be too painful and the results too meager.

Suarez asked the Jesuit visitor to make his courteous excuses to the King but to insist on reasons that were less personal to Suarez and more likely to convince Philip. He suggested that an appointment of this kind would tend to disrupt the peaceful and friendly relations then existing between the Dominicans and Jesuits in Portugal. The Society must not do anything that might disturb these relations, and it was most important that a Jesuit should not be placed in a post which had been under the control of the Dominicans for more than three decades. The Dominicans, added Suarez, had handled the work with great distinction and it was preferable that they should be permitted to continue at the University of Coimbra.

Father de Alarcon worked fast, for he believed that Suarez' reasons would be sufficiently convincing to the King. But Philip came right back with an answer on the 27th of May, only fourteen days after his previous letter, and refused to accept the excuses as sufficiently forceful. In it he told the visitor that he was thankful for the services he had done, but "the objections you make regarding the religious of St. Dominic will not cause any difficulty on their part since they do not have a right to that chair. The custom is that it is awarded either by competition or by my choice, and in the past this titulary did not belong wholly to that order. And if at the present there is no conflict between it and the Society in this realm, I will take care that nothing in the future will give rise to it. Therefore I ask you to order the said Father Francis Suarez to depart soon for Coimbra. You will inform me of his departure so that I can make out the necessary letters and rescripts." [7]

This sounded like a serious command to Suarez when he heard

[7] *Ibid.*, p. 338.

of it from the visitor, and he took his departure from Salamanca. But instead of going to Coimbra he went to Toledo to talk it over with the King himself. Where letters had failed to take hold perhaps a personal interview would convince the King that the place for Suarez was Salamanca, and the work for Suarez was authorship, and not lecturing in Portugal. Philip received him affably enough at Toledo, and was persuaded more by the emaciated appearance of the priest than by his cogent reasoning. To the other reasons Suarez added that of his poor health, and then, lest the King change his mind, he left him two complete memorials about the matter. Philip reluctantly let him have his way, wishing him God's best blessings on the work of literary composition.

In the meanwhile the ever busy Aquaviva found time to write to Suarez, agreeing entirely that it would be better not to accept the post at Coimbra. He believed that it would be to the better interest of both Suarez and the University of Coimbra if the position were filled by some Portuguese theologian, preferably a Dominican. Anxious royal eyes were then cast at Molina, who was in literary retirement at the College of Cuenca, but Philip was afraid to take a chance on a man who was under constant fire by theological adversaries. Finally, he ordered the previous professor, the learned Dominican, Antonio Domingo, to resume the course, if only as a temporary provision. This command was obediently attended to, but the old man died at the end of 1596, and the whole tiresome question was revived.

Suarez had settled down to more than a half year of uninterrupted work on his books, treating mainly the question of grace, which was then causing so much disturbance in theological circles. He anticipated a quick and successful conclusion to this enterprise when his hopes were again disturbed by a third letter which Philip sent to Father Alarcon on February 10, 1597. This time, said the King, the presence of Suarez was imperatively needed on the faculty of Coimbra. He knew and remembered all

the former objections regarding personal health, the concord
between the Orders, and so forth, "but it is absolutely necessary
that Coimbra have a man of proved virtue and great knowledge,
and I know that such a man is Father Suarez. Therefore, I ask
you to give him a formal order to take possession of this chair.
Tell him that he need not teach at the first hour, but at any other
hour that is suitable for him. And if his health does not stand
the strain, he may later give up the position."

In the face of such a plea further resistance on the part of
Suarez was out of the question. The royal suggestion that he
might change the time of his lecture to a later hour in the day
was not followed by the professor, but it was one which would
have upset a tradition going back to the earliest mediæval universities. The school day was not properly started unless the
incumbent of the principal chair on the faculty gave the first lecture in the morning. After that the other lectures could be given
at any time of the day.

For almost twenty years, then, this man of feeble health taught
at Coimbra on an exacting schedule that would have worn out
hardier men. Watt says that to read this schedule "is to be filled
with the half-incredulous awe that is produced in the ordinary
man by reading about the mortifications of the saints. The time
of his lecture, which lasted an hour and a half, was half-past six
in the morning during the summer months, an hour later in the
winter. He rose never later than half-past three in the summer,
half-past four in the winter. After an hour and a half of mental
prayer, followed by the recital of the Little Hours of the breviary,
he went to his books. By the time most people in England are
breakfasting, Suarez was settling down to a couple of hours' work
with his secretaries. He did not breakfast till mid-day, for it was
his custom to say Mass daily at eleven o'clock in the morning.
After a very light breakfast, he said Vespers and Compline, re-
cited his Rosary and read some spiritual book. At two o'clock he

anticipated Matins and Lauds of the following day. Then he settled down to five hours of mental toil before his second meal of the day. After that a short conversation with some of the members of his community, lengthy night prayers, and bed." [8]

In general outline this is the kind of life which the great theologian led from the Spring of 1597 until his death two decades later. He had tried to push off the acceptance still further in the hope that he could remain at Salamanca till his publisher there would complete the printing of his *Metaphysical Disputations*. But Philip balked at any further complications and in no uncertain terms spoke his mind to the Jesuit visitor. "Give Father Suarez my thanks, which he fully deserves, and tell him to leave immediately for Coimbra without waiting for the printing of his works. He will easily find someone at the college of Salamanca to continue this work for him."

That command came at the end of March. Suarez promptly packed up his few belongings and went to Portugal where the Jesuit provincial detained him almost a month before allowing him to start his lectures at the university. In all his previous years of teaching Suarez had never obtained the official doctoral standing so highly prized among Spanish universities. Hence the provincial of Portugal now created him a Doctor of Theology, gave him a few unnecessary instructions for carrying out his new work, and sent him to the university.

But an unforeseen objection arose from the university officials themselves. The new professor had not been lecturing a month when these men took exception to the degree just conferred upon him on the ground that it was merely an ecclesiastical honor. The University of Coimbra was a civil, not an ecclesiastical institution, and according to its statutes the degree given Suarez by his new

[8] Watt, Lewis: "Francisco Suarez," in *Great Catholics*, ed. Claude Williamson, New York, 1939, Macmillan, p. 172.

superior was little more than a Bachelor's title. The Doctorate was something high and rare among these Portuguese scholars and the Spanish theologian would have to prove his mettle in a public disputation. Averse to all this bothersome red tape but willing to fulfill all the requirements, Suarez went to Evora, where on June 4, 1597, he performed a public defense of the whole fields of philosophy and theology, and calmly accepted an honor which others fervidly coveted.

Back at Coimbra for his first summer's teaching, Suarez again appeared in a public disputation, but this time in the rôle of an objector. The story in all his biographies has it that a certain Aegydius, an Augustinian friar, was aggrieved at the appointment of a foreigner to the local theological faculty and wished to discountenance him in the sight and hearing of the whole university town. The hall was crowded to the doors, for everyone, students as well as townsmen, wished to see the new and famous professor in action.

They were sadly disappointed in Suarez. Aegydius announced his first thesis, gave his complete explanation and proof for it. Suarez rose to the bait, politely and carefully made an objection. The defendant threw out the objection on the grounds that it could not possibly be maintained by a Catholic, and then proceeded to insist upon his own proposition. When he had finished, Suarez, to the astonishment of the audience, declined to comment any further and declared that as far as he was concerned the question was closed. On his return home his fellow Jesuits, who knew that Suarez was correct, upbraided him for bringing uncomfortable disgrace on himself and the Society by bowing to an adversary. He answered them by pulling out a small volume and showing them a council of the Church which was almost in the exact words of the objection he had made to Aegydius. "If I had defended this proposition," he said, "I would have disgraced a fellow religious and public professor, and by showing that his opinion contradicted the express teaching of the Church should have ruined his reputation forever."

Such graciousness was not a rare occurrence in the life of Suarez, either here in Portugal, or in the Spanish centers of learning where he had previously studied and taught. It was typical of a man who would turn down a royal invitation three times, but who would never rise to the attack if it meant personal disrepute to others.

People are not long held in ignorance of the true character of a man like Suarez. Two decades of glorious and self-sacrificing labor stretched before him at Coimbra and the Portuguese were soon as loyal and devoted to him as ever Salamanca had been. His fame rose steadily with the years, and though Philip died about twelve months later they never ceased thanking him for demanding this Spanish light for their corner of the empire.

CHAPTER XVIII

Grace in Spain

AMONG THEIR MANY OTHER DUTIES and occupations the Spanish theologian Suarez and the Italian cardinal Bellarmine found time to insert their doctrine of congruism in the theological system of the Schoolmen. But in back of congruism there is the most exciting and interesting tale of the times. It is a drama enacted in two parts, the first act taking place in Spain, the second in Rome. Up to now the finale has never been staged; and it is most probable that a fully satisfying dénouement may never be written to this dramatic controversy *De Auxiliis*. Its solution involves a knotty problem that penetrates so deeply into the divine scheme of things that it seems to elude the grasp of merely mortal intellects.

The villains of the piece—if it had any—were Molina and Bañes; its heroes were Suarez and Bellarmine, ably assisted by Vasquez and Lessius, with an occasional walk-on by practically every important ecclesiastical and civil personage of the age.

For the sixteenth century moment the story really began with Molina, but the background of the plot goes far back to the early centuries when the first Christians wrestled with heretics over the reconciliation between free will and divine grace. The Church traditionally taught without hesitation that grace is an unearned gift without which man cannot achieve salvation but to which he has not the least natural claim. God freely gives this grace before, during and after every human action, but because of the culpable stubbornness of the human will it does not always ob-

tain its supernatural effect. The difficulty arises over the fact
that grace is absolutely necessary, but at the same time the will
of man remains free to accept or reject it; and this difficulty
caused various theories outside the pale of expressed Catholic
teaching.

St. Augustine opposed heretical teaching on the question on
two fronts. Himself a onetime follower of the Persian dreamer,
Mani, who taught that there is a fatal necessity in every human
action, Augustine opposed Manichaeism. The British monk,
Pelagius, went to the other extreme by denying the necessity of
grace and exaggerating the competence of the unaided human
will. In opposing the fatalism of the Manichaeans and the liberalism of the Pelagians, Augustine used all the fire of his genius
and all the resources of his superb intellectual ability, and though
he seemed at times to overemphasize the points opposed to heresy
he has ever since enjoyed the sobriquet, Doctor of Grace. "It
needed," writes Broderick, "the calm, critical intellectualism of
St. Thomas and the great Scholastics to balance his books and
show how his account really stood in the theology of Christendom." [1]

When the Jesuits came upon the scene in the sixteenth century
this question of grace and free will was a burning issue flaming
up and down Europe. People were heading toward eternal dam-
nation or salvation because of their belief or disbelief in it, and
because of the actions which necessarily followed. It was no
mere love of argumentative erudition, of skill and subtlety in
debate that made the Dominicans and Jesuits lock wits in the
long-drawn controversy. The heretics had set the world agog
with their theories on justification, and the two religious Orders
were more anxious to settle the problem than to worst each other
in learned polemics.

According to Martin Luther a man's good works, the human

[1] Broderick, *op. cit.*, vol. ii, p. 2.

actions of free choice, could not gain merit for the future life. Eternal destiny could not hinge upon free will, for man had no free will. He taught, as Calvin likewise taught, that this destiny was predetermined by God, and that man, therefore, could not change it in even the slightest degree by his actions. In this grotesque theory man was innately vicious, he was a slave who could not do otherwise than he did, who had only to believe firmly and then sin all he wished. It was as simple as that.[2]

In the countries won over by the Protestant preachers everyone was saying that good works were foolish. A sincere act of faith in the goodness of God and in the all-embracing coverage of God's merciful mantle was all that was required of Christians. He knew human frailty, and He knew from all eternity who would be saved and who condemned. No one could resist the will of God. The preachers were themselves convinced of this handy and very immoral teaching and they found no trouble at all in popularizing it.

Ignatius Loyola saw what was going on about him as a disastrous consequence of such illogical thinking, and he handed down as an important spiritual inheritance to his followers the insistent doctrine of free will. In an appendix to the *Spiritual Exercises* he admonished them to beware the error of the heretics in belittling the importance of freedom of the will and at the same time to hold to the sane interpretation of divine grace. "We should not lay so much stress on the doctrine of grace as thereby to encourage the holding of that dangerous doctrine which de-

---

[2] The central thesis of Lutheranism, one which Luther himself called "the article of the standing and falling Church," treats of the justification of sinful man. According to it Original Sin caused human nature to be totally and positively depraved so that every action of an unjustified person is displeasing to God. Justification, by which God imputes to man the merits of Christ, can come only by faith, which is the confidence that one has been reconciled to God through Christ. Good works are necessary only as a means of exercising this confidence. They presuppose justification and are rewarded by the fulfillment of the divine promises.

nies the existence of free will. We should, therefore, speak of
faith and grace in such manner that our teaching may, with the
help of God, redound to His greater honor, and, above all, in
these dangerous times, certainly not in such a way that good works
and free will are thought to be of less importance, or even regarded as of no value at all." [3] Loyola was living and working
in the perilous aftermath of Lutheran and Calvinist heresies and
he had the sagacity to know that the members of his Society would
have to fight their errors for decades to come.

Thus, long before Molina came on the stage to fire the first
shot of the controversy, the Jesuits had been drilled in a cautious
handling of the problem, and almost to a man they rallied to his
defense when his doctrine was called into question. Molina himself did nothing hastily. He was in no wise the headstrong, impetuous, unyielding sophist that later critics made him out to be.
At Evora as early as 1570 he dictated in his classes a commentary
on the first part of St. Thomas' *Summa Theologica* and prepared
the first stages in the system which was to bear his name. In the
following years he thought much about it and then spent almost
two full years (1583–1585) in revising it for publication. Finally, near the end of 1587 he had the work passed by the Jesuit
censors, and in the following June the Portuguese Inquisition put
its stamp of approval upon it. On the historical date of December 22, 1588, the *Concordia Liberi Arbitrii cum Gratiae Donis,
Divina Praescientia, Providentia, Praedestinatione et Reproba-
tione* was given to the world. An immediate controversy raged
hotly around the book and its author, the points of which are still
a living issue.

"In the *Concordia*," writes Dr. Pegis, "Molina concludes a
long proof of his celebrated doctrine on *scientia media* with an

[3] This is Rule XVII of St. Ignatius' "Rules for thinking with the Church."
For the standard current version, cf. *The Text of the Spiritual Exercises of St.
Ignatius,* Preface by John Morris. London, 1913, Burns and Oates, pp. 124–
125.

exhortation which has, not the cold and calm impersonal tone of a philosophical discourse, but the moving oratory of the pulpit. He has succeeded in harmonizing liberty with divine prescience. Liberty is ours, so indisputably ours, that, with the help of God's gifts, it lies in our power to avoid all mortal sins, to arise from them again, to attain eternal life, or to lose it." [4] Six years later (1594) in answer to his numerous critics, Molina published another work, showing more precisely the place of the heretics in this question of human liberty and divine knowledge.

In its fundamentals the solution given by Molina is really very simple. From the trend of certain patristic texts and from the teaching of his own professor, Molina concludes that a divine middle knowledge must be postulated. All things that God knows can be placed in three categories: the purely possible, the actually existing, the free futurible. There is no difficulty about the first two kinds. In theological terminology, God knows the purely possible, that is, an event which will never take place, by means of His *scientia simplicis intelligentiae*. He knows events that are actually existing by means of His *scientia visionis*. Now somewhere between these two there is a middle knowledge, or *scientia media*, by means of which God infallibly knows those possible events whose future occurrence is conditioned by the self-determination of man's free will.[5]

From a merely local fame the Molinist solution of this difficult question brought its author to the attention of all European theologians who made any pretension at all of knowing their business. Like Suarez' *Metaphysics* of two years later, the *Concordia* was shortly published in several editions in several different parts of the continent. Molina's name and the title of his book became

---

[4] Pegis, Anton: "Molina and Human Liberty," in *Jesuit Thinkers of The Renaissance*, ed. by Gerard Smith, Milwaukee, 1939, Marquette University Press, p. 90. This is a valuable and accurate discussion by a scholar who knows Molina thoroughly.

[5] Cf. Lange, Hermannus: *De Gratia*, Freiburg, 1929, Herder, pp. 498 ff.

bywords in all the unversities, colleges and seminaries, where learned men were accustomed to foregather for discussion and debate. But the enthusiasm with which it was received was not unmixed with criticism, both constructive and destructive.

There were minor details in the book which even Suarez could not make himself accept, and though he kept his peace about them until called upon for a judgement he was fully aware of their existence from the start. Bellarmine too, when given a list of Molinist propositions which had been sent to Aquaviva, objected to four of them. But the author had himself been able to satisfy the scholarly Dominican, Bartholomew Ferreira, the Inquisition's censor of books at Lisbon. This censor gave it the *nihil obstat* by declaring that he "found nothing in it contrary to our religion. Indeed, it clarifies whatever appears at first sight to be obscure and difficult in the holy Councils, and also elucidates and explains most eloquently many texts in both the new and old testaments. I consider it therefore to be a treatise worthy of publication for the good of the whole Church."

That the other Jesuit theologians were not unanimously in agreement with Molinism is an historical fact that was only to be expected. Some of them thought he had gone too far; others believed that the matter was still too involved and obscure to be of practical application in theological courses. But Fülöp-Miller is in error when he suggests that Suarez, Bellarmine, Valentia and the other prominent Jesuit theologians gave Molina immediate resistance and that they rushed to his defense against the Dominicans merely for the sake of Jesuit solidarity.[6] It is true that Bañes and his confréres tried to make much of the "suspiciously Pelagian flavor" in the Molinist doctrine that man is enabled constantly to resist grace, but the traditional Catholic teaching, which the Jesuits naturally defended, was that the human will is free to accept or reject the means of salvation.

[6] Fülöp-Miller, *op. cit.*, pp. 97–98.

The entrance of Dominic Bañes into the question gave it a controversial impetus such as every drama of conflicting forces needs. While Suarez was teaching at Rome, many of the notes from his previous courses in Spain were being handed about by the students of the University of Salamanca. Students' notebooks from the courses Molina gave at Evora were likewise in prominent usage all over Spain. From these and other sources Bañes was able to discover the general drift of Jesuit doctrine regarding grace and free will even before the appearance of Molina's *Concordia*. Bañes consulted these slipshod notations, especially one which Suarez' students had compiled and entitled, *In Defense of the Society; Concerning Free Will*, and partially on their basis, wrote his own *Apologia Fratrum Praedicatorum*.

Bañes therein pays Suarez the dubious honor of choosing him as one of the principal butts of his attacks. "Of all those," he wrote, "who adopted and fought for the opinions of Molina, Francis Suarez ranks first, for he even wrote on his own initiative a popular treatise to defend the doctrines of the Society." He also remarks that Suarez gave the same definition of free will (that Molina had given) "in a certain manuscript which was circulated at Salamanca, and which was denounced and handed over to the Fathers of the Holy Office by some Thomists." [7] Frequently thereafter the Dominican, in the doctrinal controversies, united Suarez with Molina to show that both represented the system to which he objected. He singled him out, tried to refute him, and to show that he was one of the most important adversaries to discredit.

Bañes was by no means an unspiritual man. After the death of Balthazar Alvarez, in 1580, he was the intermittent spiritual adviser of St. Teresa of Avila, who always affectionately spoke of him as "my father." All the while he held the chair of theology at the University of Salamanca, however, he was at logger-

[7] De Scorraille, *op. cit.*, p. 350.

heads with the Jesuits. "There is no harm in mentioning, what is undoubtedly the truth, that Dominic Bañes had a spice of the proud hidalgo in his fine character. The spirit of rivalry was strong in him, and also that pathetically human tendency to consider one's own pet cause, the cause of God. He was a theologian of very great ability and like most theologians of great ability he had theories to which he was attached." [8] One of these theories had to do with the problem which Molina answered in his *Concordia*.

Where Molina, with Suarez, Bellarmine and the other Jesuits, attacked the problem mainly from the angle of human liberty, Bañes overemphasized the part which divine grace plays. The supreme dominion of God was the first postulate of his argument. He insists that God is the First Cause and Prime Mover of all things, and that a secondary cause, such as man, cannot act efficaciously unless determined by Him. Thus God's concurrence in human actions is antecedent and not merely simultaneous; it is a *praemotio physica,* which moves man not as a moral influence but in the way that necessary physical causes act.[9] But Bañes says that this does not destroy human liberty. *Praemotio physica* in the natural order corresponds to efficacious grace in the supernatural order. In the decrees of the divine Will, God foresees everything that man will do, but man will continue to act freely at all times. The chief point in the theory is that it places an intrinsic and substantial difference between sufficient and efficacious grace, the first giving man the power to act and the second irresistibly causing the action.

Six years before the appearance of Molina's book, Bañes challenged Father Montemayor, one of Suarez' former pupils, in public disputation and called the Jesuit's arguments heretical. The learned Augustinian, Luis de Leon, then took up the battle for

[8] Broderick, *op. cit.,* vol. ii, pp. 23–24.
[9] Cf. Otten, *op. cit.,* vol. ii, p. 493.

the Jesuits and in another heated disputation argued vehemently against Bañes. The populace took sides, dubbing the Augustinian a Pelagian, and the Dominican a Lutheran until the Inquisition itself stepped in and took a hand. In the beginning of 1584 both Leon and Montemayor were cited before Cardinal Quiroga and were severely reprimanded. Montemayor wrote to Aquaviva in the following year that he had simply been following the doctrines which Suarez had taught him, and he could not see why he should be censured and prevented from teaching.[10]

The same Mondragon and Avendaño, who were then objecting strenuously to the teachings of Suarez, joined with Bañes during the years 1590–1594 in trying to have the book of Molina placed on the Index of forbidden books then being prepared by the Spanish Inquisition. They did not succeed in the attempt and really got the worst of it when Molina, learning of their designs, addressed a letter to the Inquisition in which he not only defended his doctrine, but launched a scorching attack against Bañes. He declared openly that the teaching of the Dominican was directly against the Council of Trent.

At Valladolid the chief adversary of the Jesuits was Diego Nuño who told his pupils that Molina and his companions were heretics and that prayers should be offered for the conversion of Molina since he might become like the dragon in the Apocalypse who swept a third of the stars out of heaven. In 1594, first the Jesuits, and then the Dominicans, held public disputations in which they tried, with more or less rancor on both sides, to settle the issues at question. The superiors of both Orders called their subjects together and gave them to understand that these unchristian attacks and counter-attacks were not for the good of the Church and of religion. The heat of the controversy abated in general but fresh Dominican outbursts soon occurred at Burgós,

[10] For a fair treatment of this whole controversy cf. Astrain, *op. cit.*, vol. iv., *passim.*

Palencia, Valladolid, Salamanca, Valencia, Saragossa and Cala-
tayud.

In 1596, Philip II intervened and commanded the Jesuit visitor, Father Alarcon, and the provincial of the Dominicans, to
confer with the royal confessor, Diego de Yepes, in order to find
a remedy for these abuses. They decided to silence the main
speakers and disturbers of the peace. The King then ordered
that Jesuits and Dominicans should not attend each other's disputations, that only those who held the doctrines of St. Thomas
should hold chairs of theology, that neither should call the other's
doctrines heretical or false.

Naturally, when a question of such high importance is hanging fire among intensely absorbed scholars the thing cannot long
go on without some kind of settlement. The affair took on an
entirely new character when Rome decided to take a hand in it.
As De Scorraille says, "From simple authors' quarrels and monastic rivalries, it became a question of public interest and almost an
affair of state. High dignitaries, who were till then indifferent
or silent spectators, began to intervene. Philip II began to fear
that all of this theology might endanger the peace of his subjects.
There was felt a need of pacifying intelligences, and in order to
bring this peace about, a need of recourse to Rome." [11]

Letters began to pour into the Eternal City, from princes,
priests, bishops, cardinals, and even from Philip and the Cardinal Inquisitor of Spain. They were not slow in provoking an
answer from Clement VIII, who advised the Grand Inquisitor
that "these dissensions on sufficient and efficacious grace which
have arisen between some of the Order of Preachers and some
of the regular clerks of the Society of Jesus, each attached to their
opinion so that they publicly call each other heretics, were an
occasion of scandal to the faithful and of perplexity of con-
sciences. And since this question was interesting to the universal

[11] De Scorraille, *op. cit.*, p. 377.

Church, he reserved it to the judgement of the Apostolic See." [12]
The sovereign pontiff then ordered documents and writings collected from both sides and sent to Rome; and furthermore
imposed silence on both sides until the question should be settled.

It took about three years to collect the vast heap of writings,
arguments, proofs, charges and counter-charges which made up
both sides of the case. The four Jesuit provinces in Spain gave
separate opinions; that for the province of Castile and Toledo
was prepared by Suarez and Vasquez, both of whom wrote complete treatises in which they first condemned wholly the doctrine
of physical predetermination and then explained fully the Jesuit
teaching.

From all sides of Spain there poured into the Grand Inquisitor's office the findings and reports of Jesuits and Dominicans,
as well as the views of bishops and members of other religious
Orders. These in turn were sent to Italy where they were delivered in a huge wooden case on March 28, 1598. The lines were
drawn, the materials of warfare were on hand, and the battle
over grace and free will was now about to enter its second phase.
The scene had shifted to Rome, where Clement VIII could himself be the arbitrator.

In the meanwhile Suarez had used his own report on the matter as a nucleus around which he built his famous *Opuscula de
Concursu et Efficaci Auxilio Dei*. The whole of this work is
divided into six treatises, or *opuscula*, the first three of which are
substantially the report which Suarez turned in as his contribution to the Jesuit side of the controversy. It is remarkable for
the lack of any belligerent terminology which might give offense
either to Bañes or the Order of Preachers. The completed book
which comprised six hundred pages and which was still less
than a fifth of all that Suarez published on the question of grace,

[12] *Ibid.*, pp. 380–381.

was printed in 1599 when the investigation at Rome was dragging along in its second year.

Before the Pope could get his hands on this clear-headed construction of the case the Jesuits had suffered three setbacks. The Dominicans had succeeded in arranging the controversy in such wise that it would be no controversy at all. The point at issue was to be Molina's book, *Concordia,* while Bañes and his own peculiar theses on physical premotion and predetermination were not to be called into question. Secondly, the commission which was to arbitrate the affair was made up entirely of men who, while they may not have been unfriendly to the Jesuits, were certainly not in accord with Molina and his views. Finally, in January, 1598, several months before the multitude of manuscripts, so laboriously gathered in Spain, had arrived at Rome, this commission declared that the book and the doctrine of Molina must be prohibited. The judges said that he had repudiated St. Augustine and that his doctrines were in opposition to those of St. Thomas.

Clement VIII was so surprised at this over-rapid conclusion to the question that he ordered the whole case reopened when the testimony arrived from Spain. The fresh investigation lasted only eight months, the members of the committee supposedly having gone through a mass of material which Bañes himself had declared would take two years to study properly. Another adverse decision was made, and again the Pope was dissatisfied with the result. "Finally, Clement VIII was seized with such a passion for the whole case that he spent night after night in perusing the records, and, so that he might be able to decide the matter rightly, he personally made an exhaustive study of the writings of the early fathers. But when, in due course, the vast mass of expert opinions and documents which had been prepared were brought to his room, the Holy Father was considerably startled, and despairingly asked if he were really expected to read all that." [13]

It was at this juncture that the newest work of Suarez, the *Opuscula,* came into the pontifical possession, and from then onward the Pope would not allow a step to be taken in the case until he had consulted it. There is a tale to the effect that, following his usual habit of reading in bed, His Holiness fell asleep one night over the pages of Suarez. The candle by his side fell over and scorched the pages so that the heat on his hands and the smell of smoke startled the Holy Father into sudden awakening. While beating out the flame he called his chamberlain, a noble Spaniard, who quickly swept the ashes to the floor. Ruefully, Clement remarked that this scorching of Suarez' book was a bad sign for the Jesuits in their present difficulty. But the chamberlain gingerly picked up the blackened, smoking volume and opened its pages. "Perhaps it is not such a bad sign," he said, "only the edges are burned; not the text. See, not a single letter has disappeared, and the doctrine remains intact." [14]

Omens can mean anything you read into them. Whether the Pope thought the close escape of Suarez' volume was a favorable omen, or whether the whole incident is merely apocryphal, matters little. The fact is that Jesuit doctrine never, before or since, has gone through the fire of critical judgement which it experienced at this time. In the event it was left unharmed and even unchanged, but that event was to arrive only after many years. Neither the Pope nor his committee, neither Jesuits nor Dominicans dreamed that the affair would be so long drawn out.

[13] Fülöp-Miller, *op. cit.,* p. 99.
[14] Siegfried, *op. cit.,* p. 265, quoting from Massei.

Chapter XIX

Suarez and the Controversy

To a mature Spaniard in the autumn of 1598 the death of King Philip II must have seemed like the definite end of a glorious era. The old monarch had his fingers in the affairs of the empire for so many decades that people could hardly believe in the ability of his young successor, Philip III, as worthy of taking up the same tasks in the same competent manner. But death comes to all men, and it came finally to Philip, welcomed on his part, regretfully endured on the part of his subjects.

The coronation of the blond youngster who would now rule the mighty empire made little difference in the life of Francis Suarez. He continued studiously in the professorial position into which His Majesty's father had practically forced him. He was appreciatively approved by the young King, who likewise became a steadfast friend of the Society of Jesus. The end of the century was approaching. Spain's perennial enemy in England, Queen Elizabeth, would soon end her long reign. Richelieu was an adolescent with ideas in France. Shakespeare was about to appear on the scene. Men and events shifted with kaleidoscopic rapidity in all parts of Europe, but Suarez continued brilliantly and methodically at his university duties in Portugal.

What Suarez did and said during his incumbency in the important position at Coimbra has been pretty well recorded by the observations of Pedro de Aguilar. An intelligent and likeable lay brother, he had been the companion of Suarez at Salamanca and had come with him to his new post in the west of the peninsula. It is to him that we owe the account of Suarezian anecdotes and legends surrounding the great professor, the account of scrupulously made religious duties day after day, of the popularity and success attending lectures and disputations, of the sanctity and personality which made Suarez the idol of the city.

Aguilar used occasionally to slip in at the back of the lecture hall and watch the professor at his job. He noted that Suarez continued to teach in his own original manner, a way that had given him the reputation of innovator, speaking distinctly and unhesitatingly, without aid of book or manuscript, without ever glancing at the notes which he sometimes carried to class. The lay students and the seminarians of nine colleges attended his classes, and on special occasions, most of the towns-people would crowd into the hall to hear him. Naturally, the young Jesuit students at the college were his greatest admirers and they paid him the sincere compliment of close imitation. Aguilar remarks that these young men knew that they too would be expected to carry on in this kind of work in later years, and that they copied every mannerism Suarez displayed.

Among his brothers in the privacy of the Jesuit community the professor held an assured position. In his first years as a priest he had been the spiritual adviser to his fellow religious at Segovia, and here at Coimbra he was again being honored with the confidences of the younger Jesuits. They respected his erudition but they depended even more upon his therapeutic skill in assuaging their spiritual problems. In his calm and humble way Suarez could easily get to the root of such difficulties where others of a more impetuous nature blundered along unfeelingly. So, for many years his door was always open to those who wished his consoling advice, and the lay brother, Aguilar, observed that he never once turned anyone away because of the pressure of other work.

When Suarez began his career at Coimbra he was fifty years old, never in good health but with more accomplishments already in back of him than men with twice his strength could boast. He was a man of medium height, standing approximately five feet, nine inches, which was no mean size among the small statured Spaniards. He was a brunet with nothing particularly prepossessing about him except the intensity of his blue eyes. Hollow cheeks and a broad forehead, above a gaunt and graceful body, gave at first blush the appearance of a terrifically ascetical person. But a second glance showed that sparkling and penetrating eyes were a clue to the genial kindliness which made of Suarez something more than an intellectual giant. Gentility, graciousness, self-sacrifice combined to force men into a desire for closer companionship with him. The result was that his Portuguese popularity became almost as great as that which he enjoyed in the Spanish college and university towns.

Within a year of his arrival in Portugal an epidemic of the plague brought havoc to Lisbon and then travelled over to Coimbra, where on the fifth of February, 1599, the courses at the university had to be suspended. The Jesuits who were in good health elected to remain on the job, and, following the example of Loyola and his first companions, turned their residence into a hospital, administered to the sick, buried the dead, scrubbed floors, cooked meals, worked and sweated until some of them fell ill from exhaustion and the dread plague itself. Suarez at first decided to stay and work along with them but his superiors saw that such action for a man of his physique meant almost certain death. They refused to listen to his protestations, ordering him to return to Spain until the epidemic passed and the school could reopen.

Making good use of this enforced departure Suarez supervised the publication of his *Opuscula* at the royal printing house in Madrid. This was the work which the Holy Father would peruse

with such industrious impatience during the controversy on grace
at Rome. Bañes found out what was in the air even before the
book came out and he tried to get the Portuguese Inquisition to
put a restraining order on its publication. He campaigned against
it just as he had against the work of Molina but the council was
on its guard and refused to act on his petition. When the book
appeared he tried to have it condemned on the ground that it
merely repeated the doctrines contained in the *Concordia* and was
therefore cut from the same heretical cloth. On the failure of
both attempts the Dominican resorted to the perennial propa-
gandist ruse of attacking it with a widely distributed pamphlet.
He picked out twenty Suarezian propositions, demonstrated to
his own satisfaction that they were worthy of censure, and seemed
intent on provoking an answer from the Jesuit author.

Suarez held his peace, as usual, believing that since Rome had
the whole matter of grace and free will under consideration the
best course would be to await the official judgement. In his
preface he gives notice to the opponents of the Jesuits that ani-
mosity and disputatious pettiness had no part in the composition
of this work. He wished to restore peace and harmony between
the factions and was averse to any proud demonstration of polemical ability. "I am moved to write with the same charity and the
same sincerity that influenced St. Augustine. . . . I have not
written this from a spirit of contention, nor have I published it
under the influence of ill will. . . . Indeed, since our Holy
Father Clement has been pleased to make no definition in this
case, and has committed it to the free discussion of the theologians, we ought to practice that moderation which Christian
piety and the subject itself demand, to observe such sincerity of
faith and charity, such integrity and purity of religious modesty,
that we diligently avoid digressing from them even by the
breadth of a fingernail." [1]

---

[1] *Opuscula, Proemium*, pp. 1–2.

But the pressure of criticism continued on the peninsula so that Suarez took the only course his conscience left open for him. Instead of foolishly exposing himself to further abuse by a local refutation of Bañes and his pamphlet he wrote a justifying memoir, wrapped it up with a copy of the book and posted it to Aquaviva, giving him permission to show it to the Pope, if he so wished. The general was pleased with this wise move, telling Suarez: "You have acted wisely in letting the letter and memoir destined for the Sovereign Pontiff pass through our hands. Using your permission we have judged it unnecessary and inopportune at the moment to hand these writings to His Holiness. It is better to wait until the affair of Father Molina has ended. Of this case I will say nothing since others are charged with keeping you up to date on its progress and present state. We await from God the just issue it deserves." [2]

The theologian was following logical and correct procedure in outlining his position to the Pope. Bañes was taking an unfair advantage in raising doubts about the orthodoxy of Suarez concerning questions which the Holy Father was even then trying to settle. This he was doing without offering reasons or proofs against the propositions which expressed most clearly the divergences between the Jesuits and the Bañesians. Briefly and lucidly Suarez pointed out the opinions of his own school on these fundamental issues. But for good measure he took the offensive by reminding the Pope of six particular propositions of Bañes which smelled more of heresy than did the incriminated Suarezian theses.

"I am content with this general response," said Suarez at first. "My book has been submitted three times to official and serious judgement. Now, it has not been found worthy of censure, and not a single correction has been demanded. One time in Portugal the supreme council of the Inquisition examined the work and

[2] De Scorraille, *op. cit.*, pp. 427–428.

approved it without restriction, rendering a decision which abrogated a former judgement. Some Dominicans who had been charged with the first examination, attempted to prevent the *imprimatur,* but the council and its theologians disregarded these critics, many of whom were the modern followers of Bañes. Later, the council of Castile submitted it to the inspection of the University of Alcalá. Eight of the most learned doctors there, including the Rector and the two principal theologians, studied it seriously for many days, declared that they found nothing to be censured, and gave the official approbation which is printed at the beginning of the volume. Finally, when the book came to Rome, the master of the Sacred Palace thought that he ought to devote personal attention to its study, circumstances being as they were. I have authentic knowledge that certain Dominican Fathers tried hard to influence him to forbid the reading and sale of the book. But being a just man he answered that he found nothing in the book warranting such action, and then gave it his *publicetur* unconditionally." [3]

Aquaviva himself took up the cudgels in praise of Suarez' book in a letter which he addressed to all of the Spanish provincials, telling them that "on the subject of the question *De Auxiliis,* I think it would be a good idea to acquaint the bishops, where our Fathers reside, with the doctrines of the Society and the proofs which uphold them. This ought to be done; and if some of them can profitably use the book of Father Suarez, let us give them copies of it." In this way the work got around to the men outside of Rome who were anxiously awaiting the outcome of the controversy. It found many eager readers who wanted to be able to discuss the burning question of the times, and who wanted the whole affair boiled down into a concise, digestible Latin treatise.

Modestly Suarez wrote to the Holy Father, telling him, as though writing from the other end of the earth, "It is known

[3] *Ibid.,* p. 429.

even in these parts that my *Opuscula* reached the hands of Your Holiness, and was not entirely displeasing to you." What Clement thought of the work is a well-known historical fact connected closely with all angles of the raging controversy. Some of his successors on the throne of Peter were no less unstinting in their encomia.

The definite contribution to Molinism which Suarez made in his *Opuscula,* and the point which drew much attention to his work both then and now, has to do with his explanation of *congruism*. Bellarmine too, wrote on the point, and he is sometimes considered a co-founder of the system with Suarez. Actually, the distinction between congruous and incongruous grace had been made by St. Augustine many centuries before, but in this crucial dispute between the Jesuits and Dominicans at the end of the sixteenth century, congruism was newly expanded and fully developed.

Congruism gets its name from the fact that grace is efficacious because it is given in circumstances congruous to its operation. Now circumstances are only comparatively congruous or incongruous, that is, in proportion to the intensity of the grace given. But the human will is always free and can act or not act in either case. Usually, however, when the circumstances are favorable the will acts, and the grace at hand is thus called efficacious grace. If the circumstances are unfavorable, and the will does not act, the grace is called merely sufficient. Thus, the theory holds that God adapts his grace to the circumstances in which a man finds himself. If the man is situated in a place where temptations abound, the graces he receives are more powerful than they would be if he were in a more secluded way of life.

The widest modern opinion among theologians is that "among the different systems devised for the purpose of harmonizing the dogmas of grace and free will, Congruism probably comes nearest the truth. It strikes a golden mean between the two extremes of Pelagianism and Semipelagianism on the one hand, and Calvinism and Jansenism on the other, and its principal theses can be supported by clear and unmistakable passages from the writings of St. Augustine." [4]

Suarez himself succinctly sums up the idea of congruism when he proves the minor proposition in one of his syllogisms. "*Tota illa congruitas ex se solum inducit quamdam moralem certitudinem, cui absolute non repugnat, ut vocationi sit congruae liberum arbitrium resistat, adeo ut Anselmus dixerit, potuisse Paulum resistere suae vocationi, quantumvis efficacissimae; sic enim ait Matth. 6, circa illa verba: Fiat voluntas tua. Licet sit percussus Paulus, tamen voluntas ejus erat libera, ut resisteret si vellet. Propter quod Chrysostomus, hom. 31 et 56 in Matth., agens de vocatione Matthaei et Pauli, dicit, non prius Deum illum vocasse, quia praenovit tunc vocationem fuisse penetraturam ejus animam; sentit ergo non sufficere efficaciam, quam poterat habere vocatio peculiari congruitate ad ingenium vel conditionem Pauli, aut Matthaei; sed oportuisse ut Deus etiam observaret tempus, in quo praesciret vocationem illam fuisse effectum habituram, si eam daret.*" [5]

Even at this late date, almost three and a half centuries after its publication, a reading of the *Opuscula* is probably the best approach to an understanding of the battle which turned Christian Europe topsy-turvy in the days of Suarez. The first four portions of the work are especially valuable since they deal directly with the question of grace and free will, while the last two deal with related subjects. As we have mentioned, the first three *Opuscula* made up the Jesuit opinion which Suarez submitted for the scrutiny of the judges at Rome. *De Concursu, Motione et Auxilio Dei*, is divided into three books demonstrating

[4] Pohle-Preuss: *Grace, Dogmatic Theology, VII*, p. 264. Cf. also Lange, *op. cit.*, p. 499, and *passim*.
[5] *Opuscula*, I, iii, 14, 8.

how human liberty of will is dependent upon God. *De Scientia Dei Futurorum Contingentium,* in two books, demonstrates how God is able to know absolute and conditioned future events. The third *Opusculum* is the treatise *De Auxilio Efficaci,* the very core of the problem of mutual ordination and operation between man and God, and is also a brief review of the whole question with the logical conclusions that must be drawn from the arguments.

The remaining *Opuscula,* three in number, were the result of a practice imposed by the statutes of the University of Coimbra. Each year the principal professor of each of the four faculties was bound to give an hour's repetition of all the matter he had taught in his course. Or, in place of this, the professor was permitted to choose some question of current importance, lecture on that for an hour in the public hall and then answer the objections of three of his fellow professors. This was a serious obligation on the part of the head of each faculty for, if he omitted it, he was fined seventy-five hundred reis. When he performed it, as he almost always did, he was paid twenty-five hundred reis, while each of the three objectors received two hundred.

For the hour's repetition at the mid-year of 1598–1599, Suarez elected to defend a thesis, *De Libertate Divinae Voluntatis,* but the plague intervened and the college was closed six days before the disputation was to come off. He took the question, however, divided it into two parts and made it the fourth *Opusculum.* Far in advance of the next repetition he prepared the question *De Meritis Mortificatis, et Per Poenitentiam Reparatis,* and included it in this published work as the fifth *Opusculum.* The last one was only indirectly connected with the controversy on grace and free will and was entitled *De Justitia Qua Deus Reddit Praemia Meritis, et Poenas Pro Peccatis.*

This account of the Suarezian method in the building of a book is a clear indication that the great theologian got the most out of everything he did. Where others would have been content merely to give their lectures, Suarez made his lectures serve a second purpose by putting them out in the printed page. Where others would sit down to write a book, Suarez would first try out the material in the class room and in public disputations. In this way he had not only a double fruitfulness in all his work but also a double check on the tenability and orthodoxy of his theological arguments.

The scenes changed abruptly, and often there seemed to be a dead stop in the action of the play as Dominicans and Jesuits argued in Rome. The former insisted that the whole matter was simply a question of the orthodoxy of Molina's book. Therefore, the Jesuits were to stand as the accused. But the latter declared with equally vehement insistence that the controversy turned on the point of divergence in the whole teaching on grace and free will.[6]

Before either side got very far, Molina, the original cause of all the dispute, died at Madrid, October 6, 1600. He was sixty-five years old and had just been called to assume the newly founded professorship of moral theology at the college of Madrid, an appointment which proves that he was not at all in ill-repute among his religious brethren. The report had been spread in Spain that the Roman commission had condemned him and that the populace had burned him in effigy. Bellarmine, when he heard of the rumor, reassured the Spanish Jesuits that there was nothing to it. A few months later the Spanish nuncio quashed the story in Spain but in the meanwhile this, and similar tales, impeded the Jesuits in their ministry in Poland, Italy, Germany and France.[7]

Four years later, Banes, the old lion of theological battle, died

---

[6] Pastor, *op. cit.,* vol. xxiv, devotes a whole chapter to the Controversy on Grace, pp. 281–366. Cf. also vol. xxv, pp. 229–250.

[7] Astrain, *op. cit.,* pp. 294–304.

at Medina del Campo, supposedly asserting with his last breath that he believed everything he had ever written on the question of grace with the same firmness that he believed in the unity and trinity of God. The story is probably unfounded. The man was too astute a theologian to confuse a mere theory with a dogmatic truth, for neither Jesuits nor Dominicans pretended that the theories connected with the controversy on grace were on the same level with the great truths of faith.

The controversy did not end with the death of Molina and Bañes, nor with that of Clement VIII in 1605. The matter made no progress when Leo XI was elected and died in the same year. It was finally up to the new Pope, Paul V, to put a stop to the affair. From the beginning of the *Congregatio de Auxiliis,* officially started in 1602, there were eighty-nine meetings. Of these, seventy were held under Clement VIII, none under Leo XI, and nineteen under Paul V.[8]

The weary discussions came to an end on the feast of St. Augustine, August 28, 1607, when the Pope called nine cardinals into his presence and asked them what should be done about it. Four of them, Pinelli, Givry, Bianchetti and Arigoni, were in favor of further discussions. These four, together with Bufalo and Taverna, despite the interminable arguments that had been presented on both sides of the case, still had no clear concept of what the controversy was all about. Bernerio was strongly in favor of the Dominican side of the question, while Bellarmine and Du Perron were as equally decided on the Jesuit angle. A week later the Pope told the consultors and theologians to go home. He would inform them of his decision in the matter if and when he made it.

"Thus, after a continuous controversy lasting eighteen years, this dispute over grace terminated without any definite decision. Both Orders were enjoined to instruct their members strictly to

[8] De Scorraille, *op. cit.,* vol. ii, pp. 496–498.

abstain from any discussion of the question of Molinism, and peacefully to await a final decision by the Holy See: this final decision, however, has not been issued up to the present." [9] Each side could hold its own opinion but neither could assail the other for false doctrine or heresy.

In his quiet retreat at Coimbra, Suarez was able to note the amazing change of public opinion which took place at the conclusion of the controversy. Previously people had begun to think that the Jesuits were suspect of heretical leanings, but now, by some strange process of illogic, they believed that the Society had been vindicated. The book of Molina had been arraigned before the tribunal, and the Jesuits had not been condemned. Public manifestations of joy occurred under Suarez' gaze in Portugal, but in other parts of the peninsula magnificent masques and firework displays were held. At Salamanca, Suarez' old university town, huge posters carrying the inscription, *Molina Victor!* were hung up everywhere to inform the populace of the trend of events. In typical Spanish fashion, the Jesuits at the College of Villagarcia permitted a monster bullfight in celebration of the occasion. This later event, in the judgement of Aquaviva, was going a little too far, and he ordered that the rector of the college be reprimanded before his community and temporarily removed from office.

Aside from these external and purely superficial manifestations of the climactic controversy, there remains the lasting fact that current Jesuit doctrine on grace and free will stems from it. In 1613 Aquaviva decreed for all the Society the system of congruism which Suarez, Bellarmine and the others had worked out, and which would probably never have appeared were it not for the exigencies of the Dominican-Jesuit conflict. Ever since that time Jesuit professors have been more or less at one in the matter.

[9] Fülöp-Miller, *op. cit.,* p. 100.

CHAPTER XX

The Philosopher of Law

WHEN THE EPIDEMIC drove Suarez out of Coimbra he was still hankering to get back to the quiet of his literary compositions. During the several months of 1599 remaining after the publication of the *Opuscula* at Madrid, he went to Avila, spent some time with the Jesuit community there, and then returned to his favorite city of Salamanca. Family troubles kept him there for a while and opened again what he considered an opportunity for relinquishing the honorable professorship in Portugal.

It was not that the great theologian was unwilling to work on the tasks assigned to him by superiors, that he was too lazy or incapable to perform the job. All of the contemporary evidence points to the contrary. But like any man with a thorough understanding of his own abilities, Suarez knew that he could best express the depth of his genius through the medium of theological books. To get things down on paper was a passion with him, and whether he was teaching, travelling, convalescing, or whatever else he may have been doing, he never failed to write down his ideas and plan their publication.

But a member of a religious Order in the Catholic Church is not his own employer, nor can he, except within certain limits, develop his life and use his talents and time in the way he most wishes. Thus in the late Fall he was back again at Coimbra, convinced that he could best serve God by doing the bidding of his superiors in the way and at the post where they sent him. He took up again the matter which had been interrupted by the

237

plague, and then continued for the rest of the year and through the following school term his treatises *De Deo*. Aquaviva wished him not only to teach in Portugal but also to follow his own desire in the matter of preparing books for publication.

A year or so later Suarez thought that the term of professorship which the late Philip II had suggested had reached its end, and he again asked whether he could not be allowed to retire. The Jesuit general wrote to him in August of 1601 and in July of 1602. He personally desired, wrote Aquaviva, that Suarez' health would permit the continuance of a work so important for the service of Our Lord and of universal benefit to the Church. He approved even more the writing of theological books and Suarez' retirement from teaching, which would make that writing easier. But this was an inopportune moment. The enemies of the Society were watchfully suspicous of every doctor and every doctrine among the Jesuits, and it would not do at all to give them an opening for criticism by replacing the eminent Spanish theologian with someone who might not be either so cautious or so capable as Suarez.

Furthermore, urged the general, the hold which Jesuit teaching had taken at Coimbra was just now at a state of development where it needed the expert nurturing of a most learned theologian. If another professor were to take over at this advanced stage he might interrupt the steady prestige built up since the arrival of Suarez, and might even put the whole thing back where it started. In the meanwhile Suarez should keep his eyes open for a likely successor among the younger Jesuits at Coimbra, consult with both the provincial and with Aquaviva himself, and then groom his candidate to take his place in a year or two.

On a matter of such importance as the replacement of a university's head theologian, no move could be made without royal consent and approval. The King was adamant. Letter after letter went to him from Hurtado de Mendoca, rector of the university, and invariably there came a negative reply. Philip III followed his father's example regarding the respectful awe in which he held Francis Suarez' learning; and in almost all matters concerning faculty personnel his word was law. Neither university officials nor religious superiors would dare to cross the royal will, nor were they desirous of doing so.

Finally, however, after almost two years of negotiations (1604) the King wrote to Aquaviva informing him that the tired professor of theology had himself asked for release on the score of ill health and for the sake of uninterrupted authorship. "But his lectures and his great knowledge contribute so much to the general good of the schools that I do not believe I can permit it." A compromise could be made, said Philip, if Father Christopher Gil, a man of good reputation and much knowledge, were appointed as assistant to Suarez. The present incumbent should keep his position for three years more, while Gil would carry whatever lectures, public disputations, and other duties, the head professor could not perform. Then he was to be promoted, if not immediately into Suarez' chair, at least directly in line for that honor. "Therefore," concluded His Majesty, "I request you expressly to order Father Gil to leave as soon as possible and to neglect nothing for the successful performance of the duties attendant on that position." [1]

Gil was not the youthful man whom we might expect to see placed in preparation for Suarez' position. He had already been teaching philosophy and theology for twenty years both at Coimbra and Evora and was at this time at the Jesuit headquarters in Rome. Suarez probably recommended him to Philip III, for he knew Gil as an erudite and polished dialectician. On the occasion of Suarez' doctorate examination at Evora, Gil had taken part in the proceedings and had so impressed the examinee that

[1] De Scorraille, vol. ii, p. 48.

he remarked that Gil, rather than himself, ought to take the chair at Coimbra.

Aquaviva sent Gil to Coimbra, where he arrived in the latter part of 1604, but the whole arrangement caused more disturbance than it was worth. Suarez had been forced by illness to quit his teaching the year before. He went to Valladolid for a while and then to Madrid, and before he could return to teaching, was called to Rome. In the meanwhile Francis Carreiro took Suarez' place and would not give it up when Gil finally arrived. There were mutual recriminations, disruptions of the university statutes, appeals to the King. Aegydius, the Augustinian, who had at first opposed Suarez and later became one of his best friends, also entered the picture when Philip said that he should substitute for the morning lectures and Gil for the evening lectures. When Suarez returned two years later they were still arguing about it.

The malady which forced Suarez to give up teaching in July, 1603, was the same one which had made of him a semi-invalid ever since his attempt at strenuous social work in Segovia. His lungs were in such poor state that he could scarcely breathe, let alone lecture daily to a group of several hundred students. When sufficiently rested, in June, 1604, he was called to Rome to answer certain charges preferred against him because of his confessional doctrine, published in the second volume *De Sacramentis* (1602) and in another work *De Censuris* (1603). This incident forms a separate chapter in the story of the great theologian, one which, at first, cost him the utmost anguish but which finally justified him before His Holiness Clement VIII.

While these works were being printed Suarez was teaching in his classes the doctrines which have made his reputation a permanent thing throughout the non-Scholastic world. For two full years, 1601–1603, he lectured on questions *De Legibus*. These appeared in published form only ten years later and have given Suarez a prominence in the modern world as an outstanding philosopher of law, just as his *Metaphysics* have given him a permanent place as a deeply speculative thinker. The modern law of nations stems largely from him. Francis Vittoria was its first expounder, Francis Suarez its prime philosopher, and Hugo Grotius its systematizer.

Dr. Scott places Suarez in his correct position in this trilogy when he says that "The contribution of Suarez to the epoch-making exposition of Vittoria are the analysis and definition of the general and specific kinds of law, their origin, their nature, their various forms of categories: the law natural in its several manifestations, the law of the state in its individual capacity, and the law of the states in their international capacity—in other words, the law of nations. . . . From a different approach, they reached a common goal—the establishment of a single and universal standard of right and wrong in the relations of individuals within the state, in the relations of states with one another and in the relations of the international community composed of these individuals and of these states." [2]

Suarez gets right down to cases, and in so doing he does not hesitate to differ from St. Thomas, just as he had not hesitated in other matters when his keen discrimination pointed out that a difference of opinion was called for. All authority comes from God; therefore all law derives from Him, either directly or through human legislators. Thomas had been satisfied to define law as a kind of rule and norm according to which one is induced to act or is restrained from acting. This was too broad and general for the purposes of the Spanish theologian because, unless it was explained and modified it would apply to irrational creatures as well as to men and would include counsels as well as precepts. Suarez, in his moral system, says "strictly and abso-

[2] Scott, James Brown: *The Catholic Conception of International Law*, Washington, 1934, Georgetown University Press, pp. 128–130.

lutely speaking, only that which is a measure of rectitude, viewed absolutely, and consequently, only that which is a right and virtuous rule, can be called law." [3]

Thus the theologian started out most logically with the definition of the thing which he was to treat in both lecture and book. During the two years in which he taught this legal course he divided the subject into two main headings, and redivided these into five sections each. Thus when he came to publish the work ten years later he followed the general pattern of the course, converting each section into a book so that the complete treatise comprises ten books, a total of almost twelve hundred pages (in the 1856 Paris edition).

The first book, then, besides giving the definition of law and its necessary distinctions, treats of law in general, the causes that make law necessary and the effects which follow it. Here also he treats, in the dignified march of Scholastic terminology, preceptive, prohibitive, permissive and punitive laws, and then asks whether any other categories need be added to these. The second book is probably the more important of the decade, for as Scott remarks: "The second of the books of *De Legibus* is for us Suarez' *magnum opus*, dealing as it does with the eternal law, the natural law and the *jus gentium*, in the consideration of which he assumes his rightful place as the founder of the philosophy of law in its various phases, including the law of nations." [4]

Suarez says that the "eternal law formally consists in the free decree of God, who resolves upon the order to be followed, either in general, by all parts of the universe in respect of the common good, . . . or in particular by all rational creatures in respect of their free actions." The natural law, however, "consists formally in rational nature itself in that it does not imply a

[3] *De Legibus,* I, 1, 6. Suarez admits, of course, that irrational creatures are subject to some law, but not in this sense.

[4] Scott, *op. cit.,* p. 138.

contradiction and is the basis of *honestatis* in all actions." The *jus gentium,* the only term then known for international law, is explained by Suarez as a human, positive law derived, like civil law, from the natural law.[5]

This second book of Suarez' legal work is a veritable gold mine for the student or lawyer who is looking for the foundation of modern theory and practice. It drives right down to the root of all law, follows the implications naturally contained therein, and does all this in the mode of the philosopher—the wise thinker who puts order and sense into whatever he writes. He handles questions that are continuously before public scrutiny: the observance of agreements, liberty and slavery, private property rights, the binding power of natural law, and so forth. Here then, is the principal basis for his perennial reputation as the foremost philosopher of law. In another place we have seen the roots of his flourishing name among speculative philosophers. In various other works he makes manifest a justification of his repute as a great democratic thinker and champion of human liberty.

The implications of Suarez' conception of natural law are so many and so varied that they cannot be permitted to escape notice. Without them the rest of his legal treatises are liable to lose their force, if not their meaning. "In his legal system natural law is to be looked upon as the foundation upon which he is to erect his structure of justice, national and international. National justice expressed in the form of law and applying to individuals within the state is, as it were, the first story of the structure, upon which international justice, binding alike individuals as such and individuals grouped in states, can be said to rest. International law, therefore, is based, so to speak, on two firm foundations. But the more fundamental of these foundations is natural law, the law of the human being as such, which he inherits but

[5] *De Legibus,* II, 3, 6; II, 5, 2; II, 19, 3.

does not make, for it is the basis of the law of the individuals forming the state, with such additions as may be made by the proper agency of the state from time to time to meet their special needs." [6]

The third book is concerned chiefly with the positive human law itself, that is, the civil law which men, through their regularly constituted authority, are capable of making for themselves. Driving back to first sources Suarez proves that this power of lawmaking is given immediately to human beings by God, the author of all nature. The common and true opinion in this matter, says the theologian, is that "this power is given immediately by God as the author of nature so that men, as it were, dispose the material and effect the subject capable of this, while God, as it were, contributes the form by giving this power itself. . . . God does not give this power through any special action or concession distinct from creation. Some have said that it ought to come through a revelation, but that is a false opinion for it would not then be a natural power. Therefore it is given as a property flowing from nature, indeed, as a medium of natural reason showing that God has provided sufficiently for the human race and has given it the power for its conservation and its proper and necessary government." [7]

In this same book he delves into the mooted current question regarding the right of the Catholic Church to make laws and impose them upon all Christians. He discusses, on the other hand, the practice of princes in attempting to oblige the Church to follow their civil laws. He asks and answers the questions whether laws are both positive and negative, what kind of promulgation is necessary for civil law, when a law begins to place an obligation on people, whether civil laws can bind in conscience, whether the willing acceptance of the people is necessary before a law can bind, whether the laws of a nation must be obeyed by

[6] Scott, *op. cit.*, p. 157. [7] *De Legibus*, III, 3, 2–5.

visiting foreigners, in what way just civil laws may oblige ecclesiastical persons, and finally, whether the lawgiver is himself
bound to follow his own laws. This third book is the longest of
all in the series which Suarez dedicates to the laws.

Following the same precise logical arrangement, Suarez takes
up the matter of positive canon law in the fourth book and does
much to clarify the problems then surrounding the power of the
Church over its subjects. The concluding section of the first half
of his course *De Legibus* is dedicated to "the variety of human
laws, and especially to penal and burdensome laws." This fifth
book handles the different divisions of civil and canonical laws,
all of which, in the opinion of Suarez, present their own peculiar
difficulties.

In the second year of the course on the laws, when Suarez re-
sumed the subject, he concentrated upon the question which was
of immediate practical concern to Christian citizens. After the
law is established, its various subdivisions made, its acceptability
understood by all, what could be said regarding its interpretation?
Who is entitled to interpret the law, change it, or even abrogate
it entirely? "From its very nature a human law would not be
just and reasonable unless there were implied certain conditions
or exceptions. Therefore from the justice of the human law,
considering the natural condition of the material in which it oper-
ates, it necessarily follows that its obligation in particular cases
sometimes ceases, not from an extrinsic lifting of the law but
from the change of its material or circumstances." [8] This is called
Epiikia, or equity, and its application as a special ability dates
back to the theories of Aristotle. It is the mind of Suarez, as of
all just legal experts, that the exception amends the law. If the
lawgiver were present when some exceptional circumstances
arise he would immediately note that his law does not apply, or
that it should be changed in this or that way. Thus the mutation

[8] *Ibid.,* VI, 6, 4.

of the law, its logical interpretation, or even its abrogation, is a complement and completion of the law rather than a weakening of it.

Besides the arbitrary making of a law there is also the potent factor of custom, which indeed may be said to be the starting point of all human legislation. It was the source of much of the law and continues to be the influence behind national and international modern law; hence it is not to be wondered at that Suarez gave over the whole seventh book to "unwritten law, which is called custom," investigating its origin, nature, and effects. Custom preceded every known code of law because before there was writing, people were following customs, and it followed the inception of written law because we see it always with us at the present day. Usage, habit, and custom, notes the theologian, are practically the same, but the important point is that they all result from free human actions, that is to say, without voluntary action they cannot arise. Following the author and lecturer through his scrupulous analysis of custom and the necessary part it plays in correct legal and juridical processes would lead us far afield, but there is an interesting sidelight or two worthy of discussion here.

He insists that whatever form custom may assume its constant element must always be its moral character. "From the beginning, the conception of the Spanish School was that of the morality of law, and therefore the custom with which its members dealt could not be immoral—or indeed unmoral—for morality, in their conception, was the essence of good law whether natural, statutory, or customary." Furthermore, "as a result of the labor of lawmakers throughout the centuries, certain definite prerequisites of form and expression have come into use for written statutes, but, as Suarez, points out, 'in the law of custom, there is no special form, sensible and external.' There is indeed nothing except those actions which constitute custom, and these, continues Suarez, 'in so far as they are tokens of consent, may be called the unwritten words by which this kind of law is engraved upon the memory of men.' " Finally, ignorance of custom is no excuse for its infraction, provided that the custom is known by the majority of the people. This majority, by general agreement, says Suarez, "excludes women entirely, on the ground that they can exercise no legislative authority . . . and all men below the age of twenty-five years. However, I cannot find any basis in law or any justification in reason for the exclusion of the last two groups." Scott enthusiastically comments on this passage by remarking that "Suarez is rightly considered as a great theologian and philosopher, and a no less great jurist, and these qualities his various works demonstrate beyond the possibility of successful contradiction, but in the quotations which we have just made of his exact language, Suarez proclaims himself as a feminist in a day when feminism was hardly a dream, let alone a hope." [9]

In the eighth book the theologian goes into a detailed and lengthy discussion of privileges, defining them from every angle, dividing them into every possible kind, real and personal, perpetual and temporal, negative and positive, for the common good, for private benefit. He is interested in the good of privileges and in their harm, who can give them and who take them away, how they are originated and how lost. The whole problem was not at that time the fanciful speculation which we might now consider it, for Suarez lived in an age when there were highly privileged men in both Church and state and much of a jurist's time was spent in defining and limiting the rights of these people.

The last two books treat specifically of the divine law, the ninth on the old law, the tenth on the new. These are by no means the least significant parts of the work, for Suarez him-

[9] Scott, *op. cit.*, pp. 223–227.

self originally entitled the whole a *Tractatus De Legibus Et Legislatore Deo,* but since he necessarily treated of the Divine Lawgiver throughout the whole treatise he confined himself to less than two hundred pages in the last two books. Suarez seeks the beginnings of the old law even beyond the days of the Mosaic code. He proves the necessity and obligation of that law before the coming of Christ and definitely speaks of the time when the old law and its obligations ceased to exist.

The new law of Christ, the Divine Lawgiver, is the appropriate goal to which the entire treatise directs its ultimate attention. Here is a code which binds the whole world and all its inhabitants, which is perpetuated in the law of grace, and which is perfection itself when compared to the ancient law. Fourteen well-founded and philosophically sound excellencies of Christ's law prove that it is supereminently above that which existed before His Incarnation.

Beautifully and devotedly Suarez concludes the treatise with the words: *Nam licet suo tempore utilis fuerit [lex Hebraica], cum tamen salvare homines non posset, nec ad beatitudinem introducere, vana esset, nisi per Christum compleretur, qui et sanguine suo januas coeli aperuit, et initiavit nobis viam novam, relicta lege gratiae, per quam illam consequi et in Sancta Sanctorum aeternae beatitudinis introire valeamus.*[10]

[10] *De Legibus,* X, 8, 18..

CHAPTER XXI

At Odds with Orthodoxy

COMPLICATING his chronic physical ailment there came to Suarez about this time a distressing mental worry which accentuated his rundown condition and reduced him to a semi-invalid. A passage in his latest work was condemned by a committee at Rome. "The news soon arrived in Spain," comments Coleridge, "and caused Suarez intense pain. He at once executed the order, as far as it lay in his power, and endeavored to preserve his usual external serenity; but the effort was too great, and he became for a time dangerously ill." [1] This combination of physical and mental disability was the illness which forced the theologian to give up his course in 1603 and to spend some time in recuperation at Valladolid and Madrid.

The theological hot water in which he found himself involved came out of two works, *De Poenitentia*, and *De Censuris*, which Suarez published successively in 1602 and 1603. While complaining that he had neither sufficient time nor adequate health to perform the simultaneous task of teaching and writing, he actually made a remarkable success of both. In his lectures he was devoting all his time to the subject of law; outside of classes he was spending time in correcting proofs, arguing with printers, corresponding with censors.

The *De Poenitentia*, an enormous volume more accurately entitled by its author the *Commentarii Ac Disputationes In Tertiam Partem D. Thomae*, was almost a year in the process of printing.

[1] Coleridge, *op. cit.*, p. 177.

In November of 1601 Suarez was writing to a friend that "My employment of itself requires a great deal of labor. Pray that it will all be pleasing to Our Lord. The business of printing does not go very quickly in this country, hampered as it is by a lack of material. If my volume, *De Poenitentia,* a part of which has come from the press, is delayed, the main reason is because they are short of paper. They have begun again and I hope that it will all be finished by the end of August [the following year]. Then only can they get to work on the *De Censuris,* and I trust that with God's help and your prayers it will turn out well." [2]

The printers at Coimbra were not used to the Suarezian kind of book. They were disconcerted at its magnitude, halted at every point by its scrupulous insistence on accuracy; and their facilities both in presses and paper were not always adequate to the demands of such enormous tomes. Undoubtedly they tried hard to keep the author satisfied that the book was moving forward—no matter how slowly. Withal it took them longer than Suarez foresaw, the first work appearing in September, 1602, and the second just a year later. At the tempo of modern printing presses and mass production of books this length of time would have been murderously expensive and entirely out of the question. But to publishers at the beginning of the seventeeth century such lack of speed was not only customary but even highly profitable. There were fewer books, and those that did appear were long and eagerly anticipated by subscribers and customers.

Suarez himself admits that this enterprise of his got somewhat out of control, even though he points out that brevity, after all, is a relative thing. This subject of Penance (and Extreme Unction) which he hoped to complete in one book, flowed over into two large tomes, and was even at that in his estimation a brief treatise. In his foreword to the reader [3] he remarks that both the speculative and practical angles must be treated and that previous

[2] De Scorraille, vol. ii, p. 52.   [3] *De Poenitentia, Ad Lectorem,* pp. i-ii.

opinions must be recalled and commented upon. Principles must be applied to cases, and particular cases must be traced back to their principles. In short, the theologian must be something of a historian, moralist and canonist. The result is that the plan of putting it all in one volume became impractical, and two tomes had to be written, the first including Penance, Extreme Unction, Purgatory, Indulgences and Suffrages, the second dealing only with the Censures. Putting it all in one volume, he remarked, would make it a work of unreasonable proportions, *insanae magnitudinis*.

The Spanish theologian is more famous for clarity than for brevity, and he exemplifies this fame by making a departure from the customary method of handling the subject of penance. Instead of confounding the virtue of penance with the sacrament, he makes a separate study of each. They are, of course, intimately linked, since the sacrament supposes the virtue and the virtue is false unless it tends to the sacrament, but it is a happy decision to take them one by one. If for no other reason than a methodological one, Suarez made a progressive step in so arranging his work.

Another distinctly successful innovation is the Suarezian catalogue and discussion of Church censures. By censure the Church exercises in the *forum externum* the same power of the keys which she exercises by penance in the *forum internum*. It is to the advantage of the confessor to know the juridical power of the Church and its right of punishment for he is frequently called upon to act as the interpreter of this power and right. Suarez shows himself preëminently the canon lawyer in the way he handles the general question of censures, and the specific questions of excommunication, suspension, interdicts, irregularities and so forth. The practical precision and careful wisdom he brings to bear upon the discussion of these things make of the work a valuable guide book for the ecclesiastics of his time.

Suarez himself had a couple of painful experiences in going to confession, and these incidents were sufficient to enlighten him on the distressing need for more accurate preparation on the part of his contemporary fellow priests. On one occasion he confessed to an assistant parish priest in an obscure village, and was astounded to learn that the man could not get through the formula of absolution without the help of his penitent. The Jesuit thought he ought to mention the fact to the priest's superior, the local pastor. But this worthy person astounded the theologian even more when he said: "I know my assistant is stupid and I have told him over and over again merely to hear the sins of his penitents and then send them over to me for absolution."

In another Portuguese village Suarez wanted to follow his usual custom of confessing before celebrating Mass. His exact and innocent revelation of conscience made the confessor curious to know who this virtuous priest was. He asked him his name but Suarez modestly replied that there was no need to reveal it. The priest insisted that he at least be told what position his penitent held among the clergy, and again Suarez refused to inform him. The confessor then became angry and would not give his penitent absolution, whereupon Suarez quietly went to the altar and said Mass without it. [4]

The *De Censuris,* then, was peculiarly pertinent to the times and practices which surrounded the author on all sides. A cursory glance at the work is sufficient to prove that Suarez supplied an ample antidote to these abuses, provided only that the clergy could be brought to make use of it. As late as 1863 an opinion published at Rome has it that "The treatise *De Censuris* is the masterpiece of Suarez as a canonist. Profound study of ecclesiastical laws, new theses broadly laid and solidly proved,

[4] Cf. Coleridge, *op. cit.,* pp. 180–181.

sound appreciation of difficult points, these are the principal qualities of that admirable book. We find them also in the greater number of the canonical questions that Suarez has touched upon, above all, when there is question of the Pope, his power, his laws, and of obedience to his decrees. Suarez investigates all the decisions given by the Holy See, and the resolutions coming from the Cardinals, and he hastens to modify the opinions he has taught when they are not in harmony with the apostolic decrees and with the responses of the Sacred Congregations. His works include many examples of this fact." [5]

The general belief is that Suarez was the very essence of orthodoxy; and it comes as a great surprise to most people to learn that one of his works was interdicted and that he himself fell under the censure of excommunication. The easiest explanation is that he was the victim of circumstances and that he was never formally guilty of a false teaching, but there is more to it than that. The question at issue was that of confessional practice, one that had dogged the footsteps of many a teacher before Suarez.

Peter Lombard in his *Sentences* argued that "The perfection of Penance consists of three things: sorrow, confession, satisfaction—*compunctio cordis, confessio oris, satisfactio operis*." [6] But added to these—and good Catholics have always known it— must be the absolution pronounced by the priest. But not all good Catholics know of an ancient and honorable opinion to the effect that in cases of necessity the priest and penitent need not be present to each other. This opinion, condemned by the then reigning Pontiff, is traced back to Pope St. Leo, who told Bishop Theodore on June 11, 432, that the benefit of penance and abso-

---

[5] *Analecta Juris Pontificii*, IV, ii, col. 2182. Cf. also De Scorraille, vol. ii, pp. 54–55.

[6] *Sententiae*, IV, 16, 1.

lution should not be denied to a person who died before the priest could arrive but who had previously signified to witnesses his intention of confessing.[7]

The same matter has made a more modern appearance in the question of confession and absolution by telephone, whether the sacrament is thus licitly and validly administered, whether persons are present to each other when they speak across the physical distance which separates telephone instruments. The flood of controversy which accompanied this angle of the same question helps us to understand the furore caused in the days of Suarez.

Some ancient theologians had asserted that in case of necessity the penitent could mail an account of his sins to the confessor, who could in turn send back his absolution in the same way. At the end of the sixteenth century, however, there were not many who maintained this position, but they were numerous enough to cause trouble for the Society of Jesus. Preaching at Toledo in 1594, the Jesuit Juan Jeronimo openly favored the opinion, and supported his doctrine by quoting several Dominican theologians. Of all times and places Jeronimo picked the worst ones for an assertion of that kind. Some Jesuits personally thought that the confession of one's sins could be sent to the confessor by mail, but all believed that absolution had to be administered in the presence of the penitent. The Dominicans howled their immediate opposition to Jeronimo, and the versatile Avendaño exploited the statement as the common Jesuit doctrine of the times.

The attack on the Jesuits for this indiscreet and erroneous view of one of their priests soon spread outside the peninsula. At Florence, Italy, Nicholas Lorini carried on the attack and even purported to explain why the members of the Society should hold such doctrines. According to his theory, the Jesuits wanted to hold on to the idea of confession and absolution by letter so that

[7] Cf. Migne, *P. L.,* 54, 1013.

during the summer time they could keep contact with their beautiful penitents who spent several months in the pleasant hills of Tuscany. Wealthy and refined society ladies were not easy to obtain as penitents, and the Jesuits did not relish the thought of turning them over to other priests even for one confession. Of course, the Italian theologians of the Society easily refuted these charges on every point. Lorini then announced that he would justify them from the pulpit, but in the meanwhile diocesan authority imposed silence upon him.

Both at Alcalá and Coimbra, Suarez taught the theory which was common at that time. Even while mutual recriminations were being hurled broadside among his fellow theologians he placidly held to the well-founded prevailing opinion. "It was universally taught that in the case of necessity, the material integrity of confession was not necessary; a penitent unable to do more might confess in a general way, or by some signs of interior penitence; and if the priest did not arrive until after the penitent had lost his senses or the use of his faculties, he might absolve him on the testimony of bystanders who had heard him beg for absolution, or who knew his desire to receive it. This opinion led on to another—that confession might be made by letter, and after that the penitent might be lawfully and validly absolved by the priest, without further confession, when he came into his presence." [8]

The discussions raged back and forth, in some places even gaining more attention than the long drawn-out controversy on grace and free will which was going on at the same time. As in all cases where actual practice touches people most intimately, there was only a slight step from criticism of doctrine to abuse of personality. Secular priests and other religious orders entered the fray until it became imperative for the Holy See to hand down a definitive decision. After due deliberation among the

[8] Coleridge, *op. cit.*, pp. 175–176.

theologians and Cardinals, the Holy Father "condemned and prohibited as at least a false, rash and scandalous doctrine the proposition that 'it is permitted sacramentally to confess one's sins by letter or messenger to an absent confessor and to receive absolution from that same absent priest,' and he decrees that hereafter this proposition must not be taught in public or private lectures, sermons, and assemblies, never in any case defended as a probable opinion, printed or in any way reduced to practice." [9]

This pontifical decree was issued on June 20, 1602, and did not reach Suarez at Coimbra until about mid-summer. There were still several months remaining before the *De Poenitentia* would be completely off the press but the portion of the work in which Suarez treated the matter was already set up and printed. He called in that portion and pondered it carefully. In the nineteenth disputation he had proposed the question "whether sacramental absolution could be given to an absent person," and remarked that there were two opinions: the first, that both confession and absolution could be had in necessity between absent persons; the second denies that "the sacrament can be consummated between absent persons, even in extreme necessity, and consequently a priest cannot absolve unless the penitent is present. This opinion is commonly attributed to St. Thomas, but I do not find it expressly in his works. . . . He teaches, however, that there can be confession by letter but does not say the same about absolution." [10]

A little further on in the same disputation he asserts that he had taught this latter opinion at Alcalá in 1588 and at Coimbra in 1598. When he got the work back from the printer he inserted at the end of this section the decree of Clement VIII,

[9] Denziger-Bannwart: *Enchiridion Symbolorum*, Freiburg, 1913, Herder, pp. 338–339.
[10] *De Poenitentia*, XIX, 3, 5.

soberly remarking that the Holy Father "adjoined excommunication *ipso facto* incurred and reserved to himself, for those who violate this decree, besides other punishments to be enjoined by the judges." [11] Thus the theologian takes the statement of the Pope as a confirmation of the doctrine which he himself had taught and written about absolution. He then turned to the revision of the section in which he dealt with confession itself, calmly unaware of the storm of trouble he was about to bring down on himself.

In the last section of the twenty-first disputation Suarez distinctly taught that confession, in a case of necessity, could be made to an absent priest. He tripped over his own dialectic skill in trying to square this with the pontifical decree and in trying to interpret the mind of the Holy Father. The decree had distinctly forbidden confession to an absent priest *and* absolution from that same absent priest. This could be one proposition or two according to whether the *and* is understood conjunctively or disjunctively, *complexive* or *divisive*. Suarez said he thought the mind of the Holy Father was that he condemned those who taught confession and absolution could both be had *in absentia.* Thus the theologian understood it as one single proposition. Taken singly, both propositions would not be condemned; therefore, the confession itself could still be made by letter, but absolution never. "Nevertheless," concludes Suarez, "I submit this assertion to the judgement of the same Pontiff, together with everything else that is contained in this and my other works." [12]

The theologian finally sat back content that he had done a good job in catching the work before it got out. For once he was not disturbed over the slowness of printing. He had been able to get back the copies of proofs already distributed to some of his friends in Castile and Portugal, but he had reckoned without the old watchdog of orthodoxy, Father Bañes. This agile contro-

[11] *Ibid.,* XIX, 3, 15.   [12] *Ibid.,* XXII, 4, 10.

versialist gleefully reported to his friends at Rome that the Jesuit Suarez was in the wrong again, that he had dared to interpret the opinion of the Pope in a way in which it could not be interpreted. In the beginning of October he wrote that "a certain premature interpretation had been printed and distributed without the knowledge . . ." of His Holiness.

Bañes followed the theory that you could weaken any enemy if you kept at him with a large enough assortment of bludgeons. This was simply another stroke to weaken the Jesuit side of the argument *De Auxiliis*, and it was not long in producing its effect. Cardinal Aldobrandini, Secretary of State under Clement VIII, wrote to the nuncio at Madrid: "His Holiness wishes that Father Suarez' interpretation of the recent decree on confession by letter be examined in the Congregation of the Holy Office. I will inform you of the decision as soon as I learn it." The committee appointed to make the investigation of the Suarezian text consisted of a Capuchin and two Dominicans and everybody was saying in Rome that Suarez could not hope for much favor at their hands.

The merest insinuation of such proceedings against him was enough to throw the theologian into a panic. He was forlorn; he was ill in both body and mind. The nuncio, always friendly to Suarez, wrote to Aldobrandini from Valladolid: "Father Francis Suarez is here with me and is troubled with a deep confusion, believing that he has irritated the Holy Father by his interpretation of the decree on confession. . . . He is a venerable religious, very humble and peaceable, and enjoys a great reputation in this country." That was written on August 17, 1603. Suarez' friends were busy on his behalf. Three days later Philip III himself wrote to the Pope, highly commending the theologian and asking as a special favor that His Holiness hurry the decision of the committee, expressing the hope that the reputation of the professor and the authority of his doctrine might remain intact. Many other petitions were sent to Clement on behalf of Suarez, one of them in typical feminine fashion by the Countess de Lemos who bluntly put the question: "If Your Holiness does not honor and defend a man whose whole life is spent with such rare examples of virtue, with such constancy, with so much glory to his Order and for the service of the Church, who will hereafter have the courage to do what he has done?" [13]

Some of these letters had not time to reach Rome before the decision of the Congregation was announced. On the last day of July the Holy Father together with the cardinals, after having examined section four of Suarez' twenty-first disputation, and compared it with the sense of the previous pontifical decree, announced that the book was interdicted until expurgated and corrected. The corrections, as well as all future books by the same author, were to be submitted for approval of the Roman Congregation of the Inquisition. Furthermore, Father Suarez, for the sake of his conscience, was to be notified of this decision because of the excommunication contained in the said decree.

The blow had struck. The rigorous and painful sentence of excommunication made an outcast of the champion of orthodoxy. "The titulary of the first chair of one of the greatest universities in the world and the most illustrious theologian then in the peninsula, he who had vowed his life for the defense and progress of the sacred science and who could now do nothing for this great work if his doctrinal honor and that of his Order suffered this stain; saw himself condemned for his doctrine by the vicar of Jesus Christ, placed in the ranks of other suspects, considered an excommunicant, and perhaps even cited to Rome to defend himself there like a heretic before the tribunal of the Inquisition!" [14]

The great theologian, however, was not completely abandoned

[13] De Scorraille, vol. ii, pp. 70–71. [14] *Ibid.,* pp. 72–73.

to his fate. Hundreds of letters and recommendations streamed in to the Holy Father at Rome, from clergy and laity, from priests, bishops, cardinals, from the nuncio in Spain and from the King himself. The nuncio, who appreciated him as he deserved, advised Suarez to go to Rome and lay his explanations before Clement, but the Spanish Jesuit was too sick to move. Feverishly Suarez wrote a long memorial in explanation of his doctrine and in absolute submission to the papal decrees. Aquaviva urged him to come in person, but it could not be done at the moment. Several painful hemorrhages reduced him to extreme feebleness and for a while his confréres were in despair of his recovery; but the man refused to die with himself in disgrace and his Society in dishonor. Gradually he recovered sufficiently to heed the words of Philip who had been employing his ambassador to Rome, the Duke of Escalona, in behalf of the theologian.

In March, 1604, the duke wrote to His Majesty, telling him that he had finally persuaded the Pope to listen to Suarez and to have the whole case reconsidered by the Inquisition. The ambassador then added that he was now working on the members of the Inquisition in the hope of bringing them around too. But for the second time the book of Spain's greatest theological writer was found to be at fault, and the same section of the work was again condemned.

Finally, at the end of April or beginning of May, Suarez himself went to Rome, got a favorable audience with Clement, wrote up his side of the question again, and was able to obtain a reëxamination in the summer of the following year. On the 14th of July, 1605, the general congregation of the Holy Office reaffirmed the previous decree, and to make matters worse, six days later condemned another part of the same work. On August 18th, the same Holy Office again examined the matter and again condemned Suarez' interpretation. Altogether there have been seven separate investigations both during the author's lifetime and after his death, and all come to practically the same agreement. To this day the decree of Pope Clement has not been revoked.

This seemingly rough and repeated treatment is not so dire as it would at first appear. Suarez was attempting the virtually impossible when he asked the vicar of Jesus Christ, the supreme arbiter of the whole world, to retract a decree which he had solemnly pronounced. The remark: *Roma locuta est, res finita est,* Rome has spoken, the affair is settled, had as much force then as it has to-day. The pontiffs have but rarely rescinded their written orders, and to have a Pope cancel the order of his own predecessor is an even rarer occurrence.

As a matter of well-attested fact there was an outside chance that Clement would make an exception in the case of Suarez. He had stated orally that he had not intended to include the case of a dying man whom witnesses saw begging for absolution. Such a man, declared the Pope, could be given absolution even though he was no longer capable of using his senses. In modern confessional practice there is never any doubt about this. A priest will always give absolution to a dying man even when there is no way of positively ascertaining his previous sentiments of contrition.

In his naïve good faith Suarez had the notion that he could move the mountain of tradition. In the course of a little over a year he composed fourteen brochures, memorials and letters, some of them running into the size of a volume, in order to justify his position. Always willing to submit to better judgement, he was hard-headed enough to expect that such judgement would be forthcoming to break down his own cogent arguments. To the day of his death he was not convinced that his adversaries and the Pope himself had been able to supply tenable argumentation to oppose his case. Several times he went through the whole case, taking up, discussing and then rejecting, every other historical and theological argument but his own.

But it was all to no avail. The theologian's biographers are generally of the opinion that death surprised Clement just as he was about to render a decision in favor of Suarez' interpretation of the confessional decree. There is no extant proof for the opinion. The reign of Leo XI was too short for any action on his behalf, since he was crowned Pope on Easter Sunday, April 10, 1605, and died seventeen days later. Then the energetic Cardinal Borghese took up office as Paul V, and before the end of the year persuaded Suarez that he would do nothing to remove the stricture of Clement.

The official ecclesiastical documents on the case sound extremely rigorous but the personal relations between Paul and Suarez were of a most affable kind. Spain's foremost theologian was most welcome at the papal court in those days of stress and worry. He was consulted frequently about the difficulties then present, the controversy on grace, the incipient revolt of Venice, the progress of the heretics on the continent, the attitude of the new ruler of England. "It is supposed," says Siegfried, "that at this time the offer of the Cardinalate was made to Suarez, as is inferred both from the testimony of his grand-nephew to Anton Deschamps, S. J., and from the letters of Paul V, preserved in the Suarezian family, tendering him the honor. Doubtless his humility no less than his preference for the professorial duties led him to decline the offered distinction." [15]

The evidence of a proffered red hat is too flimsy to be reliable. It may be one of those wishful suppositions that abound in ancient biographical tales and make a rocky road for the path of historical criticism. "Professorial duties" held no special attraction for Suarez; he was always trying to get out of the theologian's chair so that he could devote himself to writing. But, if the car-

[15] Siegfried, *op. cit.*, pp. 267–268.

dinalate loomed before him, he would undoubtedly have preferred even his professorship to that high ecclesiastical position. And this for any number of reasons: he was a Jesuit, and Jesuits do not, according to rule, aspire to Church dignities; he was a scholar, and scholars prefer private study to public business; he was a Spaniard, and Spaniards traditionally stay on the peninsula rather than in any other place in Europe.

During Suarez' stay at Rome there is record of an astonishing event which has withstood too much analysis to be put down as mere conjecture. The charity of authors has withheld the name of a certain religious who was most vociferous in denouncing Suarez' teaching on the validity of sacramental penance for a person destitute of consciousness who had previously signified a desire of receiving it. He was only one of many who openly dubbed the doctrine contrary to faith and argued against it before the congregation of the Inquisition. The man was taken mortally ill in the street one day and before losing consciousness asked urgently for a priest and absolution. The streets of Rome were always full of priests but it happened that the one who arrived first at the death scene recognized the man and declared that he could not give absolution since its reception under these conditions would be contrary to the dying man's will. He died without the sacrament, a victim of his own rigorous opinion, more dogmatic than the expressed belief of the Holy Father himself.

The Spanish theologian concluded his sojourn in the Eternal City in the Autumn of 1605, and then travelled back to Portugal where he took up his interrupted work at the beginning of the new year.

CHAPTER XXII

Return to Portugal

IN HIS JOURNEY both to and from Rome Suarez did not even remotely resemble the tourist who inexpertly dallies along the way, wastes time in gazing at monuments which he immediately forgets, or keeps a diary on net mileage and chance acquaintances. The theologian was a unique traveller even for his own time and his own religious profession. The route was common enough: up through France, stopping at Bordeaux, into the plains of northern Italy, thence to Rome. On the way back he made a quick jaunt to Lyons (in twelve days) and then went directly to Spain through Catalonia. It was not the route but the manner in which he travelled it, that made all the difference.

It was with no lightsome heart that he had made the Romeward trek. Under the cloud of false doctrine he could hardly be expected to trip joyously to his tribunal, but the man did not let melancholy trick him into mental inactivity. The journey was a perfect opportunity, he thought, for the composition of that long planned treatise *De Deo*; so he took along the necessary reference books, a large supply of foolscap, and the ever-faithful Aguilar. As he jogged along on his horse through strange towns and countryside he reflectively dipped into the vast storehouse of his memory, mentally noted the line of argument he would follow, and then drew his personal conclusions. Stopping before nightfall Suarez and his secretary would take a hurried meal at some hostel and then jot down as many pages as they could before retiring.

Ever a miser of his minutes Suarez was able to complete the whole treatise in this way. When he got back to Coimbra he could turn over to his printer a work of almost nine hundred pages, entitled *De Deo Uno et Trino,* divided into three separate treatises, the first in three books, the second in six, and the last in twelve. It was at first supposed to be a commentary on questions 1–43 of the first part of St. Thomas' *Summa,* but turned out to be, like most other Suarezian compositions, a series of disputations in logical order. The first treatise dealt with the divine substance and attributes; the second was on divine predestination and reprobation; the last on the mystery of the Trinity.

But there were many other duties to perform besides the composition of theological works. In the Eternal City his stopping place for a while at least was the Jesuit novitiate of St. Andrea, which still recalled the recent memory of Stanislaus Kostka and Aloysius Gonzaga, and the longer memory of other early Jesuits. The records of this residence show that Suarez gave an alms of forty ecus in 1605, but do not indicate how long he stayed there. It is quite probable that he remained for the whole period for, in the back of his mind, he had planned a work on the religious vocation, with a special part devoted to the Society. Nowhere else could he have then obtained the detailed information he later incorporated into the book *De Religione.*

The rapid return from Rome to Lyon was made possible by the generous insistence of a cardinal whose name is not preserved in this connection. The slow and humble travel of a simple religious would have stretched the journey out much more than twelve days. But the entourage of a prince of the Church in those days was of the very best, and the cardinal seems to have been as honored to have Suarez in his company as the theologian was happy to cut down the time element of the trip.

All along the homeward route people seemed to know that Spain's great scholar would be passing that way. When he was with the cardinal they crowded around the carriage to get a glimpse of him and to receive his blessing. Theophile Raynaud, a young professor of humanities at the College of Avignon, was an eyewitness to the fact that the whole town turned out to give the Jesuit theologian a triumphal welcome. These friendly ovations must have heartened Suarez, weighed down as he was by the knowledge of his own failure in the mission to Rome. But once he got into Spain the crowds outdid themselves. At Barcelona and Valencia, but especially at Salamanca, the Spaniards went wild over the return of their theologian. The whole faculty of the university, dressed in academic robes and followed by an enthusiastic student body, escorted him through the streets. By some strange illogic of the Spanish mind they greeted him with shouts of *Victor! Victor!* though they must have known well that he came off second best in his arguments with the Pope.

At Madrid, His Majesty, Philip III, embraced him heartily, assuring him that every royal device had been used to make Rome change the rankling condemnation. Now that the theologian was back would he not stay at the court as the King's adviser in doctrinal matters? The theologian would not. Now that the King was in such good humor would he not release Suarez from the chair of the royal university at Coimbra? The King would not. So Suarez decided that even teaching would be better than an official sinecure at the court. Siegfried piously comments that "One who preferred the humble garb of the religious to the princely red of the Church was not to be allured by the gifts of earthly kings. The prayer that he had uttered on the one occasion was still more pertinent in the other: *Diripuisti, Domine, vincula mea, tibi sacrificabo laudis.*" [1]

One of those who tried to keep Suarez in the royal retinue at Madrid was a certain noblewoman of high virtue and low logic. The Countess Santa-Godea was herself about to enter

[1] Siegfried, *op. cit.*, p. 268.

St. Teresa's reformed Carmelite Order but she thought that the Jesuit should remain at court. Suarez bluntly told her she was inconsistent. "You belong to the court and you are about to leave it for the cloister. Why do you tell me, who am already a religious, to leave my cell for the court? Allow me to be inspired by your example rather than by your words."

But there were matters of a more serious nature to be discussed between the theologian and the King. Aquaviva had charged Suarez to investigate and report the complications that had arisen from Father Ferdinand Mendoza's rebellious conduct in Spain. It was a pretty problem in its intricate details and one that kept Aquaviva on tenterhooks for several years.

Mendoza had been in league with the Spanish and Portuguese malcontents expelled ten years previously by the general congregation of the Society, but by a sufficient display of sorrow had been treated indulgently and permitted to remain a Jesuit. A polished man of the world, he won the esteem of the Count and Countess of Lemos and the Duke of Lerma, became their confessor and accompanied them to Italy. Here he stirred up intrigues against the general and could not be reprimanded even by Clement VIII, who did not wish to offend the duke. Returning to Spain, Mendoza, was soon the most influential person at the court. Through his connections there he obtained a brief from the Pope freeing him from the supervision of his superiors and allowing him a lay brother and two secretaries in his service, and various other privileges.

The recalcitrant Jesuit now thought himself in a position to effect the very schemes for which the malcontents had previously been ejected from the Order. He conceived the idea of getting Aquaviva in his power by having King Philip invite him to Spain. The general graciously refused the invitation, whereupon the King asked the Pope to order his departure for Spain. Aquaviva told His Holiness that it was Mendoza's vengeful doing, but Clement adhered to his order, not wishing to deprive the world's most powerful sovereign of the pleasure of a visit from the Jesuit general. The Kings of France and Poland and a half hundred other important persons interceded on behalf of Aquaviva, who was finally released from the journey only by the death of Clement.

But Paul V was likewise partial to Mendoza because he wished to use the Jesuit's influence at court to arrange a family marriage. It is at this point that Suarez entered the complicated state of affairs. He privately inquired of all the leading figures in the case, interviewed the Duke of Lerma, now minister of the king, talked with Father Haller, Jesuit confessor of the queen of Spain, Margaret of Austria, and even conversed in pleasant terms with Mendoza himself. The conclusions he reported to Aquaviva were several: the religious at the court talked with too great freedom about the government; there was a chance for coöperation between Father Haller and the duke; Father Mendoza was subtly following a new tack by talking of the general in terms of the highest respect.

Suarez evidently did not trust Mendoza, and he seems to have been the first to hit upon the smoothest way out of the difficulty. If the rebellious Jesuit could be honored with a bishopric, preferably in some far-off mission country, the threat to the Society and its general would automatically disappear. The path for this scheme was cleared when Paul V issued a brief freeing Mendoza from his vows of poverty and obedience. Finally, he made him bishop of Cuzco in Peru, and Mendoza, whether he liked it or not, was forced to accept the dignity. With this action Aquaviva, as well as the superiors of Jesuit provinces on the peninsula, were able to breathe freely again.[2]

With the report carefully written and posted to Rome, Suarez could again continue his journey to Portugal. At the end of the

[2] Astrain, *op. cit.,* vol. iii, pp. 634–659.

first week of January he was at Valladolid, and by the middle
of the month finally reached Coimbra, after an absence of almost
two and a half years. The rousing welcome he there received
did not alleviate his own intimate feelings regarding his failure
at Rome. "He is not taking up his course again," wrote the consultor of the province at that time, "and does not expect to do
so for the rest of this year. He says that he cannot appear in public after the failure of his mission to Rome." [3]

From this distance in history we would judge that Suarez was
over-sensitive about the whole affair and perhaps too proud to
admit that he was in the wrong. Actually this is a false judgement. His doctrine had been, at least verbally, approved by the
Pope, and the theologian was, if anything, an objective critic
about those things. But the whole temper of the times was such
that every move by a Jesuit had to be of the strictest orthodoxy,
not only in the teaching itself but also in the reputation which
that teaching had. The condemnation was a slur on something
Spanish and something Jesuit; and Suarez was of such nature
that he was hard to satisfy with anything short of perfection.

Be that as it may, the fact is that the most prominent professor
in Portugal made himself a refugee from his own university.
The smirch on his doctrinal honor became a psychological fixa-
tion for a while and the university council met in April to discuss his case. They objected that he had no right to absent himself at will from his duties, that it was the intention of His
Majesty to use Suarez' prestige and knowledge in actual lecturing, that the rector was to call attention to such faults and invite
him back to his course. This rector was Francis de Castro, a
former pupil and devoted admirer of Suarez. Hence his handling
of the affair was more than lenient and he did not insist on the
theologian's return for the rest of the school year.

In the meanwhile Suarez was hard at work at Lisbon where

[3] De Scorraille, vol. ii, p. 108.

he was supervising the publication of the tome written on the journey, *De Deo Uno et Trino*. As usual he was impatient of the time needed by the printers to finish the work, but here at Lisbon they were not nearly so slow as at other places. The book came out in 1606.

The theologian felt that at this point of his career in authorship he had to explain the seeming confusion and disorder which attended the Suarezian works published to date. The record showed that the first two works were theological—on the Incarnation. Then he treated the sacraments partially, and followed this by the *Metaphysical Disputations*. The *Opuscula* went back to theology, and they in turn were followed by the controversial books on penance and censures. Now he was back again to the first part of the *Summa*, discussing the Trinity and attendant questions. Suarez says that all this shifting about was dictated by the exigencies of the times; he wants his knowledge to be practical and useful at a time when questions are actually before the bar of public discussion. "I merely say that a man who is a public professor of theology, although he never spares either labor or zeal, cannot always work on the same topic or publish on the same subject. He must, as in this case, attend to now one study, now another, so that he can satisfy his duty of lecturing, respond to the demands and requests of people, and solve the difficulties of current problems. . . . Hence I must now publish this, though I have in mind to finish the tomes on the Sacraments, and even before them, a work on Religion which I have practically completed." [4]

An example of Suarez' deviating to the crises of the age is shown by the part he played in the controversy between Venice and the Holy See. During the following school year, when he was back at lecturing in the university, he took time out to write a capable tract *De Immunitate Ecclesiastica Contra Venetos*,

[4] *De Deo, Lectori Optimo*, p. xv.

more than a hundred and fifty pages in folio. Suarez had a two-fold purpose in putting out this work: the defense of ecclesiastical jurisdiction and an attack on the Venetian authorities who had published his *De Censuris* in a mutilated form, leaving out all the arguments concerning papal authority.

The most remarkable thing about Venice, wrote Ruskin, was that religion was so very much alive in private life and so dead in public life. Venice was an extreme republic whose leaders believed themselves Venetians first and Christians second, and maintained that citizenship in the republic was above baptism in the true Church. It was "in reality a monarchy tempered by assassination," [5] which defied the papal interdict of 1606, expelled the Jesuits, confiscated the property of religious Orders, threatened war against Rome, and proposed to set up a Protestant state with the help of England and the heretics on the continent.[6]

The central figure of this conflict was Paul Sarpi, a brilliant Servite friar, who had been theologian of the court of Mantua at the early age of eighteen. Wotton, the English ambassador to Venice, told James I that he was a true Protestant in a monk's habit, and the appraisal is pretty well verified by Sarpi's subsequent negotiations with heretical princes. Against the Pope, Paul V, he supplied the theological background, dialectic skill, actual pamphleteering, and diplomatic engineering for the revolutionary senate of Venice. After the open breach with Rome he instigated a veritable war of pamphlets, while at the same time mobilization for physical war was taking place in Spain, France and Venice.

Suarez was among the Jesuits who jumped into this fray in defense of the Holy See. The Cardinals Bellarmine, Baronius

[5] Campbell, *op. cit.*, p. 219.
[6] Cf. Pastor, who gives two whole chapters to this important conflict; *op. cit.*, vol. xxv, pp. 111–216.

and Caetani are likewise listed among the faithful Catholics who contributed more than thirty-eight works on the side of Pope Paul V. On the Venetian side of the controversy there were about thirty pamphlets, the most sensational of them being written by men like Pellegrini, the ex-Jesuit Marsiglio, the Senator Quirini and the Franciscan Capello. Before Suarez' *Contra Venetos* could be published for wide distribution in 1607 the differences were temporarily patched up through the intervention of Henry IV of France, Philip III of Spain, and numerous cardinals and ambassadors. The one concession the Venetians would not make, however, was the return of the Jesuits, who were then unable to go back to the city for a half century.

Sarpi was to remain a thorn in the side of the papacy for almost two decades, but the more immediate effect of his action was in the fuel he provided for James' attack on the Catholic conception of political economy. Here again Suarez would be seen rushing to the protection of the Holy Father. But in the meanwhile Sarpi's writings did their work. "They are clever, seasoned with witty sallies, and they drown the reader in a flood of arguments and texts which only a few are able to put to the test; moreover, in literature of this kind boldness in the attack invariably puts the defence at a disadvantage. Most of the ideas of Sarpi and his followers are already found in Marsilius of Padua, Wyclif, Hus and Luther. . . . On the other hand the significance of these writings lies precisely in the fact that they advocate an anti-Catholic conception of the State at the very gates of Rome." [7]

In appreciation of Suarez' work against the Venetians His Holiness sent a commendatory letter through his secretary, Scipio Cabellutius, on the second of October, 1607. On this occasion he gave Suarez the famous title, *Doctor eximius et pius,* which has ever since been associated with his name. Many men, said Paul, have tried recently to spread the dark night of error over

[7] *Ibid.,* pp. 151–152.

the liberty and power of the Church, but other faithful servants of Christ have dissipated it by the light of their sound doctrine. You are among the foremost of these; and your volume shows such labor, diligence and sound doctrine that it proves you to be an outstanding and holy theologian, *Theologum eximium exprimat, ac pium*.

These were melodious words in the ear of Suarez, coming as they did from the very Pope who had refused to unsay the official words of papal condemnation regarding that small section of the *De Poenitentia*. They are historically important in that they demonstrate without the slightest doubt the high estimate in which His Holiness held Spain's greatest theologian. They certainly lightened the burden of anguish from Suarez' heart, for he is henceforth less fractious about the question of doctrinal honor, and he gets down with greater cheerfulness and vigor to the business of teaching.

All was going well again at Coimbra. Suarez was now forced to exchange rôles with Father Gil by taking the place of his own substitute. Gil was badly racked with rheumatism, stomach trouble, and several other physical maladjustments during the autumn of 1606, and he could no longer take even occasional burdens of lecturing in theology. Thus Suarez got back in stride again and did not miss a lecture for almost three years. In the menwhile Gil died—January 7, 1608, completely done up at the age of sixty-six, as much from his brilliant and scholarly pursuits as from the constant grind he subjected himself to in hospitals, prisons, and local mission work.

Besides the *Contra Venetos*, which had to be penned during hours spared from the preparation and delivering of lectures, Suarez was busy for these three years on the composition of his *De Gratia*. This was not a supplement to the previously published *Opuscula*, for the latter were directly concerned with particular problems arising from the famed controversy over grace and free will. Other pressing duties interfered with the printing of the *De Gratia,* and the theologian was himself never able to get around to it though the manuscript was ready long before his death. The three large volumes of the work were published posthumously, the first and third in 1619, and the second not until 1651. The more important reason for such delay was an aftermath of the recent controversy. The Suarezian doctrine on grace was fought every step of the way by those who were opposed to the lucid and logical presentation of the Jesuit case, and they effectually prevented the *imprimatur* on the second volume until the middle of the century. It was finally printed at Lyons.

The contents of these books were the subject matter for Suarez' courses at the university from 1606 to 1609. His classes were constantly attended with an overflow audience, people jostling each other for positions, crowding the aisles, and even hanging about the windows, so that the regular students had sometimes to fight for their own prior rights. Grace and free will were the topics of talk in every patio and room of the town, and when the rumor came from Rome that the Jesuits had won the controversy the Portuguese were more eager than ever to hear the whole doctrine expounded by the great doctor of Coimbra. Suarez was lionized, for everyone seemed to think that the local hero had supplied the main reference book, the *Opuscula,* for learned cardinals and savants at Rome.

CHAPTER XXIII

Plots and Plans

IT IS GENERALLY SUPPOSED that a man passes into old age at about sixty; that he is ready then to ease his own portion of daily human toil and to shift it to the backs of younger and more energetic men. But Suarez was not a predictable specimen of the generality of humankind, being an exceptional man and requiring the treatment accorded to exceptions. He had reached his three score of years and there were still two magnificent performances before him: the famous *Defensio Fidei* against King James, and the less famous but equally important work *De Religione*. In 1608 the great theologian quietly celebrated his sixtieth birthday at Coimbra by publishing the first part of that work. The second part appeared in the following year; the third and fourth came out posthumously in 1624 and 1625 respectively.

In the fashion of the times he prefaced the work with a laudatory dedication to Alphonse Castelbranco, Bishop of Coimbra, saying that he had meditated over it these many years and that he now thought it ready to offer to the world. He seems to have had a genuine affection for this ecclesiastical superior. "I believe," he writes, "that no one can be ignorant of your great love of religion, since all your cares and endeavors tend to this one end, that divine worship should especially flourish in your diocese. . . . Your favours to me have been so many that I cannot possibly recount them here. From the first day on which I set foot in this city, I had you alone as a special Mæcenas of my studies; you not only granted authority and honor for my books, but also stirred me to further writing by your kind words and helped with generous deeds toward their publication." [1] The bishop was an apt recipient for such words and for a book of this kind since he truly fostered the Church and the various religious Orders, including the Jesuits, in Portugal.

In preparing this work Suarez was very careful to distinguish between the virtue and the state of religion, for he was writing to an audience of men and women who thoroughly understood religion as a very part of their lives. The virtue of religion, he pointed out, is a habit by which men practice internal and external acts of the true worship of God. "But the term religion is applied in a special way to signify a peculiar state and manner of living in which some of the faithful join together to worship God more perfectly." [2] Thus the whole field of investigation falls into a natural division of which the theologian takes full and logical advantage. Except for the problem of divine grace, Suarez gave more pages to this matter in his published works than to any other.

Under the flail of experience, both within the religious Order of which he was a member, and outside that Order, in the general Catholic life of his age, Suarez gained an all-embracing perspective fitting him precisely for this task. Perhaps it is for that reason that the *De Statu Religionis* has made such tremendous impact upon the minds of religious men and women who have read it. Perhaps for that reason, too, it is the only one of his works to appear, more or less completely, in an English translation. At Oxford, in 1884, the Jesuit father, William Humphrey, brought out a digest of these treatises in three volumes, in the preface of which the translator declares, "I have aimed simply at giving the marrow of the doctrine of my author, separated

---

[1] *De Religione; Illustrissimo ac Reverendissimo, etc.,* pp. v-vi. Suarez gave the complete work the title, *Opus de Virtute et Statu Religionis.*

[2] *De Religione,* I, 1, 2, 7.

from the dry bones of controversy." [3] The translation, though it runs to about eleven hundred pages, is indeed merely the marrow of Suarez' doctrine on the subject, for it comprises less than a fourth of all the matter published in his own *De Religione*.

One of the beauties of perusing the writings of Suarez is the absence of impassioned pleas for this or that favored idea, or of truculent denunciations against persons and notions with which he does not agree. You can be certain that anything he penned was the result of mature deliberation, and the style in which he wrote it is as nearly free of equivocation and obscurity as the medium of language permits. All of this is signally verified in his monumental work on the religious state where, if he is ever to do so, he should let himself go. Calmly and thoroughly he starts from the fundamental notion of perfection, tracing it through the different precepts and vows by which it is reached, through the various religious Orders of the Church where it is best achieved, and finally discusses most competently his own Society of Jesus.

The Jesuits were in need of some such book in the early decades of the seventeenth century because they were suffering almost continual attacks. There were men who declared the Order irreligious and anti-Catholic; some objected to its name, others to its digression from ancient monastic living, still others to its flair for external activity. Against all of these charges there was now a ready reference of rebuttal in the clearcut explanation of the Society which Suarez embodied in his work. It was at the same time the first philosophic examination of the Jesuit system, helpful to both superiors and subjects within the Order, as well as to those who contemplated admission to it.

Here, for example, the curious could find out that the Jesuits

[3] Humphrey, William: *The Religious State, A Digest of The Doctrine of Suarez, Contained in His Treatise, De Statu Religionis.* London, 1884, Burns and Oates, vol. i, p. v.

were something more than a group of learned men. Writes Suarez: "After learning there comes teaching, which is the end of learning; and in this also the Society omits nothing which can in any way be of service to its neighbours. Not to speak of preaching the Word of God, it occupies itself in teaching in the Schools the Sacred Scriptures and Scholastic Theology, also in solving cases of conscience and, if need be, taking part in controversies concerning the faith. It descends also to the teaching of liberal arts, and down even to the first rudiments of Latin. By these beginnings it reckons to arrive at greater things, nor does it count these things small without which great things cannot be done. Finally, by private counsel and by public teaching, whether by word of mouth or by means of the press, it strives by all means to aid all men, aiming at nothing save the good of those who are taught, and thereby the greater glory of God." [4]

As far back as 1564, when Suarez was a novice at Medina del Campo, there were men like Melchior Cano and Gaspar de Zuñiga, who made it one of the duties of their lives to discredit the Jesuit Institute and the Ignatian *Spiritual Exercises*. The young novice made careful notes in provision for the time when he could publicly explain and defend the exercises, probably deciding even then that this work should be apologetic rather than polemical. With studied restraint the theologian included three chapters on the exercises in his *De Religione*, a kind of commentary and justification of their doctrine, method and practice. As a true philosopher he saw that he must deal intellectually, rather than emotionally, with this prime ascetical weapon of the Jesuits, and the vogue enjoyed by the book among his confréres tends to demonstrate that he successfully did so.

By the publication of these volumes Suarez immediately appeared as the first authority of his age on matters pertaining to religious congregations and practices. The result was that he was

4 *Ibid.,* vol. ii, p. 388.

thenceforth consulted not only on questions strictly theological but also on a variety of religious difficulties, some of them only remotely connected with members of the established orders. They ranged from local wonders like the "letters of Our Lady" to international problems like Mary Ward's famous Institute.

There was, for example, the strange affair of the leaden tablets of Granada which unfolds before the reader more like a novel than a serious religious question. Still it was enough to disturb the southern Spaniards for many decades, arouse their emotional piety, and almost turn the case into a cause of national honor. Suarez was commissioned to make an inquiry. He did so with characteristic caution, and found the thing a hoax from beginning to end, though he prudently refrained from shattering the people's credulity by an over-blunt criticism.

In essence, the fable is this. In the spring of 1588 some workmen, demolishing a small house adjacent to the cathedral of Granada, came upon a leaden casket. In it were a relic of the martyred saint, Etienne, a bit of kerchief used by Our Lady to dry her tears at the foot of the cross, and an astounding parchment with a history as exciting as that of the Moors themselves. It was a prophecy of St. John the Evangelist, translated from Hebrew and Greek by Denis the Areopagite, given by him at Athens to St. Caecilius, who had it translated by his disciple Patricius into barbarous Latin for the early Spaniards. The prophecy was signed by Patricius and it foretold the future appearances of Mahomet, Luther, Anti-Christ, and continued right up to the Last Judgement. Seven years later the discoverers of these treasures supposedly found another; this time they unearthed a number of leaden tablets together with the bones of the Apostle James, of his Arab convert, Ctesiphon, and of some other martyrs.

These new relics should have been suspect from the first, especially the tablets, upon which were inscribed jumbled words in Arabic, Latin, and some other undecipherable language. Seventeen tracts traced the origin of Christianity, a mixture of true doctrines and strange errors, of oriental fact and fiction, of Christian and Mohammedan apologetics. One of them is particularly artless in relating a conversation between Our Lady and St. Peter, in which she foretold that these tablets would be revealed after an age of revolts, heresies, and wars; and that an Arab king together with a zealous Christian people would restore the pristine faith. In the meanwhile a copy would be preserved in Spain.

One wonders at the credulity of people who could let themselves be taken in by so evident a fraud. Yet enthusiasm for the discovery spread from the simple laity of Andalusia up through the ranks of the lower clergy of Spain until some of the bishops themselves took it seriously. Pedro de Castro, Archbishop of Granada, wrote to Suarez in 1600 asking him "because of his knowledge, virtue, prudence, and renown, to be the arbiter" in the affair. The theologian dodged the possibility of giving offense, and declined the invitation on the score of pressing duties. Another Jesuit, Esteban de Hojeda, evaded the task under the same plea; while a third, Roman Higuera, informed the archbishop that illness made it impossible for him to follow through the investigation.

Thus, without benefit of Jesuit council, the committee deliberated the matter and unanimously confirmed the authenticity of the leaden tablets. Clement VIII commanded that the tablets be sent to Rome for inspection, but De Castro replied that if he moved them out of Spain he would have a popular uprising on his hands. The affair dragged on in an unsettled way for several years, with the archbishop continuously trying to get Suarez' pronouncement. The latter always had good excuses, particularly in the fact of his trip to Rome, his publications, and his lectures in Portugal. In 1608 he again told the prelate that he could not come to Granada "to venerate these holy books, relics and all these marvels."

The delicate situation taxed Suarezian diplomacy, but the theologian handled it tactfully in two treatises which politely praised the strong faith of Spaniards in the discoveries but declared it as quite probable that the tablets were not genuine. These treatises have never been edited and remain in manuscript form in the archives at Granada.[5] In some of his personal correspondence and in several passages of his works he mentions these leaden tablets but never admits either the authenticity of the tablets themselves or the plausibility of the doctrines they contain.[6]

Suarez did not have the last word on this worrisome problem, for it carried on through many years of acrimonious debate, investigations and condemnations. In 1632 the tablets were taken from Granada to Madrid, whence ten years later they were sent to Rome. In 1665 several oriental experts made a Latin translation of the original and handed it over to the Roman Inquisition. At long last, in 1682, after almost a century of argument, a brief of Innocent XI condemned them as full of errors, heresies, borrowings from the Koran, and with no claim to miraculous origin. Historical scholars attributed their composition to two Moors of Granada who sought by this novel means a reconciliation between the Christian Gospel and the Mohammedan Koran. Thus was vindicated Suarez' cautious approach to a problem which, if mishandled, could have brought him a great deal of grief.

Another matter in which the theologian was called upon to exercise his wise judgement was the process of beatification of Teresa of Avila, then going forward at Madrid. The details of

[5] De Scorraille, vol. ii, pp. 142–148.

[6] For example, in discussing the Immaculate Conception Suarez refuses to accept the testimony of one of these tablets entitled, *De Domo Gloriae et Domo Tormenti*. Cf. his work under the general title, *De Ultimo Fine, Tractatus Quintus*, IX, 4, 40, published posthumously by Balthazar Alvarez in 1628.

his part in the affair are tantalizingly meager, but that he did have a part in it is beyond question.

Suarez made a trip to Madrid from Coimbra in 1609 for the express purpose of attending to some of the internal business of his province. While he was there he took occasion to remind King Philip again that his promised term of professorship at the university had long since run its course and that he now wished to have his release. As usual His Majesty put him off, pointing out that the university had great need of him and showing him a letter just received from the university council itself petitioning for his retention in the principal chair of theology. Suarez submitted with what grace he could muster. It is at this time that the King is supposed to have asked him to study the case of St. Teresa.

At any rate, Suarez gave his testimony regarding the works written by the saintly Carmelite reformer. He furthermore mentioned that he himself had met and spoken with Teresa, and that he was acquainted with and approved, Ribera's book "on the life, the miracles and the revelations of the said Mother Teresa." The beatification process had been ordered by Clement VIII as early as 1604, and all of Spain was eager to see his order accomplished in fact. For more than five years witnesses had been called to Madrid and even to Rome, and it is in this way that Suarez came into the picture. Paul V finally beatified this extraordinary woman in 1614.

When and where Spain's greatest theologian made the acquaintance of Spain's greatest religious reformer is still a matter of open conjecture. The most probable guesses point to Segovia, Salamanca and Valladolid. In 1574 Teresa came to Segovia to found a convent there, and in one of her letters written from that place, mentioned her relations with the Jesuits. Suarez was then teaching philosophy at the college in that city, and was likewise the spiritual adviser of the community, in which latter capacity he may well have come into contact with the holy Carmelite. Four years previous to that, Suarez was teaching at Salamanca at the same time that Teresa came there to establish another foundation. Finally, between 1577 and 1580, when the theologian was giving his first courses on the *Summa* of St. Thomas at Valladolid, the nun made several journeys to that city.

The more zealous among Suarez' biographers have attempted to make a strong case of the apparently casual connections between these two outstanding personalities. The historical fact seems to be that when Teresa mentioned the different theologians she had consulted in difficulties of conscience she was talking mainly of the Dominicans who highly approved her work and who gave her every possible assistance. The Jesuit, Alvarez, was for a while her confessor; Suarez was a personal acquaintance. But beyond these facts there is little to argue that the Jesuit gained his knowledge of mystical theology from the Carmelite, or that the latter profited in any great degree from contact with Suarez.

A couple of years later (1611) Phillip III again called on his old friend to take part in the official furtherance of a saint's cause. He asked Suarez to act as his attorney and representative, with the Augustinian Aegydius, and the professor of law, John de Carvalho, in the process of canonization of Queen Elizabeth of Aragon, wife of King Denis of Portugal. It was a difficult job, and it was weighed down with an intricacy of legal details in the arrangement of which Suarez was peculiarly fitted. Whether or not he was the instigator of the cause is a doubtful point, even though Descamps claims that "It was at his advice and according to his counsel that the Catholic King, Philip III, asked of Pope Paul V the honors of canonization of the Queen Elizabeth." [7]

[7] Descamps, Antoine, *Vida del Venerable Padre Francisco Suarez,* vi, 1., quoted by De Scorraille, vol. ii, p. 155.

· The Portuguese needed no one to induce them to a devotion toward Elizabeth, whom they had long venerated as the Holy Queen. She was the great-niece of another Queen Saint, Elizabeth of Hungary, and was renowned in those parts during her life as a capable peacemaker, and after her death in 1336, as the Patroness of Peace. In those ages, as in every age before and after, war was a harsh and horrid monster. Portugal was itself a contender and a bone of contention on the Iberian peninsula, but the imminence of warfare was always accompanied by prayers to the Holy Queen; and the people were gratified that she sometimes prevented it by her powerful intercession. They made pilgrimages to her tomb, just outside the city of Coimbra; and the university celebrated an annual solemn feast upon which occasions one of the professors regularly gave a panegyric in her honor.

Suarez was always at heart a pacifist, so that at Coimbra he developed a rational appreciation of Elizabeth, "that illustrious princess, virgin of Aragon, Queen of Portugal, mother and step-mother of all the other kingdoms of Spain." The business of the process which the royal committee conducted began in February, 1612, and ended about the middle of the year. In March the official representatives of the King, Suarez, Aegydius and Carvalho, attended the exhumation of the Queen's body, which was found preserved from corruption and redolent of a pleasing perfume. The body of the peace-loving monarch is still venerated at the royal Clarist monastery founded by her, and where she passed her last days. The judgement of the committee being formed, it was officially witnessed, sealed and sent to Rome. Queen Elizabeth was raised to the altars of the Church by Pope Urban VIII in the year 1625.

Numerous similar problems and questions were presented to the critical judgement of the theologian during the last decade of his life but perhaps the most interesting is that of Mary Ward and her companions, whom Pastor erroneously calls "Jesuit Sisters." [8] But the mistake in using this title is an easy one to make, for the women actually fancied themselves Jesuitesses and were sometimes called by that name at the time of Suarez. Now, if there is one phenomenon which has never appeared, and which will never appear—if the Society of Jesus has any say in the matter—it is a congregation of Jesuit nuns in the Catholic Church. When Mary Ward opened her first house on the continent at St. Omer in 1609 the Jesuits encouraged her in her work, but they maintained in no uncertain terms that any connection or similarity between her Institute and the Society was purely a figment of the imagination. There has since been no danger that other feminine founders would try to emulate Mary Ward.

"For five years," writes Maisie Ward, "the one house of the Institute was in St. Omer, but in the years that followed it spread over Europe amazingly. In 1614 they took a house in London, which instantly became a center of missionary activity. Then came foundations in Liége, Cologne and Trêves. By 1621 the Institute was in Flanders, Bavaria, Austria and Italy. In that year she first applied to Rome for approval of the Rule. But the Rule was a storm centre." [9] This Institute and Rule had been a storm center long before Mary Ward brought it to Rome, and it was the calming of that storm that Suarez tried to accomplish.

Mary Ward was a young Englishwoman of only twenty-four years when Suarez first heard of her (it seems) from the bishop, James Blaise, who helped her found the new congregation. Her primary object was the education of English girls who were otherwise unable, because of the persecution at home, to obtain a desirable Catholic training. There was nothing novel in that laudable purpose, but the manner in which she hoped to achieve

[8] Pastor, *op. cit.*, vol. xxvi, p. 347.
[9] Ward, Maisie: "Mary Ward," in *The English Way*, New York, 1933, Sheed and Ward, p. 249.

it was distinctly original. The members made two years of novitiate, pronounced the religious vows, had one Superior General for the whole congregation, had no enclosure, choir, or religious habit. "In this now explicit design of enabling women to do for the Church what men were doing in the Society of Jesus, Mary Ward was attempting something of stupendous difficulty. . . . By taking the Jesuit Rule she infallibly awakened the opposition of their opponents. But neither did she secure the support of the Jesuits. A few of them stood by them through thick and thin— Fr. Lee, Fr. Gerard and others. But most of them thought the 'Jesuitresses' [*sic!*] a tiresome and useless addition to their own difficulties and were eager to disown them." [10]

Wise indeed were the large numbers of Jesuits who were eager to disavow any such connection. They remembered well the advice of Loyola himself who had some sorrowful experiences with "Jesuitesses" in his own time, and who ruefully remarked that a few women caused him more trouble than the whole Society of Jesus. Isabel Roser was one of three Barcelona women for a short time under the direction of Ignatius Loyola; but after that affair blew up other women got the same idea, and even some Jesuits seemed to favor it. "The resistance of Ignatius to these feminine projects of Spain and Portugal was absolute. . . . Ignatius was inflexible, and answered negatively . . . never again was there question of an order of Jesuitesses to be realized." [11]

Suarez was direct and to the point in answering the questions put to him regarding the novel Institute of Mary Ward. As usual, he was all for authority, and thought that the best thing to do would be to take it out of diocesan examinations and send it to the Holy Father. His opinion was asked on three specific points:

[10] *Ibid.*, pp. 249–250.

[11] Dudon, Paul: *Saint Ignace de Loyola*, Paris, 1934, Beauchesne, pp. 640–641, where he has a competent appendix entitled, *D'un Ordre de Jésuitesses (1543–1547).*

Does the new Institute provide a pious and licit way of life? Has the Bishop power to approve and confirm it? May it be considered a state of regular life, and are the members vowed to a stable and lasting manner of life?

His reply was published only in the last century under the title: *De Institutu Virginum Anglarum,* by Monsignor Malou, together with several other previously unedited works. The theologian answers the first query affirmatively. The Institute, as it has been described to him, has an excellent motive in its designs for the promotion of the Christian life, and it uses means which are in the abstract most laudable. Considered in this philosophical approach, Mary Ward's scheme should be approved, but its practical application is a thing of an entirely different nature.

Suarez was not so gentle in handling the two other questions. The bishop was not the source of approval and confirmation for strange institutes like this, nor in fact for any congregation of religious men and women. Two councils, the Lateran under Pope Innocent III, and that of Lyons under Gregory X, expressly forbade the creation of new religious Orders without the consent and approval of the Holy See. Now, continues Suarez, this prohibition is open to interpretation, strict or lenient. Did it mean that none could, without papal authorization, inaugurate new congregations of men and women, making vows and living like religious under a common rule? Or, did it allow these groups to be formed, and simply prohibit them the title and privileges of religious orders until they had been recognized as such by the Holy Father? The theologian takes the first view, explaining that the Councils and Popes wished to prevent associations that would not conform to piety and custom, a thing which could not be controlled under the second and more lenient interpretation.

Finally, Suarez is of the opinion that the Institute, though it may be praised in many respects, is at least dubious as to the religious state of women vowed to follow it. There are certain peculiarities which demand the attention of the Pope, since only he can properly pronounce on them. These are, he points out, such things as exemption from cloister, freedom to travel about from place to place, and the exercise of the apostolic life. The first of these peculiarities is entirely contrary to the known will of several pontiffs; the second is liable to lead to many dangers and abuses; the third swerves from the opinion of the Apostle Paul who would not give women in the Church the right to teach, *mulieres in ecclesia taceant.*

The theologian died a decade and a half before Mary Ward's dream came to a shattering conclusion under the impact of a papal bull, *Pastoralis Romani Pontificis,* in 1631.[12] But it is interesting to note that the official objections were cast along the lines on which he had warned the Jesuitesses. The association had been formed "without the authorization of the Holy See; they have not put themselves under the protection of the cloister, and have on the contrary adopted a kind of life and ministry which are not suitable for women; finally in spite of the warnings given them, they have remained obstinate in their first design, going so far as to use words not conformed to sound doctrine." All was finished with Mary and her followers; the convents were closed, the women sent to religious Orders or back to their homes; she herself was condemned by Pope Urban VIII as a heretic, schismatic, and rebel, to be imprisoned in the convent of the Poor Clares at Munich.

Maisie Ward, with insular petulance, suggests reasons for the failure of this seventeenth-century religious novelty. "Mary was

[12] The time element of these events plays tricks with the certainty several authors show in reporting them. De Scorraille, vol. ii, p. 256, following Malou, suggests that the Bishop of St. Omer requested the judgement of Father Suarez. Campbell, *op. cit.,* p. 390, indicates that the new Jesuit General, Vitelleschi, in 1615, deputed Suarez and Lessius to study the constitutions of the new congregation. Ward, *op. cit.,* p. 259, infers that Suarez was at hand with Lessius when the Cardinals were making their final investigation of the Institute in 1630. By that time the Spanish theologian was long since dead.

English, and a document embodying the gravest charges against
her had reached Rome from England, signed by the archpriest
and all his assistants. Mary did not lack friends in Rome, but
they were not English: not one voice from her own people was
raised in her support. She wanted the Jesuit Rule; and the Jesuit
authorities would have none of her." [13] That there is more behind the collapse than English negligence and Jesuit opposition
is clear from the fact that Benedict XIV in 1749 renewed the
condemnation of Urban VIII when there was an attempt to
re-establish the work of Mary Ward; and in 1877 Pius IX approved a new institute of "English Ladies" without, however,
permitting any connection with the first institute.

[13] Ward, *op. cit.,* p. 258.

CHAPTER XXIV

Tilting at Royalty

BY WAY OF BEING EVERYBODY'S COUNSELLOR Suarez had a hand in the settling of many difficulties minor to those of the canonization of saints and the approbation of religious associations. Likewise he lent a willing pen to defend the major external issue at that time annoying the Holy See: the perennial question of England and Protestantism. What is more astonishing, all of these affairs had to be mulled over in the theologian's spare time, for he continued to be tied down to the routine of lectures until within two years of his death.

England was a hot problem, always twisting about in the back of Suarez' mind even while he placidly wrote books, settled disputes, conducted classes. Before the turn of the century Queen Elizabeth's buccaneers plagued the King of Spain, while her bishops wore down the patience of several Popes. When the Virgin Queen became senile and defeated every Catholic hope for her return to religious sanity, there arose a ceaselessly debated question concerning her successor. The Jesuits, like all good Catholics, were working night and day for the return of a Catholic ruler, and Father Parsons was particularly prominent among those who preferred a Spaniard. The debate was closed by the accession of James of Scotland to the throne of England.

James I was a baptized Catholic but a confirmed Calvinist, son of the devout Mary Stuart and with many Catholics among his high-ranking officials and representatives. He was crowned in March, 1603, and for a while boded such welcome relief from the vagaries of his feminine predecessor that the Jesuit Garnet could write to his superior: ". . . there hath happened a great alteration by the death of the Queen. Great fears were: but all are turned into greatest security; and a golden time we have of unexpected freedom abroad. . . ." [1] But Garnet wrote without sufficient knowledge of the fickle, shilly-shallying character of the new ruler, who would protest friendliness to all, while within a year he could command that "all manner of Jesuits, Seminaries, and other priests whatsoever, having ordination from any authority by the laws of this realm prohibited," leave the realm or take the consequences.

The Catholic laity too was badgered from pillar to post in every tricky way James or his henchmen could devise. Fines and sentences were passed right and left during 1604 until the famous Robert Catesby and his Catholic friends could stand it no longer. They conceived the plot of blowing the King and his parliament to their eternal reward with gunpowder so that they could assure their fellow Catholics a surcease of temporal persecutions. "Everybody is in despair," wrote Garnet to Rome in May, 1605, "and many Catholics are hostile to the Jesuits; they say that the Jesuits oppose and prevent the use of force in any shape. I dare not attempt to ascertain what their future plans are since the General has forbidden us to meddle with such things." [2] The members of the Society in England were under the double prohibition of Aquaviva and Clement of allowing any action that could be interpreted as rebellious, and the passage of time has proven that they had no part in the Gunpowder Plot in any subsequent outbreaks.

This is not the place to discuss the plot, which was revealed on November 5, 1605, a date afterwards celebrated as Guy Fawkes Day. It is sufficient to remark that more recent research has

[1] Broderick, *op. cit.*, vol. ii, pp. 148–149.
[2] Pastor, *op. cit.*, vol. xxvi, p. 131.

brought to light certain suspicious circumstances which make the ancient Protestant version of the story untenable.[3] Father Garnet was martyred for refusing to reveal what he had learned of the plot under the seal of confession. That was on May 5th. Twenty-two days later the Parliament passed a sheaf of disastrous anti-Catholic laws, including the Oath of Allegiance, which outdid the enactments of Queen Bess' reign, and led ultimately to the political controversy in which Suarez figured so largely.

The formula of the oath was so craftily couched by the ex-Jesuit and apostate priest, Christopher Perkins, that many lay people were fooled into pronouncing it, and even some of the clergy submitted to it. A quick reading of it leaves one with the impression that it is entirely innocuous, that anyone at the time could "sincerely acknowledge, professe, testifie and declare in conscience" that James was rightful King of England, that he could not be deposed by Rome, that even if he were excommunicated he could claim allegiance of subjects, that treasons should be reported, that no person has power to abrogate this oath. But highly questionable propositions were cleverly blended with fully legitimate ones, so that even the old and infirm Archpriest Blackwell, head of the Catholic Church in England, persuaded himself to take the oath (1607).

Pope Paul V sent two briefs to England, one before and one after Blackwell's sorrowful defection, declaring that the oath was unlawful and contained many things contrary to faith and salvation. Cardinal Bellarmine took a hand in trying to help Blackwell out of the difficulty, an action which provoked James even more than the cardinal's previous answer to the King's *Basilikon Doron*. The royal wrath exploded in the pages of *An Apologie for The Oath of Allegiance*, or *Triplici nodo, triplex*

[3] This was the subject of a lively controversy during the last decade of the nineteenth century between John Gerard and S. R. Gardiner. Cf. *The Month*, London, during that period and the several booklets then published by the debaters.

cuneus, directed against the two papal briefs and the cardinal's letter. Bellarmine came back with a scorching and devastating analysis of the oath, which he entitled *Responsio Matthaei Torti.* The King, in a panic, recalled the *Apologie,* revised it with the help of several bishops working day and night, and published it with a Premonition to Monarchs and Princes, but this time under his own name. Bishop Andrewes attacked Bellarmine with his *Tortura Torti;* and the cardinal in 1609, answered the King again with *The Apology of Robert Bellarmine,* in which he said: "I do not see why it should be necessary to look for equality of birth or station or power in a theological controversy, since equality of wits and learning is all that matters."

A legion of controversialists, both domestic and foreign, stepped into the fray on either side, and for a while it was anybody's fight. Three Anglican theologians, Tooker, Burhill and Thomson were taken on by the Jesuit Van de Beeck. The learned Lessius politely but ever so effectively made James prove himself a fool out of his own mouth.

"But by far the most famous and important reply to Bellarmine's royal traducer," says Broderick, "came from Spain, where Francis Suarez had been engaged on it intermittently ever since the appearance of the King's first book. The English agent at Madrid, Sir John Digby, knew what was afoot, and his letters to James during the years 1612–1613 are full of references to the progress that was being made. James was in a great state of excitement, hoping possibly that Suarez, who lived far away from Rome, would not be so stalwart on the Pope's side as Bellarmine. Sad then was his disillusionment when, early in November, 1613, he received the *Defence of the Catholic and Apostolic Faith against the Errors of the Anglican Sect, with a Reply to the Apology for the Oath of Allegiance and the Premonition of the Most Serene King James of England.* In the first two of its six books, his Majesty read one of the finest criticisms of the whole Anglican position that has ever been published. In the third he found Bellarmine's theses on the indirect power, and the sovereignty of the people, developed and defended with such powerful logic as had never been brought to bear on them before. The fourth book gave him still less comfort, justifying as it did, in the calm, progressive method of scholasticism, all that Bellarmine had written on ecclesiastical immunities. The fifth book was on anti-Christ, and the last, and worst of all from the King's point of view, was a direct attack on his Oath of Allegiance which dotted the *i*'s and crossed the *t*'s of all its former assailants." [4]

It is true that Suarez got possession of the controversial works almost as soon as they appeared. It was the English monarch's custom, even when he published anonymously, to have copies delivered to all the foreign embassies, whence they would in turn find their way to the rulers of Europe. Philip III's dependence upon the judgement of Suarez and his friendship for the great theologian explain the latter's immediate access to the documents. At Rome the King's work was placed on the Index of Forbidden Books, the penalty for reading it being excommunication reserved to the Pope. At Florence and Milan the book was accepted only to be consigned ignominiously to the public bonfire, while at Vienna and Brussels the governments refused to accept James' gift copies.

The Spanish monarch seemed at first to be of the same opinion with Henry IV, who earnestly urged that the royal and amateur theologian on the English throne should not be further baited. But Pope Paul V was not of a mind to let things rest as they were in 1608, and he gave peremptory orders that Bellarmine continue the controversy. On the other side of the Mediterranean the cardinal's religious brother was even then drafting his crushing arguments against James. Philip quickly perceived

[4] Broderick, *op. cit.*, vol. ii, pp. 235–236.

the direction of the wind and grudgingly gave his approval to Suarez' plan.

The theologian worked quickly and under high pressure—as he did on every crucial occasion—and had the *Defensio Fidei* nearly completed when he received a letter from Cardinal Borghese. The letter carries an impatient tone as though even top speed were not enough to please the Holy See in the English squabble. By refuting the book of the King of England, said the cardinal on January 5, 1610, as he has promised, Father Suarez would give great pleasure to His Holiness, just as he has won much merit by previous works. The Pope wanted to see a copy of the manuscript as soon as possible, and before its printing for general publication. Suarez wrote back that he wanted a letter from the Pope, to include in the book, to give it the strongest possible authority. For some unknown reason this request was not gratified, owing perhaps to the length of time consumed in getting the book out.

It took almost three years of delays that were sometimes comical and always irritating. Suarez could not follow the high-handed example of King James who threw the royal printer, Robert Barker, into jail when pages did not come from the press so quickly or so neatly as desired. Nor could Suarez help it when one courier lost the manuscript on the way to Rome, and another, carrying it improperly packed through a drenching rain, ruined many pages so badly that they had to be rewritten. The theologian was at the same time trying to accomplish a half-dozen other assignments, the principal of which was the publication of his *De Legibus* in 1612.

In the end Suarez had to be satisfied with the customary *imprimatur* of the Holy See and he released the *Defensio Fidei* without the papal letter he so much desired, and which he thought should have been given, since the work was, in the first place, asked for by Rome. In lieu of it, however, he gathered an imposing array of approbations. The title page of the original edition carried the *imprimatur* of the Jesuit Provincial of Portugal, of the Council of the Inquisition, of the Royal Council, and of the Bishop of Coimbra. Further than that he prefaced the text itself with the personal letters of three Spanish bishops who not only read the work in manuscript but approved it in glowing terms.

The Bishop of Lamego, Martin de Mello, wrote under date of November 24, 1612, that he had thoroughly perused the *Defensio Fidei.* Francis Suarez, he continues, ". . . an illustrious author, burning with zeal for the faith, a most eminent theologian, powerful with the strength of learning, on behalf of the struggling Church of God in England, has unsheathed his pen against the raving enemies in that kingdom of heresies. . . . I consider this work very worthy of the most learned Doctor, Francis Suarez; it should be printed and published for the outstanding victory of our faith over the heretics and for the public and widespread use of the whole Christian world." [5]

The second episcopal approbation was penned by Ferdinand Mascaregni, Bishop of Algarves, on December 6th, of the same year. He examined the work down to the last detail and found it a complete living book, "nerves, blood and spirit." His opinion of the book ". . . would become a huge panegyric were it not opposed by the well-known modesty of the studious author which is accustomed to turn eulogies into jokes, praises into wounds, and flatterers into enemies. Therefore, we must congratulate the Society of Jesus, an excellent parent, which although it has produced from its holy Institute—as from a Trojan horse—many men outstanding in religion, literature and personal probity, possesses only one eminent Doctor, Father Suarez, in this present storm. He soothes the sudden tumults of error, and

[5] *Defensio Fidei Catholicae,* p. x.

like a tireless warrior, rushes from battle to battle in a way that belies his position and years. Therefore, I agree that this work should be published so that it may cast light upon the densest darknesses of error." [6]

Six months later, Castelbranco, Bishop of Coimbra and friend of Suarez, gave his opinion of the work, being especially delighted with the way the theologian had met James on his own ground. The English King fancied himself a deep student of the writings of the ancient fathers, and he was in fact uncommonly well-versed in them, considering his status of layman. But Suarez meets him man for man: Irenaeus, Dionysius, Augustine, Jerome and the rest and, according to the bishop's approving letter, easily and clearly outclasses him. Looking for the victors in this controversy, the bishop says that they are neither Suarez nor James. "The victors are not the learned Fathers of the Catholic Church, nor Luther and Calvin, those impious deserters of the true faith. Nor is it Suarez, the religious follower of the Fathers, nor the Innovators, those unfortunate followers of Luther and Calvin; but only truth has won, as is clearly shown in this book. I think it is worthy of publishing and wide perusal to the great advantage of the Catholic Church, and I rejoice that our age has produced so great a teacher and the Society of Jesus so brilliant an alumnus." [7]

Fortified by all these permissions and approvals the author himself wrote a neat little dedication of the work to those Kings and Princes who were sons and defenders of the Roman Catholic Church. Politely he reminds them that His Serene Highness of England had also dedicated a recent work to them, inviting them to use against the Church that power which God had given them for her defense. Cleverly Suarez suggests that he is answering James as their spokesman, acting merely as the interpreter of their sentiments and fidelity. For they too desire that their

[6] *Ibid.*, p. viii.   [7] *Ibid.*, p. vii.

fellow King, James, should become again the devoted protector of Christ and of His Vicar on earth.

Throughout the work Suarez is sometimes forced to handle the royal author somewhat roughly, but he protests that this course has been urged upon him by the manner in which the King himself wrote. The title itself indicates the fullness of treatment he thought necessary in the refutation of royal error. His Majesty had not limited himself to a mere justification of the Oath of Allegiance—the original source of all the trouble— but had bolstered it with the schismatic views of his predecessors, Elizabeth and Henry, defended all the heretical practices. of his new Anglican sect, repeated once more all the arguments, prejudices, calumnies of his theologians against the Holy See, going so far as to offer a demonstration that the Pope was the anti-Christ predicted by the Apocalypse. But in patiently tearing down all of these presentations, Suarez never descends to the level of rough usage on which the King himself operated.

In the foreword to the first book he rapidly and briefly runs over the controversy as it stood at the time of writing, and then warns that his discussion would follow the cold, clear method and language of the Scholastics. He would do this "even though it is not pleasing to the dissenters from our faith; perhaps because it is most capable of resurrecting truth from the shadows in which it lies, and most effective in battling errors." Thus, while he is attacking a foreign adversary, Suarez remains always the perfect scholastic theologian, wielding the weapons of his own calling which allow for precise and telling blows. The *Defensio* is naturally a polemical work, but it never stoops to the torment of the enemy; it opposes doctrine to doctrine with the set purpose of enlightenment, guidance and conviction. It is only at the conclusion of each book that the theologian personally addresses the royal author, exhorting him to come alive to the uncontestable facts that have just been presented. And even here he remembers always to address James politely in the terms of his official title: *Your Most Serene Majesty.*

The unavoidable delays attending the publication of *Defensio Fidei Catholicae* increased beyond proportion the English tenseness over its contents. For almost two years the English ambassador at the court of Philip III in Madrid knew of the impending attack, and like a reliable military scout kept his monarch informed. If the element of surprise was thus eliminated from Suarez' assault, that of anxiety was steadily increased, and when it was finally accomplished it spread like the shrapnel of a high explosive in the camp of the enemy. Rome remained calm; the Pope contenting himself with a few words to Suarez: ". . . We shall have the pleasure of reading it, knowing that from an author so pious and learned as yourself can come only a work of great merit." Even more laconic was Bellarmine's remark: "I deeply appreciate the thoughtfulness of Your Reverence. But the book is so long; and I am extremely busy. I cannot promise to read it through." Philip III wrote the author from Madrid, September 3, 1613, telling him that the book has been received and that "You have defended with great knowledge the purity and liberty of our Catholic faith, and consequently the authority of the Roman Church which I hold in very high regard." [8]

This calm appraisal of true and solid doctrine on the part of important Catholics is in direct contrast with the uproar caused by the appearance of Suarez' work in London, and later on the continent. James I got hold of a copy about the first of November. Exactly one month later Sarmiento, the Spanish ambassador at London, wrote as follows to Philip III; "Two hours ago I was told that the book of Father Suarez was going to be burned with several others. I hastened to assure myself, and learned with certitude that today at noon, by order of the Archbishop of Canterbury, who has jurisdiction over London, a minister preached

[8] De Scorraille, vol. ii, p. 188.

in the cemetery of St. Paul's Church and in the midst of his sermon produced the book of Father Suarez together with one of
Becan [the Jesuit Van de Beeck] and one of Scioppius. After
he had informed the people of the contents, he pitched the books
down from the height of his pulpit and ordered them to be
burned. Immediately on the spot two sacks of books were thrown
into the flames." [9]

Of course, the burning of an author's book is mere symbolism,
and His English Majesty was not content with such action alone.
He appointed himself to the task of having Suarez repudiated
wherever his influence could reach. Surrounding himself with
the mantle of a martyr and protesting against the diabolic mis-
chief inherent in the Spanish theologian's doctrines, James commanded the professors of Oxford to conduct a public disputation
in defense of himself and in condemnation of his traducer.
Obligingly they complied; and Suarez had the university against
him. The next move of the distraught King was a request
of all other Kings and Princes in Europe to repudiate the
Defensio.

Philip III's compliance with this royal request is well known.
He asked the Cardinal-Archbishop of Toledo to form a committee
for an examination of the work, and after some little time the
investigators solemnly declared that "not only does the work
contain nothing but the common, true doctrine admitted uni-
formly by the doctors of the Church, but that there is nothing
therein obnoxious or ill-advised in that which concerns the King
of England." Sarmiento was accordingly advised to inform
James of this report and to tell him "how greatly Philip III desired his security and happiness, adding that the best means of
obtaining them was to show much confidence in his Catholic
subjects." [10] Thwarted by this suave disregard of his wishes,

---

[9] Magner, *op. cit.*, p. 160.
[10] Watt, Lewis: "Francisco Suarez," in *Great Catholics, loc. cit.*, p. 164.

James concentrated on the scheme of bringing both Suarez and the Society of Jesus into disrepute among the French.

Unfortunately the situation in France was such that it lent itself to the outlines of James' plans. Even before the attempted assassination of Henry IV, who had been over-friendly not only with foreign Protestant powers but also with local Huguenots and Gallicans, there had appeared scurrilous pamphlets and satirical writings against the Pope and the Jesuits. The Venetian rebel, Sarpi, had advised his friend Groslot that "The most important thing is to destroy the Jesuits; if they are defeated, Rome is lost and if they are out of the way, religion will 'reform' itself of its own accord." [11] Suarez' mention of tyrannicide in the *Defensio* did not help his case, for it recalled memories of Mariana's disturbing doctrine and the hubbub aroused by the murder of Henry IV. As a matter of fact, any defense of papal rights would have caused a storm in France at that time, and it merely happened as a coincidence that the English ambassador in Paris and the French envoy in London at that time were serving James too well.

So it was that the papal nuncio to Paris, Ubaldini, sorrowfully reported to Rome on June 17, 1614: "The lawyer Servin, who was like a demon in his hatred of Rome, made a motion in Parlement, first, that the work of Suarez should be burned before the door of the three Jesuit houses in Paris, in presence of two fathers of each house; secondly, that an official condemnation of it should be entered on the records; thirdly, that the Provincial, the superior of the Paris residence, and four other Fathers should be cited before the Parlement and made to anathematize the doctrine of Suarez; and fourthly, if they refused, that all the members of the Society should be expelled from France." [12] The

[11] Cf. Pastor, *op. cit.*, vol. xxvi, pp. 26 ff.

[12] Magner, *op. cit.*, p. 161. Quoted also by Campbell, De Scorraille and others.

measure was not passed in its totality but the book was none-the-less publicly consigned to the flames and virtually condemned as it had been in England. When James learned of the incident he instructed the Archbishop of Canterbury to spread the news as widely as possible by means of the Anglican clergy. The more rabid among the Calvinists desired public celebrations but Sarmiento uneasily guessed that the united action of the English and French in this affair might grow into a united resistance against Spanish power.

Back in Coimbra the source of all this agitation and international complication was placidly going about his duties of lecturing and writing. He was more surprised than troubled by the tragic destiny of his latest work and would have preferred that he himself be mauled about by heretics than to have disrespect shown the faith through the burning of a written book. He was conversing with his good friend, Father Sebastian de Barradas, on the day the news came to him regarding the condemnation of his book in London. Sadly, and without a trace of indignation, he remarked: "May it please God that the fate of my book might also be mine, and that I may confirm with my blood and my life the doctrines which up to now I have defended only with my pen." [13]

The hot and eager disputes now going on all over Europe concerning his doctrine interested Suarez less than the fact that at least one heretic had been converted because of the *Defensio*. A young cleric of Oporto had been receiving the pages of the work as it came from the printer, and had been helping Suarez in their correction. Without the author's knowledge this priest read the proofs to a young Englishman deeply interested in the controversy who was staying for a while at Oporto. The truth about the Catholic Church thus gradually unfolded before his eyes so that he came to Coimbra and asked to be received into the

[13] De Scorraille, vol. ii, p. 218.

Church. Suarez took a childlike delight in telling Aquaviva about the conversion, remarking that good fruit had been produced from the work. "Our Lord has accorded me a very deep consolation, concerning a young Englishman from Oporto, a convert to our holy faith, who came here this summer. In the declarations he made at the tribunal of the holy Inquisition, that the reading of this book had made him understand where the truth was; and this has been included in the verbal process of his abjuration. He has persevered and I believe that he has already entered the Dominican Order." [14]

[14] *Ibid.,* p. 221.

CHAPTER XXV

Suarezian Democracy

THE CONTENTS OF ANY BOOK which is able to cause the stir attending Suarez' *Defensio Fidei Catholicae* are certainly worthy of a careful investigation. The loudest cry was raised on the score that its doctrines were antagonistic to the state, a charge that can be made only when—as was done by the French advocate Servin —isolated statements are taken from the book without regard of their context. Suarez, like every philosophical Christian, was as much a defender of the state as he was a defender of the Church. He simply wanted to put first things first, and that he did this in a clearly inoffensive manner is attested by the extraordinary influence he enjoyed in the eyes of those jealous monarchs, Philip II and Philip III. The knotty problem here was the ancient one of the double-edged sword, the supposed conflict in the wielding of both temporal and spiritual power. In his classic *De Legibus* Suarez took an unambiguous stand in stating that "the Pope has not received from Christ any secular ruling power by divine right, neither over the whole world, nor over the whole of Christendom or any part of it." [1]

Suarez' refutation of King James is a model of orderly composition and demonstrates the deadly accuracy that can be obtained by a skillful and truthful logician. Proposition follows proposition with the pounding regularity of a scientific battering ram. In the first book he weakens the entire Anglican structure by

[1] *De Legibus,* III, 8, 10.

304

removing most of the props from under it, and in the second he tumbles the whole edifice to the ground by a few well-placed blows.

The first truth needing demonstration was the fact that England had fallen away from the Catholic Church, that the Anglicans were in schism, and that James was not, therefore, the *Defensor Fidei* he claimed himself to be. Suarez turns historian in showing that Henry VIII made the break with orthodoxy, that Edward introduced the Zwinglians, and Elizabeth the Calvinists. Now James has turned and squirmed in every direction trying to justify his position and to avoid the stigma of heresy; but every possible argument in his favor is here laid bare and refuted. The theologian concludes the first book with an apostrophe to His Most Serene Highness, and Most Prudent King, asking him to listen to the voice of the Lord, slough off his human respect, embrace again the ancient glorious title of Defender of the Roman Catholic Church.

In the second book Suarez is treading the even more familiar ground of theological mysteries which James, in an amateurish way, had attempted to explain. The King's objective had been to demonstrate that he and his churchmen enjoyed the true Catholic interpretation of the Holy Eucharist, Transubstantiation, the Holy Sacrifice of the Mass, devotion to the Blessed Virgin and the saints, veneration of images, Purgatory, ecclesiastical rites and blessings. It was child's play for the Spanish theologian to shatter these errors and to give a brief conspectus of the truth. Concluding again with a petition for His Majesty to come back to the fold, Suarez asks: "Are you afraid that you will suffer some human loss, that your authority will be lessened if you subject yourself to the Roman Pontiff? Rest assured that the Roman Pontiff seeks you, not your possessions; for obedience to the faith does not diminish a realm, but rather increases a temporal while it prepares an eternal kingdom, the keys of which were committed to the Roman Pontiff who is therefore solicitous of your welfare. So that you may believe this fact, the following book will show that your right and power are your very own." [2]

The third book did not please James I any more than the first and second, for it combated his clumsy theory of the divine right of kings. But this book has put Suarez on a pedestal of immortality among political students, who have written under his image the title: *First Modern Democrat*. The title is not fully deserved, for Suarez was not an innovator. His claim to fame in this regard lies in that he was the first and foremost author to expose in an unmistakably classic text the old Scholastic theory of the origin of political power.[3] This third book is a classic not in the sense that modern men refer to it in hushed tones—and never read it—but in the sense that it is still a source of the greatest practical utility. People read it and study it. Never before or since has anyone put the question and its solution in a more orderly fashion, and the current vogue of Suarez' book is an objective criterion of its modern worth.

Suarez' pivotal proposition, then, was the ancient Catholic opposition to state absolutism in favor of democratic control by the people. The whole doctrine is summarized in this wise: Political power is an *essential attribute* of the people, who constitute a corporate entity; it is radically and fundamentally *inalienable*, but for convenience and efficiency it may be transferred, by and with the *consent of the community*, for such time and under such conditions as the people deem expedient for the common good.

[2] *Defensio Fidei Catholicae*, II, xvi, 13.

[3] The theory that monarchy is not a divine prerogative is found in patristic writings as well as among the Scholastic forerunners of Suarez. In the sixteenth and seventeenth centuries it was common knowledge among Catholics. The divine right of Kings was a Protestant idea at that time. O'Rahilly has checked sixty important Scholastic predecessors of Suarez who maintained the doctrine of popular supremacy and government by consent. Cf. O'Rahilly, Alfred: "The Sovereignty of the People," *Studies*, Dublin, March, 1921, p. 43.

The ultimate test of the juridical validity of any system of government is the consent of the governed.[4]

Thus was the Spanish theologian diametrically opposed to the central thesis of the English King. With a prejudiced pedantry James and his Protestant defenders perpetrated a major fallacy in their assertion of divine right when they claimed that political power came immediately and directly from God to King. All authority is from God, therefore the King's authority is from God. As O'Rahilly points out, it is as though the capitalist should argue that all property is from God, therefore his property is from God. Suarez argues cogently and emphatically that the people stand between God and the King, that political power is given immediately by God to the community as a whole, that it is then distributed by the consent, tacit or explicit, of the people. "Natural reason shows only that this political power is necessary in the whole community, and not in one person, or in a senate; therefore in so far as it is immediately from God, it can be understood to be only in the whole community and not in any part of it. . . . From natural reason no argument can be excogitated why this power should be determined to one person, or to a certain number of persons less than the whole community, rather than to another; therefore from the force of natural concession it is immediately only in the people."[5]

Coming down to concrete application of political power, Suarez claims therefore that wherever it is legitimately exercised by a king or senate it is exercised only by the free delegation of the citizens. Naturally, modern nations are too unwieldy to allow the immediate administration of authority by all the people; thus for the sake of expediency they hand it over to a particular man or set of men. Representative democracies were even

---

[4] *Ibid.*, p. 49. The italics are mine. Cf. also Suarez, *Defensio*, III, 2; where in several places he refers to the antiquity of the thesis and mentions some who taught it.

[5] *Defensio Fidei Catholicae*, III, 2, 7.

then had in concrete examples, he points out, in the republics of Venice and Genoa where the people kept the supreme authority for themselves while they exercised it through elected delegates.

He throws an attractive bait to the royal theologian when he admits that "it is not altogether true to say that a king depends on the people for his power, even though he has received it from them, for he can depend on the people for his coming to have the power and not for its preservation if he has received it fully and absolutely." But even this remark about a king's full and absolute power is adroitly explained by Suarez when he warns that there is always a bilateral *contract* existing between people and king. Thus the authority that is actually transferred by the people is held by the monarch in virtue of a political contract which binds both the ruler and his subjects.[6] The alienation of power is not undemocratic. It can in certain circumstances be revoked by the people as even the divine rightists must have admitted in the case of James I's son and successor, King Charles I.

Since Suarez was simply restating in clearer terms the ancient heritage of political teaching, it is doubtful whether he could have anticipated the world-shaking results of this third book of the *Defensio* (and of the similar treatment he worked out in the *De Legibus*). He could see, indeed, the English brand of absolutism exemplified before his eyes, but he had no way of foretelling the full-blown kingly absolutism which would immediately precede the French Revolution, nor the various types of liberalism which would then follow right up to our own times. It was impossible to know that even certain Scholastics, like Taparelli, Rickaby, Cronin and others, would go so far in their criticisms as to misinterpret some of his fundamental concepts. Nor, again, that the founders of the American form of democracy would—

[6] *Ibid.*, III, 3, 3–4.

unconsciously it seems—pattern their Constitution on his and on Bellarmine's doctrines.

In an age of brilliant authors and thinkers, Suarez was far and above the most competent exponent of juristic affairs, but since he could not forestall objections that would arise centuries later it is foolish of us to expect that he answered every conceivable objection in so many words. It is a fact too that many of the later English writers took over his theses almost bodily without ever acknowledging their source of information, while at the same time they claimed to be writing against all "Jesuits."

The famed Thomas Hobbes is a prime example of this unethical and contradictory practice among the English political theorists. In his *Leviathan,* which appeared in 1651, he made his only —and contemptuous—reference to Suarez by asking: "When men write whole volumes of such stuffe, are they not Mad or intent to make others so?" This was a broadside at the *Disputationes Metaphysicae,* which many others of Hobbes' ilk, untrained in Scholastic precision, found somewhat beyond their intellectual comprehension. But he significantly fails to acknowledge that his *De Corpore Politico,* which appeared in 1640, was to some extent a plagiarism of Suarez' proposition that government depends on the agreement of the people. Thus it was that the connecting link was broken between the great seventeenth-century exposition of Catholic democracy and the acceptance of the Declaration of Independence in the following century. Ironically, the influence of Suarez came to America through the English Whigs and Puritans who had no qualms of conscience in attributing to themselves the democratic doctrines which they lifted bodily from the Spanish theologian.[7]

"We hold these truths to be self-evident," agreed the signers of the American Declaration of Independence, "that all men are

[7] Cf. McNamara, S. J.: *American Democracy and Catholic Doctrine;* Ryan, J., Millar, M.: *State and Church.*

created equal, that they are endowed by their Creator with certain inalienable rights, that among these are life, liberty, and the pursuit of happiness. That, to secure these rights, governments are instituted among men, deriving their just power from the consent of the governed. That, whenever any form of government becomes destructive of these ends, it is the right of the people to alter or abolish it and to institute new government."

A close parallel can be drawn from various statements in the third book of the *Defensio* of which the Declaration is a summary, but more than a decade before the work was published Suarez had been teaching in his classes that "from the nature of things all men are born equal; hence there is no reason why political jurisdiction or dominion should be attributed naturally to one person rather than another. . . . Political power did not arise until several families came to form an autonomous community. Since that community did not come into being by the creation of Adam or through his will, but through the will of all who formed it, we cannot reasonably maintain that from the nature of things Adam had political primacy in that community. It is not due the progenitor, by force of natural right, that he should be also the king of his descendants. But neither have we any reason for saying that God has given him this power by special gift of providence, since there is no evidence of this fact in divine revelation. . . . We conclude that no man has power of political jurisdiction immediately from God. Therefore this power, by force of natural right alone, resides in the community of men." [8]

The political doctrine of Suarez is of such supreme importance at the present time that it calls for a brief summation here. In its barest outline it is contained in the following points: (a) God is the source and sole determining cause of the essential nature of civil society and sovereignty; (b) the proximate causes

[8] *De Legibus*, III, 2, 3–4.

that have brought men to live together in a civil community are different, according to time and conditions, but authority is always there as an essential unifying principle; (*c*) civil society originates in the free consent of the people who form that society, which consent is a proximate cause of its existence; (*d*) the people may transfer their own political power so that the form of any government is monarchic, aristocratic, democratic, or any other legitimate form; (*e*) the people cannot give up the right to change the subject of authority or the form of government should the common good demand such change.[9]

It is noteworthy that the biographer, De Scorraille, who has written more fully and more competently on Suarez than anyone else, and who in other things goes along approvingly with his hero, deserts him in this one doctrine of political sovereignty. He reproduces with apparent agreement the many objections hurled against the Suarezian consent theory, those from the moral order, from history, from politics, from logic. "This is not the place to give a lesson in natural law," he says, "but it is apropos to observe that this scholastic doctrine was criticised much more at a later date than at that time. Modern philosophers have opposed serious objections to it." But all of these objections have been answered in various places by the more recent defenders of Suarez, and it is as unnecessary as it is impossible to deal with them here.

The third book of the *Defensio*—really a mine of political information—likewise takes up the absorbing topic of the two supreme powers, the temporal and the spiritual. Do Christian kings enjoy supreme power in civil and temporal matters? James I had claimed supreme power even in spiritual affairs, but Suarez interrupts the controversy to investigate whether he has it first

[9] Cf. Thomas F. Wallace's interesting interpretation of Suarez' theory as contained in specific portions of *De Legibus* and *Defensio*. *Proceedings of the American Catholic Philosophical Association*, "The Political Philosophy of Suarez," 1931, St. Louis University, pp. 96–105.

in merely temporal matters. "Although, as I said, we have no quarrel with the King on this point, nevertheless he often complains that Catholics deny the jurisdiction of Christian princes and the obedience due to them; therefore I think we should not overlook the question at this point, because by its solution it will be clear that *the royal power of Christian princes where it is in agreement with natural law, is preserved in its integrity, according to Catholic doctrine."* He cites the weighty opinions contrary to this, but then remarks that "Christian kings do possess civil power which is supreme in its own order. . . . They recognize no other as their direct superior within that same temporal or civil order, upon whom they inherently depend in the exercise of their own power." This is proved by the fact that there were many temporal kings, as those of Spain, France and England, who are individually and entirely free from the temporal jurisdiction of others.[10]

So much for the royal right to temporal power; but what of the Pope's similar right? Suarez proves that His Holiness does not enjoy *supreme and universal temporal* power, but that his power does extend over the Roman kingdom, or patrimony of Peter. Now the title to complete domination could have come through positive divine right only if Christ Himself had made some such gift to Peter, who passed it on legitimately to his successors. But Christ did not do this, as is evident from history and ecclesiastical tradition; "therefore no supernatural evidence can be given in support of such direct and temporal jurisdiction of the Pontiff, and it is false to attribute it to him since he cannot enjoy it except through some supernatural title." [11]

But these truthful concessions do not force Suarez to soften his blows when he comes to the very heart of the controversy with the King of England. It is his forthright contention that the Pope may use coercive power against kings, even to the ex-

[10] *Defensio,* III, 5, 3–7.   [11] *Ibid.,* III, 5, 14.

tent of deposing them from their kingdoms, if there is adequate cause. In the twenty-third chapter Suarez gives numerous proofs and examples of the papal power to inflict punishment of a temporal as well as spiritual nature, for "ecclesiastical correction and punishment consist, not in a spiritual censure alone, but also, at times, in affliction of the body; and accordingly, the pastors of the Church may resort to temporal punishment for the sake of spiritual welfare." [12]

Reason itself teaches us, as the Spanish theologian reminded the Anglican monarch, that the possession of such coercive power by the Pope is necessary, if we are to keep the proper order of things. It is necessary for both the correction and the punishment of temporal princes so that they can make amends for their injuries and give satisfaction to God and to His Church. It is necessary too for the adequate protection of the prince's subjects, whose eternal salvation is endangered by evil rulers.

Besides the discussions of democratic theory and of the relative powers of kings and popes, there is another most interesting question brought up by Suarez in this book, and continued in the sixth book of the *Defensio.* It is the question of tyrannicide, which naturally finds place in an argument against His Majesty of England. The killing of kings was commonly advocated in those times; and only a perversion of the truth can attribute this advocacy exclusively to the Jesuits, whether because of Mariana's unfortunate book, *De Rege,*[13] the contentions of Bellarmine and Suarez, or the false charges that the Society was in back of several royal assassinations in the sixteenth and seventeenth centuries. Among the Protestants, tyrannicide was vigorously preached. John Knox, for example, asserted that it was the duty of the English people to condemn Queen Mary Stuart

---

[12] *Ibid.,* III, 23, 13.
[13] Cf. Laures, John: *The Political Economy of Juan De Mariana,* New York, 1928, Fordham Press; especially the chapter on Tyrannicide, pp. 61–70.

to death. Luther taught that the community might condemn a tyrant to death, while Melanchthon went even further by preaching that the murder of a tyrant was man's best offering to a just God.

Now Suarez gradually worked up to a treatment of this problem as he approached the climax of his work in the sixth book: a direct attack on James' Oath of Allegiance. The fourth and fifth books lead the way, the former justifying at great length the right of ecclesiastical immunity, about which the theologian had written so trenchantly against the Venetians. James had ruefully declared that a third of his subjects were withdrawn from his authority by this immunity; but Suarez calmly proceeded to a definition of its limits, and ably demonstrated the reasons and advantages inherent in the exemptions which clerics in every Christian realm enjoyed. The fifth book was discomfiting to the royal theologian and quoter of Sacred Scriptures since it treated that unique and personal phenomenon, the anti-Christ. Subtly Suarez tells the King that the efforts of the anti-Christ will all be directed to a destruction of the Holy Apostolic See, and that anyone who dares attack the Pope of Rome is *ipso facto* a precursor of that evil genius, and is preparing the path for him.

Thus finally in his piercing analysis of the King's Oath Suarez comes to the thorny and highly controversial question: Is it permissible for a private person to slay a tyrannical monarch? He does not assume that James is a tyrant in the sense that he came by his authority unjustly and by force; it is rather that this legitimate King is ruling in an oppressive manner. "Even though a prince govern tyrannically," admits Suarez, "he cannot licitly be murdered on private authority." The heretics Wyclif and Hus had contended that a prince who commits a mortal sin loses his sovereignty and can be brought up for trial by his subjects. But the Council of Constance, held in 1415, almost two centuries previous to this controversy, had condemned the proposition that: "a tyrant may and should licitly and deservedly, be slain by the agency of any of his vassals and subjects, even though this be effected by means of secret snares and subtle blandishments or flattery." [14]

The Spanish theologian goes even farther than that when he speaks of the dignity of rulers, and asserts that the life of the prince should be preferred to one's own. The prince represents God in that he is exercising the authority which ultimately comes from God. If he is a capable monarch he is in the unique position of one who is indispensable to the welfare of the community and whose preservation is consequently more important than that of an ordinary subject. Actually, however, it is permissible for a private person to kill the lawful monarch only on the grounds of self-defense, and this reason will not be present unless the king begins an unjust war upon his own kingdom and inflicts violence on his subjects. But if the prince in question is a heretic the case against him is somewhat stronger.

Suarez remarks that it is most displeasing to the King of England to hear this opinion. But, referring to his arguments in the third book, he asserts the proposition to be most true: that the punishment of deposition and the deprivation of power may be imposed upon a temporal monarch. The community as a whole may unseat the king, and in this extraordinary procedure the people are supported by the authority of the natural law. The Pope by his direct power may depose a king in the case of a spiritual crime, like heresy, when the general welfare of the Church requires it. Again by his direct power he may punish temporal crimes when they are temporarily injurious to a Christian kingdom; and by his indirect power when the actions of the prince are noxious to the spiritual welfare of Christian souls.[15]

Now the matter of king-killing again comes up when Suarez decides how the punishment is to take place and who is to exe-

[14] *Defensio*, VI, 4, 2–3.   [15] *Ibid.*, VI, 4, 15–17.

cute the lawfully passed sentence. The power to impose a just
sentence presupposes the power to execute the punishment included, but no private person can take to himself the right to
slay the king unless he were commissioned by the community
or its lawful representatives. He will then be acting in the name
of the state and on public authority. Likewise, when the sentence
has been imposed by the Pontiff, the deposition and slaying can
be achieved only by the person, or persons, appointed by him.
Thus, while Suarez surrounds the proposition with all the necessary and legitimate conditions he adheres steadily to these two
fundamental points: a tyrant may be legitimately slain; the slaying cannot be done by a private person and on private authority.[16]

Driving remorselessly to the conclusion of his work against
the King, the theologian proves that the Oath of Allegiance cannot be taken by Catholics because it is an excessive assumption
of power, an injustice against morality, and an error opposed
to the true Catholic doctrine. The Pontiff not only can but must
prohibit the English Catholics from taking such an oath; they
may not coöperate with the Anglican heretics in their public
worship, and they must be considered as the victims of a real
religious persecution. In his peroration he tells the King that
all of this argumentation has been written in the spirit of charity;
and he offers to supply even more proofs, fuller explanations,
and lengthier answers in the event that the King or his ministers
are not entirely satisfied with this work. Needless to say, the
King was more than satisfied that all had been said. In lieu of
logic he answered with the only weapons he could wield: direct
and abusive physical action.

[16] *Ibid.*, VI, 4, 18–19.

CHAPTER XXVI

Other Works and Days

FAME IS A FICKLE jade in any age and Suarez discovered her changing aspects on several occasions during the hectic months following publication of his *Defensio Fidei Catholicae*. Many times in the past the theologian had taken on all comers, fellow Jesuits, fellow Catholics, heretical Christians, telling them off one by one. Now again his fame turned to infamy in the eyes of critics. Fire-eating Protestants were, of course, the principal objectors, but there were other antagonists, and these within the folds of both the Church and the Society. Mainly their complaint centered on the treatise about tyrannicide, asserting that the theologian went against the known wishes of Pope Paul V and his predecessors in the mere fact that he mentioned the mooted subject. Claudius Aquaviva, too, and his forerunners had been chary of the question ever since both the assassination of Henry III and the attempts on the life of Henry of Navarre had been attributed to Jesuit machinations.

Most serious, it seemed, was the charge that Suarez openly flouted the Jesuit general's recent decree regarding the discussion of regicide. But the theologian had an airtight defense. In the first place, Aquaviva's prohibition had not been promulgated in his province; thus it did not bind him even if he had been aware of its existence. Anyway the work against King James would not have been complete without the inclusion of this proposition. Secondly, at Coimbra, as well as throughout the whole Iberian peninsula, the theory of king-killing was an object of free and frequent debate. No one prevented it there, and everyone agreed that Suarez had simply repeated the ancient and approved Scholastic doctrine on the matter. Finally, his manuscript had undergone a searching scrutiny at Coimbra by official censors, and a double revision at Rome by representatives of both the Pope and the general. If there was any error in it they should have made the discovery and the complaints at that time.

So he was clear of that attack. He fully demonstrated once again that he was as jealous of his obedience and prudence, as a religious member of the Society of Jesus, as he was careful of his honor and integrity as a theological luminary of the Catholic Church. In the few remaining years of his life he was singularly at ease with his own fellow Catholics.

In the school year, 1613–1614, Suarez taught the highly important theological course, *De Fide,* later incorporated in the posthumously published work *De Fide, Spe et Charitate.* During the following year, his last in the lecture hall, the subject matter of his course bore the attractive title: *De Infidelibus et Haeresibus.* If there was one man then living who could competently teach this course, it was Suarez himself; for he knew intimately the ideas and practices of such people, from the Jews and Moors in Southern Spain, the Venetians in Italy, Huguenots in France, and Anglicans in Britain. It was in a sense a vindication of his whole controversy in defense of the Catholic Faith and included a dissertation on the English and French reactions to the *Defensio.*

Fortunately there have been preserved at Lisbon two interesting documents, memorials in which Suarez broke down the decree of the French Parlement on his work. The first is a Spanish translation of the decree, underlined and carefully annotated in Suarez' own hand, and showing the numerous errors it contained. The other is a treatise in which the theologian sits in judgement over his judges and logically comes to the decision that he must condemn his own condemners. His opponent had been all-embracing when they charged that his work "contains pernicious and scandalous doctrine in matters of faith; and consequently it merits to be condemned and prohibited by the Church, as it bears in itself the proof." [1]

Suarez stood in the lecture hall at the University of Coimbra, brilliantly excoriating the magistrates of Paris for their blind subservience to James I. These French Catholics had made a botch of theology, approving doctrines condemned by the Church and condemning authors approved by the Holy Father. They had lacked respect toward the prelates and doctors who praised the *Defensio,* and were particularly unfortunate in censuring the Bishop of Algarves' remark about the crown King Clovis sent to Pope Hormisdas. Suarez placed them on the horns of a dilemma when he said: "If they deny this fact they are like the heretics who are ever ready to question ecclesiastical authority; if they reject the interpretation the Bishop puts on it they are antagonistic to pontifical authority." [2] Servin merits Suarez' special attention, for the French advocate had criticized him for quoting examples of depositions of kings other than Spanish because he "wished to show that the kings of Spain were exempt from the so-called pontifical jurisdiction to which he submits the others." The theologian countered with a denial, asserting that as far as he knew none of these Spanish kings had ever deserved to have pontifical authority exercised against him.

Arguments and discussions of this nature may be considered in the light of a private quarrel between Suarez and his opponents. Sometimes they remained thus, and the theologian was

---

[1] De Scorraille, vol. ii, p. 219.

[2] Actually, Clovis made his submission to St. Remigius, Bishop of Rheims, when he was baptized on Christmas Day, 496. The King of the Franks was born 466 and died 511. St. Hormisdas became Pontiff only three years later, reigning from 514 to 523.

able to overcome his detractors by the mere force of his cold logic; but at other times—as we have seen—they became the common property of popes, kings, cardinals, and religious leaders. These disputes were personal things and frequently enough they were personally aggravating simply because of the precious time they wasted in Suarez' well-husbanded years.

There was a conflict of another sort, however, upon which the theologian did a great amount of speculation and writing. This was the matter of physical warfare, upon which his theories are so lucid and illuminating that they deserve a large space in a modern world that has not yet learned to keep the peace. As a man of peaceful disposition he was naturally averse to human killing, whether in organized war among nations or in disorganized feuding among private persons. He abhorred war but loved justice. The combination of the two fascinated him throughout all his writings on political economy but, strangely, he gave his clearest exposition in a place where we would least expect to find it: the treatise on Charity.

Suarez was mediæval-minded on the question of armed warfare. But the technique of both land and naval battles was undergoing a rapid change at the close of his life. The world had experienced almost a century of continual warfare, most of it in the old style hand-to-hand fighting; even the relatively recent Battle of Lepanto had been fought in this way. The method of the Armada did not differ greatly from that of Don Juan. Rebellions among the English subjects, religious wars on the continent, the defense of the Christians against the Moors and the Turks—all of these had occurred within the span of a long lifetime; and now Europe was on the threshold of the Thirty Years War.

In his *De Legibus* the Spanish theologian must have seen that the scholastic concept of war was being gradually outmoded, that even Catholic rulers were abandoning the principle of remedial and retributive war for the unjust practice of war as a national policy or expediency. Consequently he bent even greater effort toward bringing out the true doctrine, asserting that no war can be just on both sides, and that the power of declaring war is a power of jurisdiction which pertains to vindictive justice. It must always be considered a punishment meted out to alien malefactors. As Professor O'Rahilly remarks: "It refuses to allow us to glorify war as a positive 'policy' or to see in it the natural expression of man's higher nature . . . war, no more than slavery, is not natural to man. It is true that a righteous war may enlist sympathy and inspire generosity; but the legitimacy of such enthusiasm and coöperation is strictly conditioned by the existence of wrong and injustice. Thus the approval of war is not absolute and unlimited but hypothetical and provisional, it can never be dissociated from the attribution of grievous injustice and sin. For it is only in a fallen world that war can be envisaged as necessary or desirable; the battlefield is the extreme assertion of criminal jurisdiction." [3]

From the start it must be understood that neither Suarez nor any of his great Scholastic predecessors ever considered war as anything but a last resort, a crude and clumsy means which must be employed only after more rational attempts at the enforcement of justice have failed. "Men should be able to institute some means of satisfaction, or to give that power to some third ruler, an arbiter." [4] This is the belief of Suarez, and in another place he argues that Christian princes need not have recourse to war since they can always use the Pontiff to settle their differences justly.[5]

The theologian argues that although war, theoretically speaking, is not intrinsically evil, it may be undertaken "only in cases

[3] O'Rahilly, Alfred: "The Catholic View of War," in *Studies*, Dublin, June, 1918, pp. 228–229.

[4] *De Legibus*, II, 19, 8.

[5] *De Fide, Spe et Charitate*, III, 13, 5.

of extreme necessity, when no alternative remains," that is, only in those very rare cases where, if the evil of war were avoided even greater evils would result. But a legitimate war, whether defensive or aggressive, must always be hedged about with certain conditions; and it is improbable that these stringent conditions have been fulfilled more than a half-dozen times in the history of the world.

The rules of honest warfare, therefore, are enumerated by Suarez as follows: First, the war must be declared and conducted by lawful political power. Secondly, there must be a just cause for its inception. Finally, it must be conducted in its beginning, prosecution and conclusion, or victory, on a basis of uniform and prescribed equality. If any of these conditions are not fulfilled the war is unjust and *a fortiori* contrary to charity. It is immoral if some of the people, contrary to the supreme temporal authority in the state, institute it; if even the rightful authority wages it for the sake of the "balance of power," or some other political or economic advantage; or if there is undue brutality on the part of soldiers either during the war or after it. In those days a theologian could still write for the benefit of Christian nations to the effect that the Pope has indirect power in temporal affairs and should therefore be consulted as an umpire in international disputes.[6]

This papal tribunal had often served as a kind of mediæval Peace Palace of The Hague (now again unhappily inoperative) but the Pope had no means nor any desire to force himself upon contestants for their arbitration. At such a court, however, a regular law suit would be followed, according to which whole nations could be judged and punished, and the advocate would be a true international lawyer. "Although Suarez was both a moralist and a theologian," notes Scott, "he was also a lawyer to his fingertips, because in his day law was an integral branch

[6] *Ibid.*, III, 13, 2.

of theology, the theologians alone having a philosophy of law and the practising lawyer merely a precedent or text of the law. . . . And it should be repeated in this connection that the only justification for war during the middle ages was the absence of a court between the states for the redress of an injury received." [7]

In our present day there is much agitation for a popular referendum to decide whether or not a nation should go to war, which means nothing more than that the question of war should be brought before the tribunal of the people so that they may decide whether or not the war is just. Suarez contributed some illuminating thoughts to this modern proposal, declaring that there are really three groups of persons to be considered: the administration itself, that is, the ruling prince or senate; the generals and other chief men of the state; and finally, the combatants themselves (among whom would be included practically the whole citizenry under modern warfare).

Suarez is obsessed with the idea that a judicial inquiry should be held before the disaster of war is allowed to occur. Therefore the supreme authority in the government is obliged to ascertain the state of the question, learn what his own rights are and whether these rights have been infringed. Knowledge is necessary here, and the prince, or senate, should seek the advice of learned men, weigh the case carefully with them, and then commit the nation to war only if they decide that their case is just. The second group, the generals and other leading men, are obliged to study the justice of the proposed war, though their obligation is not so serious as that of the governmental administration itself. If the war is just they may participate in it; if it is unjust they may not.

Now the third group is the most numerous, the rank and file of soldiers who were not called upon to give advice and counsel when a war was being contemplated. In Suarez' day most com-

[7] Scott, *op. cit.*, p. 443. Cf. the whole of chapter twelve.

mentators believed that the mass of the army was not obliged to
investigate the causes and morality of war, but simply to follow
the decisions of the sovereign and his counsellors. Many moderns take the same stand, holding logically that it is impossible
for each individual to weigh the matter judiciously and to come
to a proper decision, the idea being that the responsibility lies
solely with the ruling authority. But conditions have certainly
changed since the age of Suarez. Literacy and improved com-
munication have made possible a knowledge of world conditions
that was out of the question at the beginning of the seventeenth
century. And even Suarez made the significant remark that the
soldiers could not morally allow themselves to fight if they
knew that the war was clearly unjust. Since to-day practically
every person in the nation may be conceived to be an active participant in a modern war, that principle must be applied to all,
and not merely to the men in the army.

Many of the wars previous to the time of Suarez had been
fought with a large proportion of professional soldiers, or mercenaries, and it is only natural that he should devote some consideration to their status in a moral or immoral war. Mercenaries
no longer play a large part in modern warfare but, connected
with this problem, there is another of the utmost twentieth-
century importance. It is the current problem of the sale of arms
to belligerents; and the theologian had some passing comments
to make on its advisability and morality.

Where it is impossible to ascertain which side of the conflict
is just, says Suarez, that is, where one is in doubt about the justice of either party he may sell arms to both. But there is this
significant risk attached to selling arms: if it turns out that the
purchaser is fighting in an unjust cause the seller of armament
has incurred a liability for the injury caused to the nation with
justice on its side. Thus the neutral who is out to make war profits
is really in a quandary unless he knows positively and without

the slightest doubt that the belligerent whom he is assisting is waging a just war. If he sells to both parties he is committing a manifestly immoral act since the principle always holds that justice can be on the side of only one of the belligerents. In other words, "He must either sell to one party only, assuming the dangerous task of judging the merits of the controversy, incurring the enmity of the other party, and, in short, losing his neutral status—for the neutral, as a neutral, should not and indeed cannot assume the role of friend to one belligerent and of enemy to the other—or, if he treats both parties alike, furnishing arms to both, he cannot avoid the consequence that he has contributed in no small measure to the waging of an unjust war, often doing more harm, as Suarez says, than the soldiers themselves." [8]

Preoccupied with these and similar thoughts attendant upon the great struggle against James and the English heretics, Suarez came to the close of his teaching career at the University of Coimbra. One day near the end of July, 1615, he appeared in the class room as usual, took up the subject matter where he had left off the day before, and proceeded to give the final arguments in defense of the Catholic position against schismatical and heretical errors. But this day was different from all other days in the lecturer's life for it marked the official close of more than forty years of teaching.

The news of Suarez' approaching retirement had spread over all the city and everyone expectantly awaited this last lecture. When it came it seemed no different from the others, thousands of them, that had been delivered year in and year out by the eminent Jesuit. But the hall was packed with his legions of admirers who respectfully and tensely waited for the master to sum up his arguments, embellish them with the authority of the

---

[8] *Ibid.*, p. 466. Suarez treats the question of military participation on the part of soldiers, and that of selling armament in *De Fide, Spe et Charitate*, III, 13, 6.

Fathers and of reason itself, and to conclude with the customary admonition that "all truth is contained in the Church; for she was founded by the source of truth Himself." Tumult broke loose in the audience. People rushed to the dais to kiss his hand, to congratulate him, to assure this sixty-seven-year-old professor that there would never be any one to take his place. The old man was overwhelmed by the Latin exuberance of the people. There were tears of emotion in his eyes as they escorted him in a triumphant procession back to the Jesuit residence.

Suarez' realization of his long-petitioned retirement did not mean that he would spend the rest of his days in elegant idleness. Nothing was farther from his mind. The evening of life was growing late and the disabilities of his mortal body had warned him too often that death could not be far in the distance. There was a mass of literary composition still to be attended to, projects that had lain dormant simply because there was no time for them. There was also the public duty which devolved upon him in his capacity of consulting theologian. There were so many things to be done and so little time in which to do them.

The theologian's letters to his friends during this period of so-called retirement are indicative of the strenuous routine he followed. He wrote to Father Albornoz in the Summer of 1615 that he had put the finishing touches to his monumental *De Gratia* but that its printing had not yet begun. The third part of *De Religione* was likewise ready for publication, while the fourth part was now in the hands of the Jesuit general at Rome. It happened, however, that he would not live to see either of these works printed and published. The death of Aquaviva complicated things for a while, and then the other usual delays, to which Suarez was long accustomed, held back the work. In fact, none of the remaining works of Suarez were published between 1613, when the *Defensio* appeared, and 1617, when the theologian died.

Steadily progressing through the revision of an immense amount of material at hand, Suarez was able to put several philosophical manuscripts into final form. They were respectively, the *De Angelis,* a highly speculative and metaphysical treatise on the spirit world; the *De Opere Sex Dierum,* a thorough study of Creation; and a careful psychological work entitled, *De Anima.* Several other works included in Vives' edition *Opera Omnia* were assembled by him in their entirety, but were later edited by Father Balthazar Alvarez, his friend and literary executor.

In these last years the theologian was consulted on almost every major question that came up for decision in Spain and Portugal. The Archbishop of Coimbra and the King of Spain were constantly asking his advice and opinion on every question from the Immaculate Conception and Predestination to the comparative civil rights of clergy and laity. By means of letters and memorials Suarez contributed a vast amount of literary work and erudition which has never been edited or published. Some of it was later collected and edited under the title *Consilia et Variae Quaestiones,* but the greater portion of it has perished or is still lurking among the inaccessible documents of libraries. A conservative estimate of the theologian's complete literary output would compute it at upwards of twenty-one million words. In terms of modern literary forms this would account for more than two hundred and eighty novels of seventy-five thousand words apiece. Truly a gigantic task for any author, but when we consider that all of Suarez' work was done in the highly precise and technical fields of theology, philosophy, and law, the comparison between him and a modern novelist limps badly. *Prolific* is a weak adjective to apply to him.

CHAPTER XXVII

The Sweetness of Death

IN THE ORDINARY COURSE of human events a man does not deliberately set about the business of dying, yet Suarez, in the Spring of 1617, contemplated some such process in preparation for the end of his days. "The remainder of his life," says Siegfried, "was devoted to study and prayer; or perhaps we should put it the other way, to prayer and study; for how deeply soever he loved knowledge, and no matter how ardently he pursued it, he was ready to abandon it all rather than sacrifice one hour of intimate communion with God. He devoted six hours daily to prayer and contemplation, three in the morning and three after his frugal midday repast. He took no food before noon, and kept three days of strict fast weekly, besides those of the vigils of the festivals of Our Lord, the Blessed Virgin, and some of the Saints. His moments of greatest joy were those he spent at the altar. Repeatedly he was seen wrapt in contemplation, his body uplifted from the earth, and bathed in a bright light." [1]

Naturally a man who so cherished prayer would be expected to demand more and more time for it as he approached the hour of death. But the Spanish theologian was an obedient man as well as a prayerful one. He made a fervent retreat in April of his last year, during which he was strongly tempted to give up all thought of his literary work in order to give all his time to the contemplation of eternity. For a while his conscience was in

[1] Siegfried, *op. cit.*, p. 269.

suspense: the books were calling for completion, but his soul was calling too for the unbounded satisfaction of complete prayer and meditation. As in other similar quandaries Suarez knew that the will of God could be made known to him through his superior, God's representative on earth. Consequently, before the end of the retreat he made a general confession of his entire religious life to his rector, Father Antonio d'Abreu, and asked his advice concerning the decision which he felt ought to be made by him.

The Jesuit rector solved his difficulty with ease, telling him that these great talents of his clearly demonstrated what God wished him to do, that his vocation was to defend and explain the truths of Catholicism, that his previous works and successes obliged him to continue in the same way to the end. To follow out the decision was easy, and the theologian worried no more about the temptation.

He decided to take his manuscripts and secretary to the more salubrious climate of the Jesuit novitiate at Lisbon, and to work there during the summer. On the way to Lisbon he stopped for a short visit with his friend, Rodrigo da Cunha, Bishop of Portalegre, who wished his advice on several ecclesiastical problems. Thus, for the last time, he departed from Coimbra where he had spent almost the whole of two decades in the brilliant service of the Church and the Society. He spent a few days with the prelate en route, where he found the bishop's problem to be the serious one then current in Portugal, the conflict between civil and ecclesiastical jurisdiction. He mapped out a course of action for the bishop, took his leave from him and arrived at Lisbon about the beginning of June.

At Lisbon Suarez walked into one of the most disgraceful entanglements it had ever been his misfortune to encounter. The tranquillity he hoped to find at the novitiate there was almost immediately dissipated by his being drawn into the famous affair

of the interdict. It all started with the conflict between Church
and state over property and civil rights, and ended only after
Suarez' death and through the instrumentality of his juridical
knowledge.

In previous times, both before and after Philip II added Portugal to the Spanish empire, the Church had enjoyed a more or
less complete immunity from the civil power, maintaining its
own ecclesiastical court and pursuing its own fiscal policies. But
in 1610 a Portuguese edict was passed by which the approval of
royal authorities had to be obtained before monastic and ecclesiastical property could be acquired. The Pope energetically remon-
strated through the papal nuncio at Madrid and was able to
obtain a temporary suspension of the decree. In 1614 Paul V
sent an Italian bishop, Attavio Accoramboni, to Portugal in the
capacity of collector, with instructions to have the decree revoked
and to prevent further meddling in Church affairs on the part
of the civil authority.

The Portuguese were stubborn; the collector would not budge
an inch; and the whole affair came to a climax just as Suarez
came to Lisbon. Against all precedent in Catholic countries a
young cleric had been thrown into prison. The official responsible for the action was summoned to the ecclesiastical court to
explain this open violation of the clergy's immunity. He refused
to come; was summoned twice more, and on his constant refusal,
was excommunicated by Accoramboni. But the civil magistrates,
on their part, then proceeded to teach the Italian collector a
lesson in Portuguese hospitality. They isolated him in his residence, seized his revenues, forbade his servants to attend to him,
even prevented the baker from delivering bread for the bishop,
and the grain-merchant from sending fodder for his horses. The
bishop was properly insulted. He went to the Marquis Da Silva,
the King's viceroy, demanding prompt and severe reparation,
threatening to use all his powers unless the affair was settled

within a week. Satisfaction was not forthcoming, and he placed the feared and drastic weapon of the interdict on Lisbon.

Now an interdict is the most serious calamity that can befall a Catholic city. All Church functions were suspended, Mass could not be celebrated, the sacraments could not be administered except in extreme necessity. It was in an interdicted city that Spain's greatest theologian spent the last few months of his life. He arrived a few days after the interdict had been imposed, and as soon as his presence was known he received a visit from the viceroy who wanted him to do something about the difficulty. Suarez got his side of the story, compared it with the version which Accoramboni then presented to him, and came to the conclusion that the interdict was entirely in accord with both the civil law and the canons of the Church. Da Silva was angry and annoyed, but from that moment popular sentiment swung in favor of the collector.

Neither side gave in. At the beginning of August Suarez was ordered by Gaetani, papal nuncio at Madrid, to reinvestigate the case and to send his findings and his personal judgement to him as soon as possible. His reply of twenty-five pages was considered so important that Gaetani sent it to Cardinal Borghese at Rome who, in turn, decided to use it in all future controversies over such matters with the King of Spain. Philip III had not at first fully understood the case, and sided with the viceroy, but after Suarez' explanation had come to him through the Pope, he changed his mind and ordered Da Silva to make amends.

But all of this happened after the death of Suarez. He was deprived of the pleasure of witnessing the end of the conflict (the interdict was not lifted till April 8, 1618) and of the further pleasure of receiving Paul V's felicitations. Cardinal Borghese wrote to Accoramboni on August 25, 1617, about Suarez' part in the procedure, calling it ". . . very fine, solid and worthy of that theologian. He deserves to be warmly praised and congratulated. The Holy Father charges you to do so. . . ." On the same date the Pope himself addressed a letter to "Our dear son, Francis Suarez, priest of the Society of Jesus, Greeting and Apostolic Benediction! The Venerable brother Octavius, Bishop of Fossombrone, Our Collector in those realms, has informed Us what you have done in the controversy between him and the secular magistrates which was instigated by the enemy of peace. He has also sent your refutation, befitting your great piety and learning, which was most pleasing to Us. Therefore We praise your work as We ought to, and exhort you in our Lord to continue to serve the liberty and the honor of God and of our Church, in which, by the divine grace you have been so outstanding. We know indeed how valuable your reputation is in extirpating the cockle. Although We do not doubt that you will do this We would not be wanting in our debt to you by failing to impart the apostolic benediction and commending you to our charity. May the Lord reward you the wages of your labors. Given at Rome from St. Mary Major; August 25, 1617; in the thirteenth year of Our Pontificate." [2]

The papal letter came too late to encourage and console the theologian. All through the heat of August Suarez was kept continually on the run, acting as mediator in the argument between the collector and the viceroy, walking from one end of the city to the other, disdaining, through some quirk of religious poverty, to use the carriage or horses provided for him. Perhaps it was a notion of added mortification—this further burden of walking when he could have had a conveyance—a self-denial which he might offer up for the speedy settlement of the disgraceful episode. At any rate it did not seem in God's providence to answer his sacrifice. "Nothing would induce Suarez to use a carriage, or even to shelter his head from the scorching rays of the sun with his hat, which it was the custom of the Portuguese

[2] De Scorraille, *op. cit.*, vol. ii, pp. 509–510.

Jesuits to carry in their hands, wearing only the berretta on their heads. He was struck down by a violent attack of fever." [3]

Sunday, September 10, 1617, was a quiet day in Lisbon. Because of the interdict there was no ringing of church bells to bring the faithful to Mass and devotions. Priests did not go about their regular duties. All remained indoors, and Suarez, as always, utilizing his time to the utmost, worked most of the day on a revision of his treatise *De Anima*. In the dusk of the evening he laid down his pen and reflected for a while on the arguments he would use in chapter twelve to demonstrate the immortality of the soul. Actually, he was never to work on it again; he never finished the thesis in this world, but two weeks later he experienced the thrill which must come to all mortal men when they open their eyes on the heavenly glory of the soul's immortality. [4]

On Monday morning Suarez was woefully weak from a combination of fever and dysentery. He could not rise from his bed and had to be carried to the Professed House of St. Roch, in the center of the city, where there were the best facilities for his care. The King's own physician, reputed the best to be obtained, was in constant attendance with three others. For a week they bled him, fed him herbs and other alleged medicinal preparations, and bled him again, until on the seventh day he seemed on the road to recovery. Everybody was happy, but the gray and wan old man smiled feebly at their rejoicing. The blood-lettings had weakened his already emaciated body, and he was the least surprised of all when he suffered a relapse. There was no physical strength left for the battle against death. The doctors gave up hope.

When he asked for Extreme Unction one of his religious brothers administered the sacrament while Suarez himself answered the liturgical prayers and suggested other prayers to be

[3] Coleridge, *op. cit.*, p. 182.   [4] Cf. *De Anima, passim.*

read. He received Holy Viaticum in private, but as he lingered on day after day he asked that he might again receive the sacrament in the presence of the whole community. It was the Spanish custom of the time to allow the reception of Holy Viaticum only once during the final illness, but Suarez had ably argued against this custom and opinion in his work *De Sacramentis,* and he was granted the privilege of sacramentally receiving the Savior once again before his death.[5]

Suarez remained serene while the whole town excitedly discussed bulletins concerning his condition. Everyone knew that he could not recover, and the consequence was that rare occurrence which seems so difficult of belief in our present prosaic attitudes. People literally flocked to the Professed House of St. Roch to get a last glimpse of their still living paragon of wisdom and holiness. Doctors and superiors would undoubtedly frown on such practices at a modern death scene, but the evidences of these happenings in former centuries are indubitable. The theologian was a public figure. He belonged to the Portuguese and Spanish just as he belonged to the Catholic Church and the Society of Jesus; and both state and Church—though officially at odds over the affair of the interdict—demanded representation at the earthly departure of their greatest hero.

The viceroy, Duke Da Silva, who had once rebuked his son for not reverently bending his knee in the presence of Suarez, was the only civil official who did not come in person. He sent a messenger with his greetings in the person of his son, Count Salinas, to whom the theologian said: "I humbly kiss the hand of the Lord Marquis for the interest he has shown in me. Tell him that I am en route to heaven, where I hope to share in the divine Bounty, and assure him that up there he will have in me a faithful servant in the presence of God." [6] These were indeed

---

[5] *De Sacramento Eucharistiae, Disp.* lxviii, 5, 3.
[6] De Scorraille, vol. ii, p. 345.

burning words in favor of a man who had been the prime cause of Lisbon's interdict and who, in an indirect way at least, was responsible now for the theologian's mortal illness.

The highest dignitaries of the Church called on Suarez during these last few days. The Grand Inquisitor of Portugal, the Archbishop of Lisbon, and the Pontifical Collector himself, came to see him. Accoramboni was the direct representative of Christ's vicar on earth, and in Portugal there was no other person closer to His Holiness Paul V. To show his devotion to the Holy See, Suarez wished to make his confession to this dignitary and to receive from him the final absolution. Accoramboni willingly granted this request, thinking for a while that the Jesuit might yet recover. But as he saw him weaken perceptibly at the least exertion, he connived with Suarez' friend and colleague, André de Almada, to bring in the best portraitist in the capital and to let him work in a hidden corner of the room. The humble theologian, however, was not so far out of his senses that he failed to notice the artist, who had only the barest outline on his canvas when he had to quit. Suarez wanted to die in peace, and this attempt was an affront to his humility as well as a source of suffering. In the event, the painter was able to complete the portrait from memory. The collector, viceroy, provincial, and many others commissioned copies; and upon these is based the uninspiring Suarezian likeness which is now extant.

If there is one place in this world where a holy man is at his ease it is on his deathbed. *Saepe a multis vocatum in dubium est, Doctior ne, an sanctior fuerit?* was a remark in one of the few written records of the life of Suarez.[7] He had amply demonstrated his holiness during life, but the acid test of sanctity is probably the manner in which a man gives up his life. Suarez gave a prime example of every one of the virtues to which he

---

[7] Cf. the brief *Vita* contained in the Vives edition *Opera Omnia*, vol. i, p. viii.

had vowed himself in religious life; he was obedient to every direction of superior and physician, modest of his person right to the last breath, poor in spirit and in actuality. Patient with himself, he was perhaps over-charitable to the bungling medicos and nurses who in those days had not yet developed bedside gentleness to an exquisite skill. Most of all, he showed detachment. "I have not a single regret," he said, when asked about his unfinished writings. "The great saints had to leave their work unfinished. There is nothing to worry about in such nothingness." [8]

The dying Jesuit spoke his filial dependence upon God when one of his closest friends sympathetically asked him whether he was in pain, whether anything at all troubled him. "By the grace of God," replied Suarez, "there is nothing at all which can now make me restless. God and I—we understand each other well; and, fortunately, I have never done anything except under the direction of obedience." [9] There can be no doubt that there was in his case as complete an understanding as can exist between the Divine Creator and one of His mortal creatures, that these words of Suarez were no idle boasting. It is one thing to master a complete intellectual science of the Divinity, and quite another thing to put that science to the test of everyday practicality. Suarez, the theologian, was also Suarez, the Theophilus.

The second week of painful mortal illness ended on Sunday, September 24th. The hours crept slowly toward eternity; there was less than a day left, and Suarez improved the time of patient waiting by dictating letters of farewell. In a hesitating voice that hardly rose above a whisper he spoke his final messages for João Coutinho, the present rector of the University of Coimbra, and for Hurtado de Mendoca, Bishop of Guarda, and former rector of the same university. It was a recognition of long-standing devotion and friendship towards these men, and Suarez

[8] De Scorraille, vol. ii, p. 346.   [9] *Ibid.*, p. 347.

could do no more than painfully scrawl his name at the bottom
of each letter.

In the afternoon of the same day the whole Jesuit community
of the College of St. Anthony came to the Professed House to
pay their respects to their famous dying brother and to beg him
to remember them at the court of heaven. It is a pious custom
which has suffered in the lapse, this Catholic practice of asking
a dying person to bring special petitions to God. The Jesuits
assembled in the sickroom then asked Father Suarez' blessing,
but he refused to give it unless each of them would bestow a
blessing upon him first. Slowly they filed past his bed and then
all sank to their knees while Suarez, with the help of a lay brother,
raised his right arm for the benediction.

When these religious brethren left him the dying man seemed
to rest, quietly absorbed in the thought of God and heaven. The
nearer he approached the end the more fervent were his prayers,
and his lips were seen to move, but the words of his aspirations
could not be understood. The priest who watched at his bedside
noticed that Suarez wanted to speak. He leaned over the bed
and caught the dying man's request for the recitation of the
thirty-ninth Psalm: *Expectans expectavi Dominum et intendit
mihi*. . . . The watcher, a former pupil of Suarez, chanted the
Psalm in the usual manner, finishing with the words: *Adiutor
meus, et protector meus tu es: Deus meus ne tardaveris*. At these
last words the theologian raised his voice slightly and said: "That
is for me! That is what consoles me!" After a few moments he
prayed out loud: *Eamus tandem, Domine, eamus!* Let us go at
last, Lord, Let us go! For a while longer he made inaudible
prayers and then lapsed into a very quiet sleep.

All through the night the Jesuits at the Professed House took
turns watching with Father Suarez, while the object of their
solicitude lay in a profound and peaceful slumber. It had all the
appearance of a trance for there was no sign of pain or struggle,

and the watchers could observe from his regular breathing that his soul had not yet departed. A short while after dawn on Monday morning he revived sufficiently to whisper: "I thought it was the end," and a little later still, "I would never have believed it is so sweet to die." Fellow Jesuits quietly slipped into the room, knelt in prayer, watched him raise his eyes to heaven and peacefully breathe his last at about six o'clock. It was on Monday morning, September 25, 1617, that God took to Himself the soul of his ablest theologian.

When the chief actor leaves the stage for the last time interest in the drama and its plot instantly collapses. So it is with the story of the great Suarez. But life went on just the same that Monday morning in Lisbon, and the lesser characters had still their part to play in the ceremonial obsequies.

The papal collector, Accoramboni, immediately lifted the interdict for the Jesuit Church of the city, and commanded that the most solemn services be held in honor of the man "who had rendered such eminent services to the Church, and shown such zeal in this affair of the interdict." The body of the theologian was at first exposed for veneration in the chapel of the Professed House, but as the crowds increased more and more, it was removed to the large public church of St. Roch. Services were held for three days, an Augustinian preaching on the first day, a Franciscan on the second, and a Jesuit on the third.

The Dominicans too, in their customary charitable way, paid due homage to the memory of their doctrinal adversary. One of them, a member of the congregation of the Portuguese Inquisition, remarked that "The Church of God has now lost the greatest genius it possessed since the time of St. Thomas." Another, well-known for his knowledge and piety, said that "Here has departed one of the most learned men of modern times." [10] The

[10] *Ibid.*, p. 350.

number of other encomiums that have been gathered by enthusiastic biographers of Suarez add little but a variation of the same
theme of veneration, praise, respect, and devotion. One of these
writers, Descamps, has given whole chapters to the testimonials
of popes, cardinals, kings, religious superiors, writers, and
others, who spoke of the Jesuit theologian in the most glowing
terms.

Similarly, there are endless testimonials to the marvellous
occurrences which demonstrated the sanctity possessed by this
light of the peninsula. One man, in the last throes of the death
struggle, touched his hand to a letter written personally by
Suarez, and was immediately restored to health. Others reported
apparitions, miracles of a physical and spiritual kind, cures and
healings. For more than a century after his death there was an
intermittent personal cultus practiced in his honor in Spain and
Portugal. Even to-day there are many who believe that Suarez
should some day be raised to the altars of the Church for the
public veneration of the faithful. Actually, his cause has never
been presented to the Congregation of Rites, either for beatification or canonization, and the honoring title *Venerable,* which is
applied to him, is traditional rather than official.

When Suarez died there were not yet any Jesuit saints honored
by the Holy See, but there were several causes then being brought
forward. Ignatius Loyola, Borgia, Xavier, Kostka, Gonzaga—
none of these had yet been canonized, and perhaps for this reason the cultus of Suarez was left to come in its turn after these
great saints. There were other delaying reasons, such as the renewed separation of Portugal from the rule of Spain, and the
later persecution and expulsion of the Jesuits by Pombal. All
of these are probable explanations for the neglect of a man who
was considered a saint by his contemporaries and who, in happier
times, would certainly have enjoyed an immense posthumous
veneration.

The mortal remains of Suarez suffered a similar disregard. They were placed with great honor and ceremony in one of the side chapels of the Jesuit Church of St. Roch at Lisbon. One of the theologian's former pupils, Father Antonio de Castro, a secular priest of wealthy and noble lineage, donated the sum of money needed for an elaborate decoration of this tomb, with the request that he should himself be buried at the feet of his former master. But at the expulsion of the Jesuits from Portugal in 1759 the Church was taken out of their control, and the new administrators built a large organ into that whole section of the Church where Suarez' body lay. Only recently, in the last decade of the nineteenth century, has all this super-structure been removed, and the chapel restored, so that the tomb of the great Jesuit is again open for the visitation of the faithful.[11]

But if other places and other people have neglected Francis Suarez, the University of Coimbra has through these several centuries borne public testimony of its appreciation to him in the form of a now weather-beaten plaque bearing this inscription:

FRANCISCVS SVAREZ EVROPAE ATQVE ADEO ORBIS
VNIVERSI MAGISTER APPELLATVS
ARISTOTELES IN NATVRALIBVS SCIENTIIS
THOMAS ANGELICVS IN DIVINIS
HIERONYMVS IN SCRIPTIONE
AMBROSIVS IN CATHEDRA
AVGVSTINVS IN POLEMICIS
ATHANASIVS IN FIDEI EXPLICATIONE
BERNARDVS IN MELLIFLVA PIETATE
GREGORIVS IN TRADVCTIONE BIBLIORVM AC VERBO
OCVLVS POPVLI CHRISTIANI SED SVO SOLIVS
JVDICIO NIHIL

[11] De Scorraille: *Le tombeau de François Suarez retrouvé*, an enlightening article in *Etudes*, for January, 1894.

Index

Date Due

Date Due			
NOV 17 '51			
NOV 29 '51			
DEC 14 '51			
MAY 14 '52			
JUN 2 3 '52			
APR 2 8 '53			
JUN 1 5 '54			
NOV 8 0 '60			
DEC 1 9 '60			
E 23 '65			

MARYGROVE COLLEGE LIBRARY
Man of Spain : Francis Suarez,
270.921 Su1F

3 1927 00114613 0

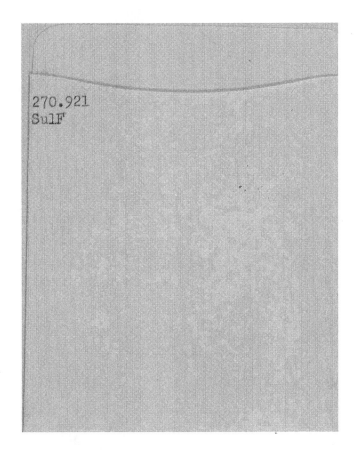

270.921
Su1F

CPSIA information can be obtained
at www.ICGtesting.com
Printed in the USA
BVHW051025100223
658264BV00004B/22

9 781013 789335